The International Theological Commentary on the Holy Scripture of the Old and New Testaments

General Editors

Michael Allen
of Reformed Theological Seminary, USA

and

Scott R. Swain
of Reformed Theological Seminary, USA

Consulting Editors

Mark Gignilliat
of Beeson Divinity School, USA

Matthew Levering
of the University of St Mary of the Lake, USA

C. Kavin Rowe
of Duke Divinity School, USA

Daniel J. Treier
of Wheaton College, USA

Joel

Christopher R. Seitz

*Professor of Biblical Interpretation, Wycliffe College,
University of Toronto, Canada*

LONDON • NEW YORK • OXFORD • NEW DELHI • SYDNEY

T&T CLARK
Bloomsbury Publishing Plc
50 Bedford Square, London, WC1B 3DP, UK
1385 Broadway, New York, NY 10018, USA
29 Earlsfort Terrace, Dublin 2, Ireland

www.bloomsbury.com

BLOOMSBURY, T&T CLARK and the Diana logo are trademarks of Bloomsbury Publishing Plc

First published 2016
Paperback edition published in 2025

© Christopher R. Seitz, 2016

Christopher R. Seitz has asserted his right under the Copyright, Designs and Patents Act, 1988, to be identified as Author of this work.

All rights reserved. No part of this publication may be reproduced or transmitted in any form or by any means, electronic or mechanical, including photocopying, recording, or any information storage or retrieval system, without prior permission in writing from the publishers.

No responsibility for loss caused to any individual or organization acting on or refraining from action as a result of the material in this publication can be accepted by Bloomsbury or the author.

Scripture quotations are from the New Revised Standard Version Bible, copyright © 1989 National Council of the Churches of Christ in the United States of America. Used by permission. All rights reserved worldwide.

British Library Cataloguing-in-Publication Data
A catalogue record for this book is available from the British Library.

ISBN: HB: 978-0-56757-073-4
PB: 978-0-5677-1654-5
ePDF: 978-0-56766-775-5
ePub: 978-0-56766-777-9

Library of Congress Cataloging-in-Publication Data
Names: Seitz, Christopher R., author.
Title: Joel / by Christopher R. Seitz.
Description: New York : Bloomsbury T&T Clark, 2016. | Series: International theological commentary on the Holy Scripture of the Old and New Testaments | Includes bibliographical references and index.
Identifiers: LCCN 2015043423 | ISBN 9780567570734
Subjects: LCSH: Bible. Joel--Commentaries.
Classification: LCC BS1575.53 .S45 2016 | DDC 224/.707--dc23 LC record available at http://lccn.loc.gov/2015043423

Typeset by Fakenham Prepress Solutions, Fakenham, Norfolk NR21 8NN

Contents

Abbreviations	vii
General Editors' Preface	ix
Foreword	xi
Introduction	1
1 Joel as a Prophet Among Prophets: The Challenge	3
2 A Canonical Reading of Joel and the History of Interpretation	13
3 Joel and Prior Prophecy	25
4 The Unity of the Book of Joel and Modern Research	31
5 Intertextuality: Joel's Character as Prophet	37
6 Who is Joel?	49
7 The Message and Purpose of the Book of Joel	53
8 The Day of the LORD in the Book of Joel	67
9 The Living God of Joel in the Lived Life of the Church	85
Bibliography	95
The Book of the Prophet Joel	99

Solemn Opening (1.1–4)   111

Part One The Day of the LORD Upon Israel (1.5–20)   129

Part Two The Unfolding Day of the LORD (2.1–27)   147

Part Three Finale (2.28–3.21)   183

Appendix I: *NY Times*, 6 March 2013   227

Appendix II: Temporality in Joel 2.3–11: The interchange of
prefixed and suffixed forms   231

Index   235

Abbreviations

AB   Anchor Bible

BZAW   *Beihefte zur Zeitschrift für die alttestamentliche Wissenschaft*

HAT   Handbuch zum Alten Testament

ICC   International Critical Commentary

NRSV   Holy Bible: New Revised Standard Version

TRE   Theologische Realenzyklopädie

General Editors' Preface

The T&T Clark International Theological Commentary series aims to offer interpretation of the Bible that addresses its theological subject matter, gleaning from the best of the classical and the modern commentary traditions and showing the doctrinal development of Scriptural truths. In so doing, it seeks to reconnect to the ecclesial tradition of biblical commentary as an effort in *ressourcement*, though not slavish repetition. Alert to tendencies toward atomism, historicism and scepticism, the series seeks to offer a corrective to the widespread pathologies of academic study of the Bible in the modern era.

In contrast to modern study of the Bible, as a collection of witnesses (fragmented and diverse) to ancient religious beliefs and practices, this series reflects upon Holy Scripture as a common witness from and of the triune God of the gospel. These interpretations will give priority to analysis of the scriptural text as such, reading any given passage not only in its most immediate context, but also according to its canonical location, in light of what has historically been termed the *analogia scripturae*. In so doing, however, the series does not mandate any uniform approach to modern critical methods or to the appropriation of classical reading practices; the manner in which canonical reading occurs will follow the textual form and subject matter of the text, rather than dictate them.

Whereas much modern biblical criticism has operated on the presumption that the doctrinal resources of the Church are a hindrance to the exegetical and historical task, commentaries in this series will demonstrate a posture of dependence upon the creedal and confessional heritage of the Church. As Zacharius Ursinus noted centuries ago, the catechetical and doctrinal resources of the Church are meant to flow from and lead back unto a cogent reading of the biblical canon. In so doing, the reception history of the text will be viewed as a help and not merely an obstacle to understanding portions of Holy Scripture. Without mandating a particular confessional position (whether Eastern or Western, Roman or Protestant), the volumes will be marked by a creedal and confessional alertness.

Finally, commentary serves to illumine the text to readers and thus does well to attend not only to the original horizon of the text, but also to its target audience(s). Unfortunately, much biblical interpretation in the modern academy (from both its more liberal and conservative wings) operates as if a sharp divide should be drawn between the source horizon and the receptive horizon. This series, however, gestures toward contextual concerns regarding how the biblical literature impinges upon, comes into confrontation with, or aligns with contemporary questions. While the series does not do the work of homiletics, the commentator ought to exposit with an eye to that end and an ear to those concerns.

In seeking to honour these canonical, creedal and contextual commitments then, the T&T Clark International Theological Commentary series will include sequential commentary on the totality of scriptural books, though the format of volumes will be shaped by the specific demands of the various biblical texts being expounded. Commentators will provide English translations or make use of widely known contemporary translations of varying sorts, but their exposition will be based ultimately upon the original language(s). Commentators will be selected for their capabilities as both exegetical and dogmatic theologians, demonstrated in linguistic and literary facility, creedal and confessional clarity, and an ability to relate the two analytic exercises of dogmatic reasoning and exegetical reasoning. Through its principles, format and selective criteria for commentators, the series intends to further sketch and, in so doing, show the significance of a theological reading of Holy Scripture in the modern era.

Michael Allen and Scott Swain

Foreword

I should begin with a word about the approach to be adopted in this first volume of the new International Theological Commentary (ITC) series. In what way is the high standard of the ICC being adjusted or augmented by use of the term 'Theological' in the new title?

For the purpose of this commentary, a 'theological' reading is one in which the most plausible diachronic observations about the text's literary coming-to-be are used as a sounding board against which to appreciate the theological achievement of the final form of the text. This dialectic also opens the text onto the long and rich history of interpretation, whose grasp of the text's present literary form and movement enabled a distinctly theological and creative evaluation of the Book of Joel's message. I do not take the word 'theological' to mean directly homiletical or applicative, so much as a species of reading which should more naturally give rise to that. Because 'history' is the achievement of the Book of Joel and not principally a speculative lens on its ingredient parts as they come to form through time, the reader should be able to move much more briskly from the exegesis to a present day hearing. In the case of the Book of Joel, furthermore, it is the argument of the present commentary that Joel has been designed to anticipate every generation of readers quite self-consciously (Joel 1.2-3) and not by means of the latter's careful finding of his or her way backwards through the cataract of time's bumpy and un-providential movements.

I am fortunate in this volume, moreover, that the Book of Joel has so few text-critical and translational hurdles to overcome. This fact may find explanation in the late date of the book and its mature and well-designed final form, which is itself deeply indebted to a long history of prophecy, upon which it draws to enable its message to sound forth.

The hallmark of the ICC has been its trenchant engagement with text-critical and translational issues. In this volume of the ITC, no less attention will be paid to a serious diachronic evaluation and to matters of the Book of Joel's development. But these will be attended to in order to shed light on how the final form of Joel functions as a commentary on the rich history that lies before it and that contributes to making it what it is in the presentation that now confronts us and directs us to its future.

I should like to take the opportunity to thank the Alexander von Humboldt Foundation for an extended research leave at the University of Göttingen that enabled the work on this Joel commentary project.

Special thanks go to my host Prof. Dr. Hermann Spieckermann who made the stay more than pleasant and our time in Lower Saxony memorable in the land of Luther.

Professor Mark Elliott at the University of St. Andrews read and commented on earlier drafts of the commentary and offered his customarily wise input. I also acknowledge with gratitude the PhD students at Wycliffe College in the University of Toronto who attended seminars on the Book of the Twelve.

I recall with fondness lectures given by Professor Dr. Jörg Jeremias on the prophets at the University of Munich in 1979 when I was a student there. His work on Joel and the Book of the Twelve has been unfailingly persuasive and my debt to his work will be registered in the commentary herewith.

My research students Nate Wall and Rob Kashow kept an editorial eagle eye on this initial commentary in a fresh series, but of course their 20/20 is not to blame for my near-sightedness. I thank them for their vigilance and help.

Joel is a special witness in the Book of the Twelve and I have tried to honor that specialness.

Christopher R. Seitz

Introduction

Surveying the recent spate – deluge, glut, avalanche – of monographs on the redaction of the Book of the Twelve and especially of Joel's specific role in that, one is tempted to speak of a 'Book of the Twelve Gold Rush'. That is, an unregulated free-for-all where anyone with mule and pan will show up to stake a claim, the only requirement being finding new and untapped space. The recent monograph of Schwesig clarifies in the preface that it was completed before being able to consult that of Beck, which appears in the very same BZAW series but only ten volumes and one year away.[1] The drive to produce a master-view and to incorporate a vast range of very different texts into a single reconstruction makes for an unbounded set of possibilities and an equally bewildering array of proposals.

In consequence, we wish to clarify at the outset that it will not be the task of a commentary on Joel in this series to wade through and set in tidy rows all the variants in this new wave of research. This can be done, of course. Yet, the threat is real that the task could overwhelm and also distract from an evaluation of Joel as a single work, *even as we must strive to receive its message in relation to books*

---

[1] Paul-Gerhard Schwesig, *Die Rolle der Tag-JHWHs-Dichtungen im Dodekapropheten* (BZAW 366; Berlin: Walter de Gruyter, 2006); Beck, M., *Der 'Tag YHWHs' in Dodekapropheten: Studien im Spannungsfeld von Traditions- und Redaktionsgeschichte* (BZAW 356; New York/Berlin: Walter de Gruyter, 2005).

with which we believe it intends to be heard. That belongs to Joel's particular character as prophecy, as we shall hope to show.

All the same, we must still think through the implications of this new approach. I have myself participated in the recent work on the Twelve, though from a different angle of interest.[2] My previous research has focused rather on new models for setting forth a genre to be called 'Introduction to the Prophets' – one that moves resolutely away from the isolating-and-dating approach made popular since the mid-nineteenth century, whereby the prophets are distinguished from one another by means of historical tools and set in a 'proper' sequential order. This became the 'canonical order' after the fashion of approaches of the last 200 years. Specialist studies of redactional layers in the Twelve have implications for the questions I have proposed, but in large measure they are very content to 'pan for gold' in their own specific region of XII research – not least because the task of re-description that it sets for itself is extraordinarily demanding in its own right.

What I will do is give a flavour of the research by isolating certain interpreters I judge to be representative of these new approaches. I will also endeavour to place more detailed discussion in a form and a place where it will not detract from the reading of the commentary as a bona fide and hopefully clarifying guide to the Book of Joel. A commentary on recent research, especially when it is as vast and prolific as is true now of work on the Twelve, is not a commentary on Joel. It stands as a challenge for this commentary nevertheless, given when it is being composed, to give proper attention to this recent wave of research, but also to do so in a way that it stands as a help in interpreting Joel and not as a topic in its own right.

---

[2] See C. Seitz, *Prophecy and Hermeneutics: Toward a New Introduction to the Prophets* (STI; Grand Rapids, MI: Baker Academic, 2007) and *The Goodly Fellowship of the Prophets: The Achievement of Association in Canon Formation* (Grand Rapids, MI: Baker Academic, 2009).

1

Joel as a Prophet Among Prophets: The Present Commentary Challenge

The present challenge for the interpretation of Joel (or any of the Minor Prophets) is finding the proper balance between a) guarding the integrity of Joel's specific witness (as an individual book within a collection of twelve books), and b) comprehending how Joel means to be heard in relation to its location within the Twelve. But more needs to be said here so as not to confuse what is meant by these two dimensions. First, 'guarding the integrity of Joel's specific witness' – what does that mean?

In the nineteenth century, it came to mean placing the book in its proper 'historical context' and attending to matters of author, dating, audience and relationship to other prophetic testimony.[1] It meant above all securing the proper sequence of the twelve witnesses in relation to one another and in relation to other prophetic works. We must constantly remind ourselves that 'the integrity of Joel' need not mean that on these same specific terms; and it did not mean that in the long history of interpretation. Jerome assumed, in a low-flying sense, that undated books were next to their contemporary neighbours; Calvin muses about historical setting (Obadiah and the Babylonian exile) and then briskly moves on; the Antiochenes are interested in what we might call historical context, but it would never occur to them to rearrange the witnesses according to some more

---

[1] See C. Seitz, *Prophecy and Hermeneutics*, 15–92.

proper or decisive order. The idea that a 'proper sequence' needed to be secured, whereby the individual witness was ranged historically before and after other witnesses and that this was decisive for an account of prophecy in general and for the witness of an individual prophetic book – this particular definition of guarding Joel's integrity, meant above all an act of distinguishing Joel and focusing on what is distinctive about this book *vis-à-vis* the other witnesses, using a species of the category 'history' as the means to do that. What emerged in consequence was the 'introduction to the prophets' genre. Here the prophets were placed in a sequence and their development and distinguishing features were plotted (including precedents available to them in the form of religious traditions, available for their use and adaptation).[2] How did prophecy begin, develop and change? And indeed why did it end? These became the controlling questions. A new 'canonical' Introduction form emerged with its own specific contours and requirements for readers and interpreters.

In this model for understanding the 'integrity of an individual witness' what proved decisive were differentiation and developmental factors. The actual literary presentation itself was judged either a neutral matter (a starting point for disentangling and rearranging) or an obscuring cataract. This was true of the larger presentation of the Twelve in a stable sequence, but also especially of the individual witnesses themselves (which parts of the single witness were authentic and which secondary would need to be determined to get at the real, specified 'historical' prophet/prophecy).[3]

At present there is a deep and sustained interest in attending to prophecy in the Twelve, according to a different model of

---

[2] Von Rad's was an especially fine example of the species. For quick reference see *The Message of the Prophets* (trans. David M. G. Stalker; London: SCM, 1968). A good modern English language example is Joseph Blenkinsopp, *A History Prophecy in Israel* (Louisville, KY: Westminster John Knox, 1996).

[3] The existence of minor variants in order (of the XII or Isaiah–Jeremiah–Ezekiel) does not affect this basic observation. More on this below.

interpretation. It is not that the historical origin dimension and development have fled the field (the diachronic dimension). By no means, rather, these are now differently evaluated as to their proper place in comprehending the literary presentation itself. That is, the larger form of the Twelve, far from being a neutral or obscuring feature, is taken to be significant and *on its own historical as well as literary (synchronic) terms*. Historical development and differentiation remain key elements in the act of interpretation, but now in the service of describing the significance of the form as it sits before us, as its own act of theological, historical and literary presentation. I have referred to this elsewhere as an 'achievement of association'.[4]

In the light of this new frame of reference, to speak of the integrity of the singular witness of Joel means something very different than on prior terms. It means, then, being able to describe what the significance of Joel having literary boundaries (a beginning, with a superscription; a content of specific character and an ending) and not being merged into a single twelve-fold book (like the lengthy book of Isaiah) means.[5] This is all the more crucial now that light is being shined so directly on matters of association and relation and cross-reference within the Twelve as a work with its own particular character and integrity. To see Joel in a fresh way in relation to the other books of the Twelve (and especially the book of Amos, for reasons to be explained) could ironically mean losing Joel as a work with its own integrity, forfeited now on terms other than the older historical contextualization. To the degree to which Joel's significance is understood to be in relation to what it says within the Twelve as a whole; or to restrict or foreground Joel's significance in

---

[4] *Goodly Fellowship* (2011), 77–103.
[5] For a discussion of the similarities and differences between the XII and Isaiah as whole works, see Odil H. Steck, *Der Abschluss der Prophetie im Alten Testament: Ein Versuch zur Frage der Vorgeschichte des Kanons* (Neukirchen: Neukirchener Verlag, 1991); Terence Collins, *The Mantle of Elijah: The Redaction Criticism of the Prophetical Books* (Biblical Seminar 20; Sheffield: JSOT Press, 1993).

relation to how reading it creates a lens on subsequent books and their interpretation; or to see portions of Joel as relevant, chiefly insofar as one successfully associates them with kindred editorial activity elsewhere – in each of these cases, we can observe a raising of the historical question from a different angle, which threatens to hold the literary presentation of Joel as a work with its own integrity hostage to a particular reconstruction, greater than the sum of the parts themselves. It is potentially to infringe on the character and integrity of Joel as this has been marked in the final form of the Book of the Twelve, where Joel is one literary witness among others equally so marked and differentiated – now not on the terms of the prior historical investigation and disentangling, but rather – in such a way that it has not been merged into a common and un-bordered single work.[6]

It is crucial that we begin our opening remarks in this way, because of the genre we are undertaking. This is a biblical commentary on a single witness. It is not a commentary on the Book of the Twelve (whatever that might be) and neither is it a commentary treatment on one book self-consciously *en route* to a 'Twelve Book' presentation that subsumes it. More on this will follow. The Book of Joel, given its discrete character as a book, must not be allowed to vanish behind a complex reconstruction of the history of the development of a twelve-book collection. It must stand on its own, and yet speak within its specific literary context as well.

Now we will look at the question of the second dimension. To read the book of Joel with its own integrity is, at the same time, to encounter – arguably more than in any other book in this twelve-book library – a clear and sustained character of association and affiliation,

---

[6] The comparison with the Book of Isaiah is telling at this point. See 'The Effect of a Middle: Redactional and Intertextual Connections between the Book of the Twelve and Isaiah' (unpublished paper, Society of Biblical Literature Annual Meeting 2013, Baltimore, MD).

built into what makes Joel what it is. This has been explained in our season of historical-critical reading as due to the book's late date. That is, the latterly appearing Book of Joel knows and is indebted to other witnesses in the Twelve (and elsewhere). In its knowing and in its indebtedness, so it could be argued and will be argued, it requests us to follow suit. The reader and interpreter of Joel, then, is a reader and interpreter of Joel's own horizon of influence – which in this case is both a matter of understanding how Joel is using other prophetic witnesses and what its relation to them in the Book of the Twelve is meant to convey, without allowing his specific literary presentation to be swallowed up in an account of the development of the Twelve in diachronic terms. We need to stay with this point a bit longer in order to be clear what we mean. It will be useful to give a specific illustration.

J. Jeremias – among others – has made a persuasive case that Joel's main theme, the Day of the LORD, is developed on the basis of his understanding of that Day elsewhere in the Twelve and that this must be grasped if his own unique portrayal of it in the literary context of his own work is properly to be appreciated.[7] The locusts and drought particularly of Amos (the witness he precedes), fund his specific description. Does that mean Joel has no genuine drought and locust plague in view for an audience he is addressing and that instead we are in the clean fields of literary intertextuality and association? Not necessarily; both factors – individuality and association – could be in play. We will have more to say about that in the commentary, for it touches immediately on the concerns we are raising here. That is, does Joel retain its own integrity as an individual witness, or is it to be

---

[7] J. Jeremias, 'Gelehrte Prophetie: Beobachtungen zu Joel und Deuterosacharja', in *Vergegenwärtigung des Alten Testaments: Beiträge zur biblischen Hermeneutik* (Festschrift für Rudolph Smend zum 70. Geburtstag; eds, Christoph Bultmann, Walter Dietrich, Christoph Levin; Göttingen: Vandenhoeck & Ruprecht, 2002), 97–111. See also note 10 below.

melded into a wider field of editorial reference and, if the former, how might this integrity be described on historical and referential terms?[8]

Yet, especially as we consider the specific character of Joel, this second dimension again raises its head. Does Joel as an individual witness seek to influence, constrain, recast – or choose the most accurate phrase you can – how the Day of the Lord is now heard in Amos (and in Zephaniah and elsewhere)? What are we to make of the sequential presentation of the Twelve considered as a whole, as a literary phenomenon? Similarly, Joel's depiction of the character of God may well be forged in a conversation with the Book of Jonah (the King of Nineveh there speaks like Joel's hoped-for penitential addressants; compare Joel 2.12-14 and Jonah 3.9). It is one thing to see this level of association and quite another to assess its significance. It is a reciprocating dimension, with one witness being influenced arguably by another and with the synchronic form of the unfolding presentation in turn affected as well.

One may pursue this point a bit further to illustrate the challenge. Rendtorff can speak of the reader of Amos knowing what the Day of the LORD is in his specific presentation (where it is introduced as if we all know what he means, or at least his own audience presumably did; see Amos 5.18). How? Because, Rendtorff argues, the reader has read Joel first, where the Day is a main theme (and according to Rendtorff, now in three different renditions).[9] But is this to evacuate what we might properly consider Amos' own specific address in his own day, exploiting an arguable vagueness so as to allow Joel to fill in

---

[8] Theodoret of Cyr in his commentary on the Twelve argues for a realistic interpretation of the locusts and drought in Joel (he refers to the alternative reading that sees the locusts as symbols for serial national powers). In so doing he links the locusts and drought in Joel to Amos 4 and Jeremiah 14–15. This same instinct arises in recent scholarship, but on the grounds of Joel's late testimony informed by the prophetic legacy available to him in Amos and Jeremiah and elsewhere. There is more on this below.

[9] R. Rendtorff, 'How to Read the Book of the Twelve as a Theological Unity', in *Reading and Hearing the Book of the Twelve* (eds James D. Nogalski, Marvin Sweeney; *Society of Biblical Literature Symposium*, Series 15: Atlanta, GA: SBL, 2000), 75–87.

the blanks? Is this what the author of Joel intended to do as well? Or does Joel know the presentation of Amos and believe he understands it quite properly and now seeks a greater elaboration based upon his hearing of Amos and other witnesses, and indeed the voice of God as he is addressed by it? And, lastly, what effect does it have on our reading of witnesses subsequent to Joel that we come to them via him (and Hosea)? Our concern is not only that Joel not be swallowed up, but equally Hosea and Amos and the other witnesses in this complex presentation.

The reason these questions present themselves is precisely because we are confronted with two realities at the same time within the Book of the Twelve. We can see Joel's obvious relationship to other prophetic works and within a consistent field of association can conjecture that he knows them and means for us to see that as well; indeed, it may well belong to the specifics of his particular prophetic vocation, as a prophet brokering older prophecy for a new day, as we shall see. And yet, at the same time, we read his book at a particular place within that larger field of association, literarily speaking. There is really no good way to speak about this dimension *in strictly diachronic terms*, because we must allow for the strong possibility of mutual enrichment, of reciprocal association, both now imbedded in what we must attend to as the character of the presentation of the Twelve in its present form.[10] Stated negatively, to focus solely on

---

[10] To see something of the challenge of the synchronic and diachronic dimension (about which further below) consider this sentence from Jeremias summarizing the matter. '… in its present position the book of Joel precedes the other books of the Twelve with the exception of Hosea … Therefore it serves a kind of hermeneutical key to the Twelve. A reader of, say, Amos and Zephaniah will have read Joel before coming to them in his or her scroll and will understand Amos and Zephaniah in line with Joel's message, though the historical Joel learned from Zephaniah and Amos and modified them both [via his own presentation]. Consequently, we have to distinguish between two different trends of interpretation. While Amos and Zephaniah strongly influenced Joel, the book of Joel by its present location among the Twelve influences the meaning of the books of Amos (Obadiah, Jonah) and Zephaniah.' He speaks of a 'process of double influence' ('The Function of the Book of Joel for Reading the Twelve', in Rainer Albertz, James D. Nogalski, Jakob Wöhrle (eds), *Perspectives on the Formation of the Book of the Twelve*

speculations regarding diachronic development can very quickly void the potential for the literary presentation as it now exists to exert its own pressure. In this presentation, Joel is its own discrete witness. It comes before Joel and after Hosea and it has a specific literary form. I imagine this is why Jeremias is reluctant to say that Joel was only composed for its place in the Twelve and in relation to it and that it had no independent life strictly speaking. He is keen to understand this context of association and indeed pursues it with intelligence and perception. But what he is getting at, I believe, is that Joel is a discrete work all the same and one must strive to understand both it and its relationship to the wider canonical context at one and the same time.[11]

A brief explanatory postscript

My own recent interest in the Twelve as a collection comes from a very different angle than the many monographs and specialist studies one can see in the bibliography at the close of this Introduction and referred to above. I have been concerned in my writing with a

(BZAW 433; Berlin/Boston, MA: Walter de Gruyter, 2012), 77. There is also the question of Joel's relationship to Hosea. The ecological effects of God's judgement is a major theme of Hosea ('grain, wine and oil' of 2.8 and similar refrains in 2.9, 2.12, 2.22, 5.12, 8.7, 9.2, 9.4, 9.14, 9.16, 14.7), and it is reproduced in its own form in Joel.

[11] In an earlier frame of reference, where Joel's relationship to other books in the Twelve had been replaced by a straightforwardly chronological presentation, it was probably important to emphasize the dimension of intentional association by referring to Joel as having no independent existence; equally Jonah. But the danger was probably real that the individuality of the witness, now understood on terms other than historical-critical ones, would begin to recede. The concern of Ben Zvi, Barton and others, to emphasize the discrete character of the books, to the extent of viewing them as unrelated and in no intentional association, probably senses the issue at stake, but exaggerates the independence of the witnesses within an obviously significant field of association provided by the canonical form. Among other essays, see Ehud Ben Zvi, 'Twelve Prophetic Books or "The Twelve": A Few Preliminary Considerations', in *Forming Prophetic Literature: Essays on Isaiah and the Twelve in Honor of John D. W. Watts* (eds James W. Watts, Paul House; *JSOTS* 235; Sheffield: Sheffield Academic Press, 1996), 125–56.

species of historical study of the Prophets which must create its own 'canonical' order and which has introduced the Prophets according to a sequential grid, whereby what is important is disentangling them, putting them in historical settings and isolating them by describing their particularities and long-term development, ending in time, so many argue, with Jonah's curious presentation.

Specialist studies of the Twelve have sought to understand the Minor Prophets as a collection, by noting lateral layers of kindred material and describing the development of a Twelve Collection with primary attention given to the larger associations and less to the works as individual achievements. I am thinking here of the publications of Nogalski and Wöhrle, and to a lesser extent Schart. There was a push-back against this approach by Ehud Ben Zvi and also some recent challenge as the 'redactional approach' has gathered steam (Barton, Perlitt, Beck, Troxel).

I find it unfortunate that the term 'redactional' implies for many the 'lateral associations' model of Nogalski and Wöhrle, for, on the face of it, it could equally extend to any model that seeks to understand the order and arrangement of the Twelve Minor Prophets, but which focuses more closely on the individuality of the works as nevertheless taken up into a larger field of association. The comparison between the tradition–historical model of Rendtorff in the Pentateuch and that of an older literary-critical/documentary model may be relevant here as well in the Twelve. Rendtorff questioned a model which did not deal with the individuality of the five finished books, whose present existence is a stable fact, as deeply ingredient in any account of their present collective shape.[12] Beck wants to use the term 'anthology' to describe the Twelve, but this does not mean that the books have nothing to do with each other; he is simply cautioning against

---

[12] *The Problem of the Process of Transmission in the Pentateuch* (John J. Scullion, trans.; Sheffield: JSOT, 1990).

ignoring the literary fact of individual works whose character as literature does not evince the larger over-arching 'redactional' connective tissue argued for in various detailed reconstructions.[13] I share that concern and in my own study of the Twelve, have never sought to produce a 'master-theory' that would align all the books according to a comprehensive editorial system that was at work within them – and so could be critically reconstructed – from beginning to end.

---

[13] Beck, M. 'Die Dodekapropheten als Anthologie', ZAW 118 (2005): 558–81.

2

A Canonical Reading of Joel and the History of Interpretation

In the sense sketched out above, a canonical reading of the Book of Joel is one *that attends to the form* – the form of Joel as we receive it and also the form of the Book of the Twelve in which it is found. Because the Book of Joel and other biblical books often give evidence of a rich prehistory, it has been deemed interesting, incumbent, or fully required to detail that history if one is to 'interpret' the present text. A canonical reading is more cautious about whether the text can yield the sort of detailed reconstruction often sought and it seeks to give proper proportion to efforts to undertake such a description. Minimally, a careful sense of the prehistory of a text, as this is critically assembled, can shed important light on the final form and what it has chosen to highlight. But a canonical reading also works with one cardinal rule: it seeks to pay attention to what the canonical form has itself given priority to and also what not to pay attention to. That is, it judges the final form as itself a proper commentary on its history of development, wherein certain features are put in the foreground and others are left in the background.

To speak of 'the integrity of Joel' is then, to acknowledge that decisions have been made to set it apart from the other witnesses with which it exists, shares important themes and indeed gives evidence of direct association and interrelationship. So, for example, however much Amos and Hosea display an important dimension of affiliation in their prehistory, the task is to understand that feature within the context of the literary presentation of two differently finalized works and to take them seriously as such on those same terms. It is from within this perspective that we are enabled to see that Hosea's critique of the cult and false worship is nevertheless also related to Amos' concern for social justice and the righteousness of God.[1] The works themselves, in their given forms, have sought to manifest matters of commonality and difference both, which doubtless goes back to the individuality of the prophet and his once-upon-a-time historical context. But the matter did not end there, for the final form of their writings shows how those who transmitted their works, wanted us both to appreciate their unique presentation and witness and also the way in which one and the same God was calling them both under his providential oversight. Sometimes to be too close to what we call 'history' is to be unable to see what God will take time to disclose.[2] Prophecy is a phenomenon in which we speak about 'inspiration', and by this is certainly meant that the prophet is given to see things and say things *whose final horizon is not for him to know completely, but is for God to make known in time.*[3] His message is intelligible, but it is always deeply associative, both because God sets the prophets among other prophets and also because he alone maintains the final 'literal sense' of what he intends finally to say. To be 'inspired' is to be taken up into this framework of knowing, such as it is.[4] That this can be a trial for the prophet is but one reason, though surely a main one, the one encountered by God, for this vocation objects strenuously

---

[1] See the fine work of J. Jeremias, 'The Interrelationship between Amos and Hosea', in *Forming Prophetic Literature,* 171–86.
[2] C. Seitz, 'Prophecy and History: The Book of the Twelve as History', in *Prophecy and Hermeneutics,* 189–219.
[3] Herein lies one of the problems of modernity's account of the centrality of 'authorial intention', critically determined. 'Book' and 'author' go separate ways.
[4] For a sensitive discussion of this matter, in the light of modern approaches, see Don Collett, 'Reading Forward: The Old Testament and Retrospective Stance', in *Pro Ecclesia: A Journal of Catholic and Evangelical Theology* XXIV:2 (2015): 178–96.

and must by that same God be commandeered and dispatched and upheld through trial (Jer. 1.1-10).

Is a canonical reading a form of pre-modern reading and does the earlier history of interpretation manifest the same interests as we note in a canonical approach? The answer is certainly 'Yes' and 'No' in equal measure.

Because the Minor Prophets circulate together in textual transmission and are counted as one book (in both the Jewish and Christian tradition), reflexively no interpreter decides to comment on only part of the collection or selects one book out and specifies more directly an approach that is appropriate for a commentary on it alone. We know of no commentary on the Minor Prophets that has a different order than what we have in English-printed Bibles, in spite of the fact that the three major uncials of the LXX can provide an order that departs from this (placing the amply superscripted books of the first half of the collection side-by-side, so Hosea, Amos, Micah, followed by Joel, Obadiah and Micah). The Antiochene interpreters, Theodore of Mopsuestia and Theodoret of Cyrus, have provided us with full, sequential commentary on the Book of the Twelve, and in the order of the present MT, though of course they are reading a text in Greek translation.[5] The same is true of Jerome, who has left us this fine narrative summary. It is worth quoting in full.

The twelve prophets whose writings are compressed within the narrow limits of a single volume have typical meanings far different from their literal ones. Hosea speaks many times of Ephraim, of Samaria, of Joseph, of Jezreel, of a wife of 'whoredoms' and of

---

[5] Theodore of Mopsuestia, *Commentary on the Twelve Prophets* (Robert C. Hill, trans.; The Fathers of the Church, Vol. 108; Washington, DC: The Catholic University of America Press, 2001); Theodoret of Cyrus, *Commentaries on the Prophets, Volume Three: Commentary on the Twelve Prophets* (trans. with an introduction by Robert Charles Hill; Brookline, MA: Holy Cross Orthodox Press, 2006). The Greek text of the Antiochenes frequently goes its own way and shows a tendency to move closer to the Hebrew textual tradition. It is frequently labelled *Lucianic*.

'children of whoredoms', of an adulteress shut up within the chamber of her husband, sitting for a long time in widowhood and in the garb of mourning, awaiting the time when her husband will return to her. Joel, the son of Pethuel, describes the land of the twelve tribes as spoiled and devastated by the palmerworm, the canker-worm, the locust and the blights and predicts that after the overthrow of the former people the Holy Spirit shall be poured out upon God's servants and handmaids. The same spirit, that is, which was to be poured out in the upper chamber at Zion upon the one hundred and twenty believers. These believers, rising by gradual and regular gradations from one to fifteen, form the steps to which there is a mystical allusion in the 'psalms of degrees'. Amos, although he is only 'an herdman' from the country, 'a gatherer of sycamore fruit', cannot be explained in a few words. For who can adequately speak of the three transgressions and the four of Damascus, of Gaza, of Tyre, of Idumæa, of Moab, of the children of Ammon and in the seventh and eighth place of Judah and of Israel? He speaks to the 'fat kine' that are in the mountain of Samaria and bears witness that the great house and the little house shall fall. He sees now the maker of the grasshopper. Now the Lord, standing upon a wall daubed or made of adamant, now a basket of apples that brings doom to the transgressors, and now a famine upon the earth, 'not a famine of bread, nor a thirst for water, but of hearing the words of the Lord'. Obadiah, whose name means 'the servant of God', thunders against Edom red with blood and against the creature born of earth. He smites him with the spear of the spirit because of his continuous rivalry with his brother Jacob. Jonah, fairest of doves, whose shipwreck shows in a figure the passion of the Lord, recalls the world to penitence and, while he preaches to Nineveh, announces salvation to all the heathens. Micah the Morasthite, a joint heir with Christ, announces the spoiling of the daughter of the robber and lays siege against her, because she has smitten the jawbone of the judge of Israel. Nahum, the consoler of the world, rebukes 'the bloody city' and when it is overthrown cries: 'Behold upon the mountains the feet of him that bringeth good tidings.' Habakkuk, like a strong and unyielding wrestler, stands upon his watch and sets his foot upon the tower, that he may contemplate Christ upon the cross and say, 'His glory covered the heavens and the earth was full of his praise. And his brightness was as the light; he had horns coming out of his hand: and there was the hiding of his power.' Zephaniah, that is the bodyguard and knower of the secrets of the Lord, hears 'a cry from the fishgate, and an howling from the second, and a great crashing from the hills'. He proclaims 'howling to the inhabitants of the mortar; for all the people of Canaan are undone; all they that were laden with silver are cut off'. Haggai, that is he who is glad or joyful, who has sown in tears to reap in joy, is occupied with the rebuilding of the temple. He represents the Lord (the Father, that is) as saying 'Yet once, it is a little while, and I will shake the heavens, and the earth, and the sea, and the dry land; and I will shake all nations and he who is desired of all nations shall come.' Zechariah, he that is mindful of his Lord, gives us many prophecies. He sees Jesus, 'clothed with filthy garments', a stone with seven eyes, a candle-stick all of gold with lamps as many as the eyes and two olive trees on the right side of the bowl and on the left. After he has described the horses, red, black, white and grisled, and the cutting off of the chariot from Ephraim and of the horse from Jerusalem, he goes on to prophesy and predict a king who shall be a poor man and who shall sit 'upon a colt the foal of an ass'. Malachi, the last of all the prophets, speaks openly of the rejection of Israel and the calling of the nations. 'I have no pleasure in you, saith the Lord of hosts, neither will I accept an offering at your hand. For from the rising of the sun even unto the going down of the same, my name is great among the Gentiles: and in every place incense is offered unto my name, and a pure offering.' As for Isaiah, Jeremiah, Ezekiel and Daniel, who can fully understand or adequately explain them? The first of them seems to compose not a prophecy but a gospel.

The quote continues with brief descriptions of these Major Prophets, followed by the writings (Psalms, Proverbs, Song of Songs, Esther, Chronicles, Ezra and Nehemiah).

We know that, elsewhere, Jerome holds the view that the Minor Prophets are in chronological order. Undated books are in his opinion to be dated with reference to their neighbours. But the fact that this is mentioned only in passing by him, shows the very different emphasis we now witness in modern historical contextualization, as compared with his conception. I mention this here, because a conclusion one can draw from it is that, in general terms, what holds the Twelve together for Jerome is that they represent a coherent temporal association. He does not dwell on how they might be related to one another thematically or intertextually, in the manner of present interest in the Book of the Twelve. Rather, his low-flying assumption of contemporaneity serves the purpose of relating them on other grounds all the same (so, Hosea, Joel and Amos are contemporaries in his understanding). It is obvious that, as he states, for Jerome, what in fact makes the collection of the Twelve significant as a whole work is what he calls their 'typical meanings', which are 'far different from their literal ones'. By 'typical' we can see that what Jerome means is their figural or prophetical potential in relationship to Christ and the Church. But in his narrative execution, it is intriguing to see that in actual fact the literal sense (in this instance, its sense located in past time and in literal address to contemporaries as cited) still helps him in his summarizing description and indeed is what is in the foreground, all the same. It is beyond the scope of this present discussion, but a close examination of both Theodore and Theodoret, would give evidence of the location Jerome occupies, somewhere between them in their historical and figural amalgamation when it comes to commentary on the Book of the Twelve as a whole.

The twin pressure of a) a manuscript tradition that differentiates a single Minor Prophet from Isaiah or Jeremiah by locating them in a stable collection of Twelve and b) loose theories of chronological and/or typical association means that, even when there is interest in the historical context of the prophet, this never becomes a matter of independent pursuit. This may also explain why the brief historical contextualizing usually appears at the very start of the commentary proper and after that recedes in importance, such as it is, until the next, ensuing individual prophet appears and needs introduction of some minimal kind. It is fair to say this same practice remains effectively in place even up to the time of the much later commentary of Calvin. And this is true even though Calvin does not hold to the view of Jerome that undated books are in the proper chronological sequence.

In sum, it is the anodyne 'pressure' of the manuscript tradition (XII as a single work) which resists an individualized treatment of the prophets.[6] The commentator who embarks on an interpretation of Hosea will not stop there, will not start somewhere else and will carry on until Malachi is completed. Though Calvin holds the view that Obadiah is a prophet of the Exile and that Habakkuk is in fact later than Zephaniah, he never uses this kind of historical information to prise the prophets apart from one another, much less to consider their historical sequentiality a factor of decisive importance in how we are to interpret them. In mild terms, it may also prevent a different and more ambitious order of speculation, in which Joel and Jonah end up, for example, as very late books. Jonah is typically regarded as the same prophet who appears in the narratives concerning the Northern Kingdom in 2 Kings and even in many of the earliest historical efforts to provide a new chronological order for the individual prophets of the Twelve, Joel still remains an early pre-exilic prophet. Other prophets rely on him and not vice versa. Similarly, Jeremiah used the

---

[6] The fact that we can point to 'alternative orders' in the LXX (the term is probably far too strong) plays virtually no role whatsoever in the earlier commentary tradition of Jews or Christians.

prophecies of Obadiah; Amos quoted Joel (so as to make clear his prophetic calling and divine warrant).[7]

What a canonical approach shares with the earlier history of interpretation is resistance to believing the manuscript tradition (XII in a single collection) lacks any interpretative significance, of the kind we see in Jerome's account above.[8] Also, it does not hold to the view that historical contextualization is the main index for interpretation insofar as the manuscript tradition nowhere has sought to preserve it. Jerome's low-flying assumption that the canon means to preserve a chronological order may be wrong, but the alternative of recasting the Minor Prophets into a different, 'more correct' order never presented itself as an option, or occurred to any interpreter, until the nineteenth century. It must also be emphasized that, in consequence of this, the prophets never became the isolated individuals they would shortly become, whose relationship, if no longer intimated in loose ways by the manuscript tradition itself, would hereafter have to be provided (if possible or desired) by theories of common traditions and subsequent editorial supplementation.

What is genuinely new in present canonical reading is the assumption that certain historical conclusions are more likely true than others (Joel is a late book indebted to other prophetic testimony). In this instance, however, it is our conviction that the manuscript tradition never intended that it be read as offering a precise chronological unfolding of twelve serial witnesses and preferred to leave the matter unmarked, as indeed it has. It has been noted by recent interpreters of the Twelve that a decision to provide (what are commonly termed 'deuteronomistic') superscriptions for Hosea, Amos, Micah

---

[7] See my discussion of the earliest critical sequences in *Prophecy and Hermeneutics* and *Goodly Fellowship*. Compare note 30 below.
[8] The Twelve appears as a single work and also when a reckoning of the total number of books is being given. In the earliest Church fathers where we find reference to it (Athanasius, Cyril, Epiphanius, Gregory, Amphilochius, Hilary, Jerome, Augustine) it typically precedes Isaiah. This is also true in Vaticinus and Alexandrinus.

and Zephaniah comes with the concomitant judgement that this has not been carried out in other places (Joel, Obadiah and Habakkuk) and so is likely an intentional canonical feature.[9] Moreover, Joel's 'lateness' is not a warrant for dislodging him and placing him on a new timeline necessary for an 'interpretation of the prophets' as a whole. He is where he belongs: in relationship to the 'prophets as a whole', as the XII itself presents this. His witness is only available in relationship to them as Book 2 of a twelve-book total form, where he follows Hosea and precedes Amos. In this case, it is precisely his *literary* placement that makes his likely *historical* location serve its true purpose as a prophet among prophets. 'Late' and 'early' find their proper meaning *as such* in the canonical portrayal and in God's time. This means that what we may see as a later witness, precisely by the decision to leave the matter unmarked in the canonical form, can now exercise an abiding theological purpose as a lens through which to see God's word to his servants the prophets, merging 'early' and 'late' horizons on a single providential plane. What we are here describing may be exactly what the phrase 'Day of the LORD' seeks to encompass and convey. We are speaking of a complex temporal conceptualization (what a LORD's *day* might mean), that must be appreciated if Joel and time in the Twelve are properly to be understood.

In sum, by virtue of its own placement in time, a canonical approach is not an imitation or repristination of pre-modern reading. It shares with such reading a concern for proper historical proportionality,

---

[9] On the decision to leave witnesses temporally unmarked, see Rendtorff's contribution to *Reading and Hearing* (2000). He writes, 'But what about those writings that are not dated? It would be too simple to say that those who put the individual writings together had no information about the time of the activity of these prophets. From that point of view, the question why the undated writings have been put where they now stand would be even more urgent. Seemingly, in most cases, there were no particularly chronological reasons' ('Theological Unity', 76–7). He goes on to discuss the placements of Joel, Obadiah, Jonah, Zephaniah, Habakkuk and Malachi, probing the theological and thematic reasons for their location.

measured against the form of the prophetic presentation itself. Because it exists in the shadow of historical inquiry, as this gathered momentum in the eighteenth and nineteenth centuries, it has had to recalibrate the relationship between a search for origins and pristine settings and the form of the presentation itself and what it has chosen to prioritize. We accept as a reasonable conclusion and not at odds with the canonical portrayal itself, that Joel is a late witness. Moreover, the Book of Joel gives evidence of various kinds of being indebted to other prophetic texts and of representing a particular species of prophecy in the light of this. The burden on a canonical reading – in contrast to that of an earlier history of interpretation – is to know how to evaluate certain historical conclusions (Joel is a late witness) in light of the canonical presentation. In this presentation, Joel appears as 'Book Two' in a twelve-book collection. Yet his main theme ('Day of the LORD') will show itself prominent right through to the very end.

One final brief word on a divergent order in the tradition (that is Joel appearing after Hosea–Amos–Micah). Although from the prologue to Joel, Cyril clearly refers to the Greek order (with Joel after Micah) and it has been argued that the original text of Cyril actually worked with this order[10] (modern translations of Cyril reproduce the MT order; see Hill), it is striking that he still uses the Hebrew order exegetically, as it helps confirm Joel's date as contemporaneous with his neighbours (Hosea and Amos).[11] The same exegetical effect

---

[10] Jennifer Dines, 'Verbal and Thematic Links between the Books of the Twelve in Greek and their Relevance to the Differing Manuscript Sequences', Albertz et al., *Perspectives*, 355–70.

[11] Cyril of Alexandria, *Commentary on the Twelve Prophets, Volume 1* (Robert C. Hill, trans.; The Fathers of the Church, Vol. 115; Washington, DC: The Catholic University of America Press, 2001). He writes: 'The divinely inspired Joel probably prophesied at the time when those placed before him – namely, Hosea and Amos – would also be thought to have done so. The Hebrews, in fact, decided that he should be ranked with them and not after Micah' (259). It is confusing to read this in Hill's edition, where Hill follows the standard practice of producing Cyril, not with the Greek order, but with that of the Hebrew. The confusion mounts when one reads Cyril's comments on Obadiah. He notes that Obadiah's oracle develops what Joel had said about Edom. In the Greek order,

is registered by Theodore and Theodoret, who do indeed have a Greek translation with the books in the order of the MT and also by Jerome. So if we are entitled to speak of a special 'Greek order' that circulates in Christian circles in the third to fourth centuries (or earlier), it remains the case that we have no Christian interpreter who sees any special interpretative purpose in its different arrangement of the first six books. Rather, the Hebrew order of books is preferred, because overall it seems for these interpreters to be chronologically sequential. This in turn allows assumptions to be made about the undated books Joel and Obadiah and Jonah, with reference to their dated neighbours.

Sweeney's serial efforts to portray alternative orders and their alleged exegetical significance, in Jewish and Christian circles respectively, falters for lack of any evidence whatsoever in the Christian reception history of the significance he alleges.[12] Indeed, the obverse is true – witness the Antiochenes, Jerome and Cyril. However we account for departures from the familiar Hebrew order, it is also far from clear that it represents a somehow distinctly 'Christian' (and not Jewish) conception. My own view is that the Greek variant order often reflects an instinct to match like with like in certain transmission circles, as a 'tidying-up' of the order now seen in the MT; so the more amply superscripted books (Hosea, Amos, Micah) are placed together (a similar move relates the former prophets to kindred narratives from the Writings).[13] This purely mechanical adaptation comes with no special exegetical significance and as we

---

Obadiah of course comes immediately after Joel; it is not separated by Amos. Yet the comment of Cyril does not obviously follow from this. He asks the reader to 'remember' what Joel had said at the close of his book and he in turn speaks of Obadiah, who 'in due course explains the manner and style of the destruction of Idumea' (135). This makes it sound like Amos intervenes, as indeed it does in Hill's translation.

[12] M. A. Sweeney, 'Sequence and Interpretation in the Book of the Twelve', in Nogalski, ed., *Reading and Hearing the Book of the Twelve* (Atlanta, CA: Society of Biblical Literature, 2000), 49–64.

[13] See my discussion in *Goodly Fellowship*, 92–5.

have seen, even those who may be working with the order (Cyril) nevertheless prefer the Hebrew one when it comes to interpretative potential. Dines' comment on modern theories of an early collection of books (serving as a precursor for the Twelve) standing close to the Greek order, as this will emerge later in the third century, is misleading. Rather, those who hold this view, also believe it goes significantly back in the redactional history of the XII and serves only as a torso on which to accommodate the additions of Joel, Obadiah and Jonah – in the order to be preserved in the MT (and much earlier at Qumran, in Greek and in Hebrew).[14] No one argues for a redactional development that moves from this precursor idea to the Greek order and indeed many are forthright, that the Hebrew order is where the editorial and interpretative significance is explicitly present; the Greek either does not understand this or has confused matters with its mechanical rearrangement. As we have seen, for a variety of different reasons, the earliest Christian interpretation prefers the order we now have in the MT.

---

[14] For a critique of the 'Book of the Four' precursor notion, see also C. Levin, 'Das "Vierpropheten Buch": Ein exegetischer Nachruf', *ZAW* 123 (2011): 221–35. See also the insightful essay of R. van Leeuwen. He gives evidence of a comprehensive wisdom redaction, which only functions properly in the Hebrew order and is disrupted in the subsequent Greek rearrangement ('Scribal Wisdom and Theodicy in the Book of the Twelve', in *In Search of Wisdom: Essays in Memory of John G. Gammie* [eds Leo G. Perdue, Bernard Brandon Scott, William Johnston Wiseman; Louisville, MY: Westminster John Knox, 1993], 31–49). '… this theological observation [concerning "who knows?" the ways of YHWH] is buttressed by a brilliant wordplay connecting not only Hosea to Joel and Jonah, but all three to the doxological ending of Micah. The pun has to do with "Who/ever" and "know" (*my…yd*') in each of the first three passages (Hos. 14.10; Joel 2.14; Jon. 3.9). The Micah doxology, like the other three, begins with "who" (*my*). But, as noted by many commentators, the opening of the Micah passage is already a pun on the prophet's name, "Micah", a theophoric name referring to the incomparability of YHWH ("YH/WH") … The Micah doxology ends the collection of the first six books of the Twelve with a description of the one whose name the wise have learned to know through God's ways revealed by the prophets' (38–9). This is an important insight on the editorial and theological structure of the Hosea–Micah order and one which will inform reading of Joel in the commentary.

3

Joel and Prior Prophecy

In the earlier history of interpretation (because the books are being read serially), it had long been noted that Amos begins and ends (Amos 1.2 and 9.13) with language that appears in Joel, the prophet who precedes him (Joel 3.16; 3.18). In the first attempts in the nineteenth century to recast the order of the manuscript tradition in terms of chronology, this residue of the earlier history of interpretation remained. The prophet Amos drew upon his predecessor Joel. Calvin actually held the view, that because Amos had refuted the charge that he was a prophet by profession, in his riposte to Amaziah (Amos 7.14-15), he wanted to assure his readers that his authority was sound all the same. He did this by quoting Joel. So Joel was the earliest of the prophets.[1]

Further, because Jonah's date could be secured straightforwardly by recourse to 2 Kings 14 (this too was a residue of the previous history of interpretation), he is therefore to be placed before Amos. By the time of de Wette, it had started to become customary to

---

[1] See the account of the emergence of the earliest critical theories in *Prophecy and Hermeneutics* (75–85). 'In the mid-nineteenth century Ewald was confident that the third prophetic book, Joel, was actually earlier than Amos or Hosea, while in our own day Joel is regarded as the last prophet or a competitor for that position with Jonah' (82). See also C. Seitz 'Prophecy in the Nineteenth Century Reception', in *Hebrew Bible/Old Testament:The History of Its Interpretation* (ed., M. Saebø; Vol. III.1; Göttingen: Vandenhoeck & Ruprecht, 2013), 556–81.

place Amos before Hosea in chronological re-castings (the former is briefer and Hosea seemed to have a longer career according to his superscription). So we find the curious order – soon to disappear – of Joel–Jonah–Amos–Hosea. The first two books in this original concept, will in time be counted as among the last.

Leaving Jonah aside for the moment, one strong argument in favour of Joel's late date was its abundance of cross-reference, not limited to the Amos links noted that came at the end of Joel and immediately resurfaced in Amos ('the Lord roars from Zion') and also at its end ('the mountains will drip with sweet wine'). In the context of this introduction, we can therefore content ourselves with the main picture.[2]

1 Joel 1.15 and Isaiah 13.6 are virtual parallels.
2 An obvious (ironic) cross-reference exists at Joel 4.10 and Micah 4.3.
3 Joel's day of darkness, gloom, clouds, thick darkness and blackness (2.2) resembles Zephaniah's day of (wrath, distress, anguish, trouble, ruin), darkness, gloom, clouds and blackness (1.15). Even though Zephaniah's is more fulsome in description, Joel glosses the Day he describes: 'whose like has never been from old, nor will be again after them in ages to come' (2.2).
4 Joel's characterization of God (itself based upon Exodus 34.6-7) finds its counterpart in Jonah 4.2 (and in various reflexes, in Hosea, Micah and Nahum).
5 The mocking question of the enemy in Micah 7.10 ('Where is your God?') appears as well in Joel 2.17.
6 Both Joel 3.5 and Obadiah 17 promise that 'on Mount Zion there will be a rescue' – Joel's version appears to register it as a quote ('as the LORD has said').

---

[2] A helpful table is provided by J. Crenshaw in his Anchor Bible volume. He notes twenty-two occasions where Joel 'frequently "cites" predecessors' (27), allowing as well that in 'some instances he probably draws on phrases at vogue at the time' (*Joel* [Anchor Bible]; New York: Doubleday, 1995).

7 The mixture of locust (*yeleq*), fire, grasshopper (*'arbeh*) in relation to a foreign enemy amassing (Assyria) we also find in a prominent position in Amos (1.4-12).
8 Joel 4.16 clearly serves to anticipate Amos 1.2 (though with a different effect there!).
9 The promise of Joel 4.18 also provides the backdrop for the lavish (and truly needed) final promises of Amos 9.13.

The point here, furthermore, is not to identify an idiosyncrasy characteristic of a single book (Joel) but rather to point to a pattern of mutual influence in the Book of the Twelve for which Joel is a prominent culminating exemplar. Obadiah's oracle against Edom (1.1-21) clearly picks up from the ending of Amos, where the promises regarding David's fallen booth are made in relationship to Edom's judgement (9.12). Yet Joel 4.19 even more clearly anticipates Obadiah's proclamation and in so doing seconds (or 'firsts') Amos 9.11-12.

Moreover, to focus on verbal linkages is useful up to a point, so as to give a general picture of what we might now identify as a new form of prophetic activity, presupposing as it does a textual base with potential for elaboration and extension ('scribal prophecy'). But the actual reality is broader than this. Because 'Day of the LORD' language and depiction is both central to Joel and because it exists elsewhere (Isaiah, Jeremiah, Zephaniah, Amos and Nahum), we can easily conceive of Joel as utilizing this depiction and bringing it into proper, final focus – for the purpose of his own individual witness and also for that witness within the Book of the Twelve as a whole. A good example of that, can be found in the admixture of drought imagery for the Day of the LORD (in 1.10-12 and probably 2.17-18) in connection with locusts (1.4), both described in conjunction with fire (1.19 and 2.3) and the metaphor of enemy assault (1.6ff. and 2.4ff.).

The combination of locusts, fire, fruit-become-judgment, darkness, the LORD at the altar in judgement – this is what the visions of Amos show us (7.1-9.4). Joel 'sees' – or is confronted by – all of this as well, including an altar where intercession, following repentance and a turning to the LORD (2.12-17), calls forth the compassionate and forgiving YHWH, as once of old following Moses' intercession (Exod. 33.12-23). Hosea concludes and opens onto Joel with something of the same basic framework (14.1-8). Joel is, arguably, that 'wise one' who penetrates into and through the Day to see the very 'ways of YHWH' (Hos. 14.9). As van Leeuwen has so clearly shown, these ways are the very disclosure of YHWH himself in judgement and in mercy.[3] There is more on this in the commentary to follow. The point here is that the Day of the LORD corresponds to YHWH's disclosure of himself in judgement and mercy and that extremely thick theological confession, unsurprisingly, links Joel to a wide range of kindred testimony.

Jeremias has sought, in a series of insightful reflections, to give more definition to Joel along these lines and in association with the Book of the Twelve as a whole.[4] He has further done so in the context of reflecting on the changing character of prophecy in Israel. He assumes, as do most interpreters, that Joel is a later witness *vis-à-vis* prophecy as a total phenomenon. Unlike earlier readings of Joel along this line that sought to locate Joel primarily in a history-of-religions or sociological frame of reference, he has instead allowed the associative character of Joel *vis-à-vis* other prophecy to receive the fullest attention. He notes that the role of the call narrative as validating the prophet and indicating his divine authority, so prominent in earlier prophecy (Amos, Hosea, Jeremiah, Isaiah, Ezekiel; probably intimated in Micah 7; Habakkuk), is not in

---

[3] See the essay of R. van Leeuwen in note 14 of Chapter 2.
[4] Detailed engagement with the work of Jeremias is undertaken in the commentary proper. Reference to two of his contributions is found in notes 7 and 10 of Chapter 1.

evidence in Joel (or Obadiah; see also, 'Second Isaiah'). One can also see evidence, it could be conjectured, that in places like Joel 3.5 the prophet is indicating his recourse to prior prophecy ('as the LORD has said'). This comes alongside the already noted feature of Joel as deeply indebted to other prophetic texts. Joel's prophetic vocation, in other words, is tied up with his association with prophecy as it exists (in stable textual form) and *as it continues to press for fulfilment*. I have argued for a similar conception in relation to Isaiah 40–66.[5] The divine council of Isaiah's call (Isa. 6) is the resource grounding further inspiration. This consists in hearing and seeing beyond the 'how long' of judgement (6.8), based upon sealed words of Isaiah now being opened for an Israel with unstopped ears, eyes able to see and hearts able at last, by God's mercy, to turn and be healed. I would argue that the hermeneutical and historical realities tied up with Joel are very close to this elaborate Isaiah enlargement, its rationale and larger theological purpose.[6]

---

[5] 'The Divine Council: Temporal Transition and New Prophecy in the Book of Isaiah', *Journal of Biblical Literature* 109 (1990): 229–47; 'How is the Prophet Isaiah Present in the Latter Half of the Book? The Logic of Isaiah 40–55 within the Book of Isaiah', *Journal of Biblical Literature* 115 (1996): 219–40.

[6] The Book of Zechariah operates in this same spirit. The testimony of the prophet emerges with reference to the long history of 'former prophets' whose words are still active and pressing for fulfilment (1.1-6 and 7.1-14).

4

The Unity of the Book of Joel and Modern Research

In the 1992 dictionary summary of Theodore Hiebert it is still possible to open a treatment of Joel with these words: 'Underlying all aspects of the study of Joel is the fundamental issue of the book's unity.'[1] Hiebert speaks uncontroversially here and the 1979 Introduction chapter from B. S. Childs would also bear his judgement out.[2] 'Literary Integrity' is the first main topic to be treated in Childs' summary of prior research. While Joel – prophet and book – were regarded as a single coherent presentation until the late nineteenth century, two distinct parts were soon to be firmly distinguished and the latter's authenticity and relationship to the former questioned.[3] Duhm put the theory in its classic form. Chapters 1 and 2 spoke of a locust plague (Eng., 1.1–2.27).[4] The final chapters came from a Maccabean author, who shifted the past focus to an eschatological one dealing with the nations and Israel's vindication (in English versions, 2.28–4.21). This same author was also an editor of the first

---

[1] 'Joel, Book of', III.873.
[2] *Introduction to the Old Testament as Scripture* (Philadelphia, PA: Fortress, 1979), 386–7.
[3] Usually cited as the progenitor of this division in Joel (Chapters 1–2 and 3–4 in the MT) is M. Vernes, *Le peuple d'Israël et ses espérances relatives à son avenir depuis les origens jusqu'à l'époque persane (V siècle avant J. C)* (Paris: Sandoz et Fischbacher, 1872). Earlier interpreters did not hold to a single view of Joel's historical location (Ibn Ezra was sceptical we could know; Rashi preferred the time of Manasseh, making Joel a contemporary of Nahum and Habakkuk).
[4] The Greek versions have only three chapters in their versification system and English translations typically reproduce this. The section 3.1-5 in the MT, thus becomes 2.28-32, as a result. Chapter 3 of the MT folds into English Chapter 2, leaving its 4.1-21 to become 3.1-21 in English printed Bibles.

part, introducing interpolations in 1.15, 2:1b.2a.10a.11b.[5] Similar views were promoted with slight modifications only by G. A. Smith (Expositor's Bible), T. H. Robinson (HAT), Bewer (ICC) and others.[6] In the modern period, Plöger and Smend have maintained this basic stance, though the former speaks of three parts (MT: 1.1–2.27; 3.1-5; 4.1-21).[7] Part Three is a supplement to a post-exilic Part One and Part Two corrects the overall picture by restricting the salvation to a portion of Israel only. More complicated theories of Joel's development are available as well, including those of Bergler and Wöhrle.[8]

Two of the more prominent examples of those defending unity – a position that is by no means a minority one in scholarship – are to be found in the 1948 study of A. S. Kapelrud and in the *Hermeneia* commentary of Hans Walter Wolff.[9] Kapelrud posited a specific setting for the book, which allowed him to argue for a single unified purpose. Joel is a liturgy designed for a repentance ritual to be conducted in the temple. It opens with a psalm of lamentation (1.2–2.18), comprised of communal lament (1.2-12), call to repentance (1.13-20), description of distress (2.1-11) and a further

---

[5] B. Duhm, 'Anmerkungen zu den Zwölf Propheten', *ZAW* 31 (1911): 1–43; 81–110; 161–204. Also, *Israel's Propheten* (Tübingen, 1916). Rothstein's translation and annotations of S. R. Driver also presented the notion of two main parts of Joel (*Einleitung in die Literatur des Alten Testaments* [Berlin: Reuther, 1896], 333–4).

[6] See Bibliography.

[7] Otto Plöger, *Theocracy and Eschatology* (S. Rudman, trans.; Richmond, VA: John Knox Press, 1968).

[8] S. Bergler, *Joel als Schriftinterpret* (BEATAJ 16; Frankfurt/Bern/New York/Paris: Verlag Peter Lang, 1988); Jakob Wöhrle, *Die frühen Sammlungen des Zwölfprophetenbuches* (BZAW 360; Berlin: Walter de Gruyter, 2006); *Der Abschluss des Zwölfprophetenbuches* (BZAW 389; Berlin: Walter de Gruyter, 2008); 'Joel and the Formation of the Book of the Twelve', BTB 40 (2010): 127–37. Wöhrle concludes his essay in BTB with this sentence, 'It is thus reasonable to suppose that the Book of Hosea was part of the exilic Book of the Four, that it was replaced by the primary layer of the Book of Joel when the Joel-Corpus was edited, and that it was reintegrated into the Book of the Twelve not until a very late stage' (134). It is hard to know whether this speculation is 'reasonable' or not, but it certainly shows a very difficult theory at work to account for the Book of the Twelve's redaction history. The key diachronic piece of the theory is displaced by the final form in major ways.

[9] *Joel Studies* (Uppsala: A. B. Lundequistska Bokhandeln; Leipzig: Otto Harrassowitz, 1948); *Joel and Amos: A Commentary on the Books of Joel and Amos* (Hermeneia; Philadelphia, PA, 1997); original, *Dodekapropheten 2 Joel und Amos* (BKAT XIV, 2, 1975).

call to repentance (2.12-18). This is followed by a concluding of the liturgy in the form of divine response, in three sections (MT: 2.19-27; 3.1-5; 4.1-21). Wolff sees instead of a social setting (liturgy) a literary symmetry linking the sections (that are similar to those of Kapelrud):

1 Lament (1.1-20)
2 Announcement of Judgement (2.1-11)
3 Call to Repentance (2.12-17).

Find their balancing counterpart in the second half of Joel:

1 Economic restoration (2.21-27)
2 Promise of the Spirit (3.1-5)
3 Jerusalem's salvation (4.1-4, 9-17).

In both Kapelrud's and Wolff's analyses, the unit at 2.17-20 becomes a central focus of the book linking both main sections. The recent monograph of Schwesig maintains this basic conceptual stance, while also relating Joel to the Day of the LORD material in the Book of the Twelve as a whole.[10]

Following the lead of Wolff, Jeremias has emerged as a strong defender of Joel's unity but now also in the service of reading Joel as a crucial unified witness within the Book of the Twelve. We will have more to say about his approach below, but a fine summary of his position is available in the 1988 TRE entry on Joel.[11] Closely tracking his conception is also the recent work of Schwesig. He sets the two major parts of Joel into a panel with the first constituting the Prophetic Speech proper (1.2–2.17) and its corresponding 'God's Response' (2.18–4.17). Like Jeremias, he is also keen to show Joel's dependence on 'Day of the LORD' language elsewhere and how Joel's presentation consequently affects how we read the books that follow.

---

[10] Paul-Gerhard Schwesig, *Die Rolle der Tag-JHWHs-Dichtungen im Dodekapropheten* (BZAW 366; Berlin: Walter de Gruyter, 2006).
[11] *Joel/Joelbuch* in *TRE* XVII (1988): 91–7.

So it is that the main feature which now affects the analysis of Joel's coherence as a single literary work is its association with the Book of the Twelve and redactional analyses of it and of Joel undertaken at the same time. Yet the work has not resolved the question of literary unity. Some believe the wider Twelve context supports the view of a complicated development of the Book of Joel as such. We noted above the tendency of this kind of approach to absorb Joel as a single literary work into a reconstruction of the Twelve as a single (and extremely complicated) total project. But for others, Joel remains a unified and coherent work whose relationship to the movement of the Twelve as a whole can only be understood when Joel is allowed to retain its literary integrity and coherence. Indeed, many of the earlier efforts to divide the book into constituent parts gathered their momentum in the context of a natural assumption that Joel was composed of a core of historical/authentic oracles, which had in turn been re-actualized and modified by an eschatalogizing editor from a later time. Once Joel is seen as a single unified project of a later period, the distance between earlier and later levels of tradition and redaction collapses and the depth of distinctions between original core and secondary levels vanishes and loses something of its critical purchase. Wöhrle, for example, is forced to ascribe some texts to a 'drought level' and others to a 'locust level' in his search for linear associations in the Book of the Twelve, without clarifying just how or why this very complicated – indeed rather tedious – textual amalgamation was to be sought via redaction in Joel in the first place.[12] The

---

[12] This also means he must find a way to reproduce a new 'early Joel' level. This 'primary level' introduces the books with which it is allied (Amos, Micah, Zephaniah). Moreover, in relation to these works it forced Hosea to be displaced from its erstwhile initial position. Apart from the extremely tentative basis for such a prehistory, what disappears as well is the clear relationship Joel does indeed have with Hosea (as per above). On this, following the lead of Schart and Jeremias, see especially now Schwesig (*Rolle*, 122). Compare as well the observations of Ronald L. Troxel, 'The Problem of Time in Joel', *JBL* 132 (2013): 77–95. Regarding Wöhrle's analysis of Joel 2.1-11, he notes, 'The assumption that we can confidently dissect a text that was created by reuse of earlier materials into successive layers is tenuous' (80, n. 9).

sociological framework that animated the conception of someone like Duhm and helped him comprehend a text's movement out of an original realm of significance and a later one of transformation, with accompanying theological meaning, has given way to abstract 'drought' and 'locust' distinctions, themselves en route to yet further 'Foreign-Nations-Layer' I and II; and 'Salvation' and 'Grace' layers of final redactional supplementation. The Book of Joel as a coherently unfolding individual work vanishes into the reconstruction's complexities.[13]

By contrast, Schart, Jeremias, Schwesig and others have allowed a later, coherently unified Book of Joel to emerge. Elements of its portrayal (the combination of features of drought, locust, fire and the military metaphor they bespeak) are indebted to and anticipate other portrayals. By seeing Joel both as a late composition and one composed in relationship to the texts that likewise take up the theme of the Day of the LORD, other explanations emerge that dampen down the need to see any potential literary difference or distinction as the grounds for positing discrete redactional layers.

We can state our view of the canonical shape of Joel in summary now. *The two parts of the book meaningfully intend to transition from a situation of natural disaster and the judgement it bespeaks in the present, toward an overcoming of that by means of repentance (2.12- 17). This presentation is intended to be normative for Israel as such, in times of coming hardship and trial and also for how she understands the final denouement of God's dealing with her vis-à-vis the nations as agents of his will.* What Joel says on this score represents the wisdom called for by Hosea's final plea (14.9), as a penetration into the ways of

---

[13] See the perceptive exchange of Schart with Wöhrle in the case of the Book of Jonah (in Albertz, ed., *Perspectives*), where he writes, '... as soon as one recognizes the satirical mood of the book of Jonah, no convincing arguments that would justify the hypothesis of two distinct literary layers remains' ('The Jonah-Narratives within the Book of the Twelve', 115). The balance between the single book and the Twelve must be carefully attended to, lest the former becomes only the occasion for a redactional evaluation of the latter.

God with his people.[14] To the degree to which this refers to a specific instance of God's judgement (in locust plague or in national assault) it is also a Day of the LORD in the widest possible sense: the means by which God makes himself known in mercy and in forbearing judgement at all times with his people.

The liturgical theory of Kapelrud may have been wrong in its details but it certainly captured the aspect of Joel that means to serve a wider purpose than any single moment in time can comprehend. This 'liturgical time' covered by the language of 'day' requires further exploration and evaluation than is proper within a section primarily dealing with the modern inquiry into the structure and unity of the Book of Joel. I will deal with this in the commentary proper and in a brief theological reflection at the close of the Introduction.

---

[14] Seitz, *Prophecy and Hermeneutics*, 126. 'And what Joel commends of these ways in his own day includes not only an audience for us to look back on, though it does that admirably. This is precisely the intention of the book in its own canonical form, as demonstrated in an introduction that picks up where Hosea left off: "Tell your children of it, and let your children tell their children, and their children another generation" (Joel 1.3). Here in unmistakable form, accentuated by the juxtaposition of Joel with Hosea in the canonical form of the Twelve, is the dynamic character of the prophetic word sought by von Rad, by another means and so passed over by him in the form the canon delivered it' (126).

5

Intertextuality: Joel's Character as Prophet

Joel joins Obadiah, Jonah, Habakkuk and Nahum as those five books without specific historical designations supplied in their superscriptions. The specific Assyrian focus of Nahum could yield the natural conclusion that the prophet speaks of the pending destruction of the Assyrian capital, Nineveh, around the time of its specific historical accomplishment. Critical in this regard, however, are its opening verses, where an obvious play on the compassionate formula of Exodus 34.7-8 appears (Nah. 1.2-3) – a feature it also shares with the above-mentioned Joel (2.13) and Jonah (4.2) and in less clear (though unmistakable) form in Hosea 1 and Micah 7.[1] How one properly evaluates this dimension requires its own special treatment below, as it is critical for an interpretation of Joel as such and in association with these other witnesses.

Habakkuk's tableau of divine judgement fits congenially in the period of the transition from Assyrian to Babylonian ascendancy in the Levant and even allowing for possible further supplementation, the book situates itself uncomplicatedly in this general time. Jonah is a special case and can be put to the side in the context of this evaluation. What can be said here, is that one must account for the reversal

---

[1] A particularly insightful exploration of the compassion formula in the opening six books of the Twelve (MT) and the theological significance of this in the light of Hos. 14.9, can be found in Raymond van Leeuwen (see note 14 of Chapter 2). See also T. Dozeman, 'Inner-Biblical Interpretation of Yahweh's Gracious and Compassionate Character', *JBL* 108 (1989): 207–23.

of God's relenting *vis-à-vis* Nineveh, such as we see this in the final verdict of Nahum. But the main issue is whether Jonah reads as an ironic *Auseindersetzung* presupposing Joel (does it object to Joel's *theologoumenon* that repentance is a bona fide way to effect God's forgiveness, on the grounds of it being too predictable and theologically objectionable an account of God's ways?);[2] or whether Joel presupposes it.[3] Whatever else may be said at this juncture, given that they are both likely late witnesses, the issue is close-run and it is likely that their historical composition and mutual influencing emerges from a similar period of time, as the Book of the Twelve achieves its final total effect. We prefer to speak of Jonah and Joel as *together* mapping out the space within which reflections on God's character *vis-à-vis* Israel and *vis-à-vis* the nations is being mutually and intentionally explored, on the basis of the revelation of that character to Moses at Mt Sinai.

Both a) the respective dating of three of these works (Joel, Obadiah, Jonah) and b) their relationship to one another, are not straightforward

---

[2] See Alan Cooper, 'In Praise of Divine Caprice: The Significance of the Book of Jonah' in *Among the Prophets: Language, Image and Structure in the Prophetic Writings* (eds Philip R. Davies, David J. A. Clines; *JSOTS* 144; Sheffield: Sheffield Academic Press, 1993). Compare as well A. Schart, 'The Jonah Narrative in the Book of the Twelve', in *Perspectives on the Formation of the Book of the Twelve* (eds Rainer Albertz, James D. Nogalski, Jakob Wöhrle; Berlin: Walter de Guyter, 2012), 109–28.

[3] See the recent discussion of Klaus Spronk, 'Jonah, Nahum and the Book of the Twelve: A Response to Jakob Wöhrle', *JHS* 9 (2009): 2–9. Spronk leans toward the view adopted here, that one must be careful to allow the integrity of the development of individual books to come into the foreground and only then make decisions about the relationship to other books (as against trying to argue for lateral redactional work, across discrete books that in turns leads erratically toward their respective final form; this leads Wöhrle to hold that Jonah has two distinct levels in its straightforward narrative line, one with a 'grace level' alongside another to be isolated literarily). Spronk holds that Jonah responds to Joel in conversation with Nahum (in respect of the key text based upon Exod. 34.6-7 they all share). For the view that Joel responds to Jonah, see H. Spieckermann, 'Barmherzig und gnädig ist der Herr ...', *ZAW* 102 (1990): 1–18. Spieckermann believes the formula is more clearly anchored in Jonah than in Joel and that formal judgement determines his conclusion. In this sense, though Spronk disagrees with him about the direction of influence, they both study the books as discrete works and reach conclusions only after that concerning the possible direction of influence. The view we hold is that in cases where the works are arguably close to one another historically, mutual and reciprocating influence may be the intentional decision regarding their association in the Twelve.

matters to determine. All are especially well-integrated works in the Twelve and all are likely later works. The former means that their composition is likely intended to respond to and exist alongside, other works in the Twelve, as integral to their individual existence. The latter means that it may represent a false trail to believe that in order to understand them we must be able to know which predates or presupposes the other; they may represent a collaborative effort to bring the growing collection of prophetic testimony into a final form. All three witnesses deal with the nations' relationship with Israel (including the special case of 'brother Edom') and this is, of course, a major theme in the Twelve as a whole. Two deal with the theme of repentance. Two speak of the 'Day of the LORD' and likely do that in relation to what has been said about the 'Day' in the prophetic witness more broadly (Hosea, Amos, Zephaniah, Jeremiah, Isaiah, Ezekiel). Their temporal proximity – now located at a later time – ironically returns us to something of the portrayal we observed in the previous history of interpretation, where they were thought of as *early* contemporaries.[4] They are prophets in association with their colleagues in the Twelve and in the Three and should be read in the light of that. They have rejoined one another in the 'goodly fellowship' of the Twelve, now on different terms of course.[5]

Jeremias has elsewhere called attention to the fact that certain characteristic features of earlier prophecy are notable for their absence in later texts. His basic point requires confirmation and

---

[4] Seitz, *Prophecy and Hermeneutics*, 78–83; 122–23; 'Reception', 564–70. Early diachronic readings saw Amos quoting Joel; Joel (and Jeremiah) quoting Obadiah; Jonah is referred to at 2 Kings 14.25.
[5] Note the opening remarks of Cyril concerning Obadiah. 'It is likely that Obadiah prophesied at the same time as Joel, and was, as it were, accorded the same vision and shared the explanation. While the divinely inspired Joel, remember, at the very end of his prophecy says, "Egypt will become a wasteland and Idumea a desolate countryside for the wrongs done to the children of Judah, in return for the innocent blood poured out in their land", the other in due course explains in detail the manner and style of the destruction of Idumea.' (135) He might have also seen the link between Amos 9.12, but his text has 'human race' (*ādām*) instead of 'Edom' (*ĕdôm*).

amplification here. The validating call narrative is missing in Joel and Obadiah, and it appears in rather ironic form in Jonah – he is called but disobeys his call, which itself becomes a major theme to be developed in the book as a whole. The absence of even the spare kind of superscription that warrants Zephaniah is not present. At the same time the density of cross-reference in later texts may suggest that these particular prophetic works operate on the basis that their vocation is to give attention to what has already been said by God to his servants, as this continues to press for fulfilment. The leitmotif is clearly present in Zechariah where the phrase 'former prophets' appears in course (1.4; 7.7 and 7.12) and where the opening chapter speaks of the overtaking word of 'my servants the prophets' (1.6), which continued to confront the generations. Striking is also the theme of repentance – now seen *as positively undertaken* – registered there (1.6).[6] Prophecy is viewed as a plural phenomenon; as a movement of some considerable conformity in perspective and reach; as having a character that can now be referred to as past, but yet alive.[7] We have already had reason to mention the Book of Isaiah as itself giving evidence of later expansion, based upon the alive and still accomplishing word of God (55.11).[8] The Psalter will grow in part by secondary expansion of core traditions attributed to David (Books One and Two) but also as organically extended to the monarchy as a totality via the agency of choral guides and other unknown agencies, which the Book of Chronicles is content to describe as its own peculiar form of prophecy.[9] Ezekiel's swallowing of a written scroll (2.8–3.4) – on which are the words lamentation,

---

[6] On the role of the former prophets and ethical conduct, see the evaluation of M. Boda, 'From Fasts to Feasts: The Literary Function of Zechariah 7–8', *CBQ* 65 (2003): 390–407.
[7] See Ronald E. Clements, 'Patterns in the Prophetic Canon', in *Canon and Authority: Essays on Old Testament Religion and Theology* (eds George W. Coats, Burke O. Long; Philadelphia, PA: Fortress, 1977), 42–55.
[8] Seitz, 'Isaiah 40–66', in *The New Interpreter's Bible* (Nashville, TN: Abingdon, 2001).
[9] David L. Petersen, *Late Israelite Prophecy: Studies in Deutero-Prophetic Literature and in Chronicles* (Missoula, MT: Scholars Press, 1977).

mourning and woe – is itself a striking adaptation of a former emphasis on the spoken word, whatever else we are to make of it.[10] The latter chapters of Zechariah, are themselves replete with cross-references to earlier texts and the night-visions of the earlier chapters, can only deliver their sense when we know where the ingredients with which they operate are originally to be found in other texts.

Prophecy then does not 'die'. It lives on in the recourse made to it and on account of the deep sense that what it says continues to speak and to address new generations, though now in a form appropriate to a much wider prophetic testimony, in developing written form.[11] Former prophets are being compared and alignments sought, due to hearing them in relation to one another.[12] Isaiah and Micah find their witness in collaboration.[13]

It has been noted, that the central theme of Joel, is the 'Day of the LORD' and, related to that, the theme of repentance. The Day of the LORD is an extremely richly attested theme in earlier prophetic texts. Within the Book of the Twelve alone, it reaches a sustained

---

[10] Does Ezekiel experience a divine 'antacid' enabling him to bear the hardship familiar to Jeremiah – a scroll of lamentation and mourning and woe – but now without the same heartburn? 'Then I ate it; and in my mouth it was as sweet as honey' (3.3). For background, see Ellen Davis, *Swallowing the Scroll: Textuality and the Dynamics of Discourse in Ezekiel's Prophecy* (Sheffield: Almond, 1989).

[11] Instead of a call narrative, later prophecy legitimates itself 'durch einen Rekurs auf schriftlich vorgeliegende ältere Prophetenworte' (Jeremias, *Gelehrte*, 99).

[12] What Jeremias describes as ingredient in the development of Hosea and Amos ('Interrelationship') has its counterpart in later prophecy's dependence on earlier prophecy, now itself associative and requiring coordination. On this phenomenon elsewhere, compare B. S. Childs, 'Psalm Titles and Midrashic Exegesis', *JSS* 16 (1971): 137–50 and C. Seitz, 'Psalm 34: Inner-Biblical Exegesis and the Longer Psalm Superscriptions – "Mistake" Making and Theological Significance', in *The Bible as Christian Scripture: The Work of Brevard S. Childs* (eds Christopher R. Seitz, Kent Harold Richards; Atlanta, GA: Society of Biblical Literature, 2013), 279–98.

[13] B. S. Childs writes, 'The present shaping of Micah's prophecy has interpreted the book by placing it within a larger context shared by the prophet Isaiah' (*Introduction*, 438). Compare C. Seitz, 'Scriptural Author and Canonical Prophet: The Theological Implications of Literary Association in the Canon', in *Biblical Method and Interpretation: Essays in Honour of John Barton* (eds K. Dell and P. Joyce; Oxford: Oxford University Press, 2013), 176–88.

crescendo in the final pre-exilic testimony (Zephaniah).[14] This is the 'former prophecy' par excellence, to use the language of Zechariah. The notion of a sustained assault from the foe from the north which reduces Judah to rubble (*Chaoskampf*) in God's cleansing judgement, is crucial for the logic of the Book of Jeremiah as a whole (its foundation is in Chapters 4–6), even though the language of 'Day' is not present.[15] Isaiah 13 is far less reticent, as the LORD assembles the nations for, 'The Day of the LORD ... like destruction from the Almighty' (13.6). Ezekiel 30 speaks of the LORD's Day in relationship to his judgement over the nations. The Day of the LORD in Amos is one that Israel could have escaped (so the 'yet you did not return to me' refrain of 4.6, 8, 9, 10, 11) but tragically refused (4.12; 5.18-20). Amos exercised a solemn vocation of intercession on behalf of God's people ('O LORD God forgive, I beg you. How can Jacob stand? He is so small'), thus twice turning back God's visions of judgement (7.1-6). But the verdict is sealed by the silencing of the very voice that spoke judgement (7.10), but also alone spoke words of intercession leading to a verdict of forgiveness (7.3; 7.6).[16] Without this, the divine judgement must have its relentless force unleashed (8.2). The divine 'way' of justice (Hos. 14.9 in relation to Exod. 34.8) God makes known to Israel as he did to a wilderness generation before.

The commentary proper will explore Joel's own Day of the LORD (DOL) presentation.[17] It is, however, important here to say more

---

[14] Most agree, including Wöhrle (who otherwise seeks to restrict the range of DOL texts available to Joel), that Zephaniah is a key text for Joel ('Joel and the Formation of the Book of the Twelve', *BTB* 40 [2010]: 127–37). Wöhrle contests the influence of Isaiah 13 on Joel, for example. See Troxel's discussion of Wöhrle and Jeremias in 'The Fate of Joel in the Redaction of the Twelve', *CBR*.

[15] On the influence of depictions of Assyrian and Babylonian (Isa. 5.26; 13.2-8; 14-16; Jer. 4–6); on Joel, see Bosshard-Nepustil, *Rezeption von Jesaia 1–39 im Zwölfprophetenbuch* (Göttingen: Vandenhoeck und Ruprecht, 1997), 297.

[16] See the illuminating essay of J. Jeremias, 'Interrelationship' (note 12 above).

[17] Jeremias is correct in understanding the use by Joel of DOL texts as wide in character and scope. So, for example, regarding Joel 2.1ff., Joel's 'description of an undefeatable, hostile enemy is full of references to former texts surpassing all of them by their combination' ('Function', 80).

about where this emphasis has come from in Joel's witness. What is clear in many of these descriptions of the DOL is the impossibility of escape. God's patience has run its course: his 'way' of mercy and forbearance has given way to and been replaced by his 'way' of righteous judgement. This has taken time. He has acted in forgiveness for the sake of his own name/way and because of the pleading of 'all my servants the prophets' (see the DtrH (Deuteronomistic History) refrain). More than any other early witness in the Twelve, Zephaniah makes clear that the Day of the LORD has now unequivocally come – however 'near' it was before – and that there will be no one who does not experience its force and fate. All creation – in whatever way the prophet means that – will experience the judgement of God Almighty (Zeph. 1.2-3). This opening coda merely serves as the starting point for an exploration of the depth, scale and range of the DOL.[18] The fate of the righteous can now only be that of waiting (3.8) for God's reversal of fortune (3.20) and for a promise made in darkness to find its own dawning in a new Day (3.11ff.). We see a similar description in Amos' Final Section (9.9-15). It will take the dawning of a new Day to reverse the effects of the Day of the LORD for Amos' generation. And only those who acknowledge the righteous judgement of God will be able to see that Day.

I have noted in the opening chapters of Jeremiah the juxtaposition of two main levels of text.[19] On the one hand unmistakable is the speech of Jeremiah to his contemporaries under and in the cloud of dark judgement: a fate Judah is to share with sister Israel, but which will be far worse for her, due to her failure to learn from it and take its lesson to heart (compare the generations in the wilderness).

---

[18] 'Zephaniah even increases [*vis-à-vis* Amos 5.18-19] this picture of death without any hope' (Jeremias, 'Function', 79). 'The wrath of God is without measure and without limit. No one can survive it' ('Function', 79).

[19] C. Seitz, 'The Place of the Reader in the Book of Jeremiah', in *Reading the Book of Jeremiah: A Search for Coherence* (ed. M. Kessler; Winona Lake, IN: Eisenbrauns, 2004), 67–75.

This also includes Jeremiah's own experiencing of the judgement he must speak forth to them: his passion in its grip; his complaint against his own commandeering by God; his cries of injustice and at time God's rebuke and God's silence; that is, the lamentations of Jeremiah (Jer. 11–20).[20] But interwoven alongside of this are the confessions of a later generation (in 2–6 and 8–15). These intercalations acknowledge the righteousness of God's past judgements. They look on the situation as described and speak words of repentance and make acts of contrition. They do not say 'evil shall not overtake or meet us' (Amos 9.10) precisely because they have chosen to walk in the ways of the LORD (Hos. 14.9).[21] They can walk at all to the degree they acknowledge the ways of God that are constituted by his judgement. And so they are given voice in the legacy that is Jeremiah's final form. Transgressors can only stumble in these 'ways' and so will perish without voice, joining the generation that died in the wilderness – in the days of Moses and in the days of the prophet Jeremiah.[22]

In this depiction we come close to the logic unfolding in Joel and in his depiction of the Day of the LORD. Jeremias has very effectively shown how in the case of DOL passages in Isaiah 13 and in Amos and Zephaniah (and we might add here Jeremiah's scenario), the key feature is the inescapability of judgement. No generation of those 'little ones' under twenty (Num. 14.29) is referred to as exempted to enter the Promised Land, as we might put it in relation

---

[20] See C. Seitz, 'The Prophet Moses and the Canonical Shape of Jeremiah', *ZAW* 101 (1989): 115.
[21] Cyril links this verse from Amos to Jeremiah as well. He writes of the referent here, 'Some of them reached such a stage of derangement, in fact, as to think that the holy prophets lied and they claimed that no predication would take effect. Jeremiah in his wisdom also confirms this in saying to God, "Lo, these people say to me, where is the word of the Lord? Bring it on"' (127).
[22] Van Leeuwen (cited in note 14 of Chapter 5). An important correlate to the deportment of sinners as Hosea 14.9 intimates this ('stumble') can also be seen in Zephaniah, 'those who say in their hearts, "the LORD will not do good, nor will he do harm"' (1.12; cf. Mal. 2.17).

to Moses' former successful intercession.[23] The wrath of God has been released.[24] This important word is central to both Zephaniah 1 and Isaiah 13 (Zeph. 1.15; Isa. 13.9). Jeremiah's foe from the north will likewise execute a thorough judgement. Like Moses before him, Jeremiah will share the fate of the people, though unlike that former generation, Joshua and Caleb will not be joined by others to enter the promised land of God's future; Baruch and Ebed-Melech alone 'escape'.[25]

I have also drawn attention to the correlation between Jeremiah and Moses in respect of the charge to the former not to intercede, in obvious contrast to Moses. The non-intercession gives rise to lamentation, including arguably that of God himself (Jer. 12.7-13). Jeremias has claimed a critical role for the 'drought liturgy' section of Jeremiah 14.1-15.4 influencing Joel's DOL depiction and this for two reasons at least. First, the language used in Jeremiah to describe the drought resembles what we find in Joel. But, in relation to our remarks above, the primary level of the text – and not the confessions from a later generation that now appear in 3.24-25; 5.18-19; 9.12-16; 9.23-24 – displays a first-person plural confession and a request for forgiveness (14.7-9) that is met by direct refusal from God and a renewed charge to Jeremiah that he not intercede.[26] All the more poignant is its repetition in 14.20-22, again followed by a second 'No'. Jeremiah receives the bitter reply: 'Though Moses and Samuel stood before me, yet my heart would not turn toward this people. Send them out of my sight' (15.1). The Book of Joel, in contrast, sees the hope expressed by the confessional supplementation of 5.18 ('But even in those days,

---

[23] Seitz, 'Prophet Moses', 9-10.
[24] See now J. Jeremias, 'The Wrath of God at Mt Sinai (Exod. 32; Deut. 9-10)', in C. Seitz, K. Richards, eds *The Bible as Christian Scripture*, 21-35.
[25] This is my argument in 'The Prophet Moses' (16-19), where Baruch and Ebed-Melech are held to be the editorially reinforced counterparts to Joshua and Caleb.
[26] Note the close proximity of Hosea's final admonition in 14.9 to the wisdom refrains of 9.12 and 9.23-24 (let the wise 'boast in this, that they know me, that I am the LORD; I act with steadfast love, justice and righteousness').

says the LORD, I will not make a full end of my people') put into full effect. Distinctive in his portrayal is the DOL in all its intensity, indeed even as without precedent (1.2) and yet, *alongside this and inside it, an enactment of intercession that leads to divine grace and rejoicing, the provision of the spirit as longed for in the days of Moses (Joel 3.1; Num. 11.29), ongoing salvation (3.5) and the full knowledge of God (4.17), even as the Day marches on to its final end.*

We will want to work through this fresh adaptation by Joel of the DOL material available to him, for at its heart is what it means for the present Book of Joel to provide the testimony that constitutes his enduring work. We can state at this point our basic agreement with Jeremias that the opening verses of Joel do not refer to a 'this' (1.2) that intends to direct us back to Hosea and refers to the audience's refusal to repent à la Hosea's final plea (Hos. 14.1ff.).[27] Nogalski has sought to read Joel in the context of Hosea to such a degree that the 'this' of 1.2 has ceased making primary sense within the book of Joel as such. It does not refer to an unprecedented assault of locusts about to be described, and in his view that is not the purpose for which the elders are assembled and addressed. Rather, they are assembled in order that they might tell future generations that 'this' has not happened in their days or in previous days – that is, the repentance called for by Hosea in the final chapter, which in turn was to have led to healing and renewed bounty (14.4-7). In consequence, he argues, Judah is enduring a plague of judgement as Hosea's Israelite audience did in their days. This is a very good example of the tendency of a specific kind of redactional approach to merge the individual witnesses so

---

[27] 'If one reads Joel in isolation [his phrase], "this" is a pronoun that can be interpreted as a proleptic reference to the devastation described in 1.4-20. If, however, one chooses to read Joel in the context of the Twelve, the antecedent can be interpreted as the extended call to repentance and its attendant promise from Hosea 14.1-8, or even the entire book of Hosea ... the open-ended call to repentance of Hosea (14.1-3) has not resulted in the fulfillment of YHWH's promise when the reader encounters the scene described in Joel 1.2-20.' (*The Book of the Twelve: Hosea-Jonah* [Smith and Helwys Bible Commentary; Macon, GA: Smith and Helwys Publishing, 2011], 217–18).

thoroughly into a field of lateral association, that they lose their ability to function as demarcated witnesses within a collection of twelve books similarly set apart. The calamities described in Joel 1 are given no grounding, he argues, because Hosea's frame of reference is assumed: no repentance has ensured, so in consequence we have judgement.[28]

Part of Nogalski's reasoning turns on the expectations an older form-critical view offered regarding oral speech, which would ask to us to understand the referent of 'this' as something not yet related by the prophet (the locust plague), but which the audience is awaiting all the same.[29] He rejects this reading on the grounds that we have in Joel a literary context in which a 'connecting function' requires a clear antecedent. It is, however, questionable if such a differentiation is really at issue here (oral versus literary), such that he finds the only conclusion possible that 'Joel 1.2 … refer(s) back to preceding material, in spite of the fact that this material appears in another book'. The most natural referent for the unprecedented 'this', is what the reader will soon learn is a massive locust plague and reflexively, this is how the vast majority of interpreters have taken it.

Yet, a more sophisticated form- and tradition-critical assessment has been offered by Jeremias, who shares the view of Nogalski all the same that one must attend to the character of Joel as distinctive from earlier prophetic texts. He notes the similarity of the opening call (1.2-3) to Exodus 10 and various psalms of recital, where what is to be reported means to effect a change on the part of those who will be addressed. The generational motif is clear in Exodus 10 as

---

[28] Nogalski summarizes his position in this way: 'The most natural reading of Joel 1.2 would therefore expect something had preceded the verse to which the "this" now refers. Hos. 14.2ff. provides the expected background for this question and indeed on two related levels – the question of repentance and of promise … By alluding back to Hos. 14.2ff., Joel 1.2ff. acknowledges that the promise has not been fulfilled, but counters [because repentance has not ensued] that the blame should be placed on the shoulders of an unrepentant people, not on YHWH' (Processes, 16–17).

[29] Wolff classifies Joel 1.2-4 as a *Lehreröffnungsruf* (BK, 22).

well as the character of what is being reported as unprecedented; this makes it a particularly rich intertextual clue.[30] By attending carefully to the literary context – a concern he shares with Nogalski – he notes a further feature that takes us beyond the following locust plague alone and which comports with his view as to the intention of the opening exhortation. The elders (pre-) assembled and addressed here are re-convened in the 'solemn assembly' of 2.15. What is the purpose of this second assembly? It is to witness the saving act of God as described in 2.18 and the consequences that devolve from that (2.19-27). As in Exodus 10.2 we have the same goal in view: 'Then you shall know that I am in the midst of Israel, and that I, the LORD, am your God and no other.'[31] On this reading, then, the double 'this' (*zō't*) of 1.2 is the unprecedented 'plaguing' that follows (not of Pharaoh and the Egyptians but) of God's own people Israel, *but also* (and again in starkest contrast to the days of Pharaoh, as well as the days of Jeremiah) the salvation that Israel experiences from within the vortex of this judgement, due to the intercession of the priests and God's acting for the sake of his name so that he might thereby be known in his 'ways' (2.27 following Hos. 14.9 and Jer. 9.24). The boast of Israel, as Jeremiah puts it (9.23-24), is this species of wisdom. 'This' is what elders are given to speak forth to all generations.

To understand the specific witness that is Joel is to attend to how previous prophetic material is being handled by him, bringing its force into play for a new composition and a new purpose, thereby raising up a new generation in its salvific wake.

---

[30] '... that you may tell your children and grandchildren how I made a fool of the Egyptians ... so that you may know that I am the LORD' (10.2). And regarding the effect of the plagues, 'something that neither your parents nor your grandparents have seen, from the day they came on earth to this day' (10.6).

[31] The distinctive phraseology belongs to the special contribution of Joel *vis-à-vis* Exodus and is the subject of the commentary evaluation proper.

6

Who is Joel?

Up to this point 'who Joel is' has been explored by endeavouring to describe what the Book of Joel is and how it is distinctive: in its own integrity, in relation to prior prophecy and *vis-à-vis* the larger Book of the Twelve. This is not a counsel of despair. The book itself says no more about Joel than that he is the 'son of Pethuel' and beyond that admits of no date or specific historical setting whatsoever. And what is *not said* belongs to the book's distinctive communication in that form.[1] The prophet Joel is his written testimony.

We have noted the absence of a call narrative. Missing as well is the usual, 'Thus says the LORD', that characterizes Israel's historical prophets and serves to suggest a live phenomenon in which a people is addressed by the speech of an individual called to that purpose ('Hear the word of the LORD, O people of Israel' as Hosea classically puts it: 4.1).[2] When we compare the equally invisible character of a prophet like Nahum, all the more striking is the wholesale absence of the use of a messenger formula in Joel.[3] Indeed, the two occasions where we find a kindred expression in Joel (3.5 and 4.8), striking is the perfective tense (*qatal*) formulation (*kaʾăšer ʾāmar YHWH*; *kî*

---

[1] Rendtorff has emphasized that the decision to provide superscriptions for prophetic books (a secondary, editorial move) means equally that *not* providing superscriptions is an intentional editorial decision as well ('Theological Unity', 76–7; and see quotation at note 9, Chapter 2).
[2] This is the ground presupposition of early form-criticism in respect of the prophets.
[3] See Nah. 1.12, 2.13, 3.5.

YHWH *dibbēr*). Because 3.5 finds a clear correspondence at Obadiah 17 it approximates a quotation; 4.8 can equally be taken to refer to a former promise.[4] The use of *nĕ'ūm YHWH* at 2.12 makes it all the more significant as an isolated occurrence, consistent with the critical role 2.12-14 plays in the drama of the book as a whole. The fact that here the compassionate formula is being registered (in its unique Joel dress) does not allow us to place even this example in the lone tally of Joel as a traditional prophetic voice, *viva voce*.

The direct address of 1.2-3 (less so its reflex at 2.15-16), it is also to be noted, consists of something that the prophet means for *others* to report subsequently (elders, inhabitants of the land) and not himself, in a way we can witness that in the texts that follow. In Joel, the narrative voice generally gives instructions about what is to transpire ('wake up'; 'lament'; 'be dismayed'; 'put on'; 'sanctify'; 'blow the trumpet'; 'return') and reports what he is given to see (1.4; 1.17-18; 2.3-11). The divine response he brokers in 2.18 is a third-person record in which divine speech arises as a response (2.19-27). This gives the Book of Joel the feel of something privately – if dramatically and coherently intended – composed. By its general descriptions it avoids being tied down to any specific historical context or discrete sociological setting. Elders, inhabitants, priests, ministers, congregation, aged, children, bridegroom – these are the characters inhabiting Joel's world of description. Are the locusts metaphors for nations or nations metaphors for locusts?[5] *When* is all this happening? This depiction characteristic of Joel is sustained without much relief, the single exception being a text many regard as supplemental (4.4-8). Here suddenly the contours of prophecy as we see it elsewhere, in more or less historically specific dress, appears – though for all that, the verses are obscure.

---

[4] 4.4-8 will require special evaluation in any event, as it appears to depart from the style of Joel we are endeavouring to characterize here.

[5] We discuss this important interpretive question in detail below. See the fine essay of Josef Lossl, 'When is a Locust Just a Locust? Patristic Exegesis of Joel 1.4 in the Light of Ancient Literary Theory', *JTS* 55 (2004): 575–99.

We will also have occasion to note that the temporal perspective of Joel is challenging.[6] Some things are reported as though they have transpired and are being presently experienced. Joel reports a locust plague that has happened and its present effects. This present reality opens onto a description that stretches into the future as Chapter 2 opens. Joel then reports a charge to the priests in the present and an action of God in response, that describes God's already accomplishment. Calvin struggles to make sense of this section of Joel. He wants the repentance and divine response to be future-oriented (see modern translations as well) in spite of the verbs in Hebrew. But as he moves to the divine promises themselves, he envisions them as something akin to 'prophetic perfect': God has already determined to do what he here says. It is a factual reality, even as it will presumably take place when the people repent (in the future). In the second main section of the book, the time frame shifts perceptibly to the future, or to a second phase of divine action after what has so far been described.

In our view this temporal ambitiousness is crucial for how Joel is meant to function as prophetic address, distinguishing Joel from what we see in his neighbours Hosea and Amos. The characters in Joel's narrative world of address, are intentionally presented without specific historical and temporal setting, not because we cannot imagine such a thing, but precisely so that the text can move from a realistic encounter in time, *through time*. This is the prophet Joel's vocational accomplishment. His anonymity serves the book's inherent, intentional purpose. It is *his book* that prophesies. The opening exhortation to tell future generations is a fact we can easily enough relate to Israel's own time, but it also points to the Book of Joel's reception history in that time. The generations to be told are

---

[6] See especially Ronald Troxel's insightful essay, 'The Problem of Time in the Book of Joel', *JBL* 132 (2013): 77–95.

in the nature of the text's purpose and intended after-life *our own as well*. Rather than asking us to recognize the bridging function of texts like Isaiah's or Jeremiah's secondary supplementation (eyes being later opened; confession being later given), as we can comprehend that in earlier prophecy, in Joel there is no original text and original audience to be first determined and then alongside that secondary bridging. It is one and the same thing being accomplished at the same rhetorical time, as what it means for the Book of Joel to function as prophecy as such. In other prophetic works, we can imagine an original act of performance and plausibly identify alongside that an act of hermeneutical extension in literary form (in Jer. 1–20). In Joel the 'original performance' and the subsequent rehearsal are on the same plane and so cannot be distinguished in the same way.

One further important implication requires to be noted in passing. When one reckons with the extraordinarily widespread and sustained use of Joel in Christian reception-history, as the appointed text for Ash Wednesday's threshold on Lent, this ought not be conceived of in the realm of 'legitimate transfer' or even 'suitable application', however much that may be true. Rather, it corresponds with Joel's deep and integral purpose as such and matches seamlessly the horizon it was composed to seek. To use the language of David Yeago from a related context of reflection, this later use conforms to the actual 'judgment' the Book of Joel renders.[7] We conclude the Introduction below with an extended example of what we mean. Our main point ought to be clear. The rich reception history of Joel properly and directly grasped its own deep internal logic. Joel reaches out for the audience as inherent to its first and final purpose, and it does this through its brilliant modification of earlier prophetic discourse, suitable for its time and for its location and purpose within the Book of the Twelve.

---

[7] David Yeago, 'The New Testament and Nicene Dogma: A Contribution to the Recovery of Theological Exegesis', *ProEccl* 3 (1994): 152–64.

7

The Message and Purpose of the Book of Joel

This chapter is purposefully titled because the message and the purpose of the four-chapter work of Joel are very closely connected. As we are here arguing, the hermeneutical purpose of the Book of Joel stands in the forefront of any view regarding its origins and 'original' message. Joel never existed without an explicit hermeneutical purpose and that purpose belongs to its own delimited character as one book among the Twelve, but also in relationship to these other witnesses. Critical in this regard is the Book of Hosea and especially the character of its final chapter.

The book of Hosea ends on a note of irresolution. God is passionately devoted to a wayward people and the opening illustration of the prophet and Gomer, serves the purpose of introducing that main theme of the book as a whole. Clear expression is given to this theme in Chapter 11's cry from God, 'How can I give you up, Ephraim, How can I hand you over, Israel?' (11.8). God is torn. He cannot but love Israel to the end, but his wrath is kindled and Israel's destruction is in view (11.9; 13.7-11; 15-16). The movement between these two poles marks the tenor of the latter chapters (11–13).[1] The final chapter, then, beseeches a people he loves to 'return to the LORD your God'

---

[1] Speaking of 11.8-9a, Jeremias writes, 'Was in V.8-9a als dramatischer Kampf zweier auflodernder Kräfte in Gott beschrieben wird, ist für Hosea jedoch kein einmaliges Kampfgeschehen mit unsicherem Ausgang, sondern zutiefst in Gottes eigenem Wesen begründet' (*Der Prophet Hosea*; ATD 24/1 [Göttingen: Vandenhoeck & Ruprecht, 1983], 146).

(14.1). Here, the prophet uses the familiar word for repent (šûb) which typically entails a turning *away* from sin, and instead twice speaks of it as a turning *toward* God himself (šûbâ *'ad YHWH;* šûbû *'el YHWH*).² In first-person address God promises in the light of this to heal his people (14.4-7). The bounty of God's blessing will then return. But the book closes with no taking up of this poignant plea from God. Hosea ends with this cry to Israel unfulfilled.³ It offers instead a prescription, in this form.

> Take words with you and return to the LORD, and say to him:
> 'Take away all guilt; accept that which is good [viz., these very words]
> and we will offer the fruit of our lips.
> Assyria shall not save us; we will not ride on horses;
> We will no more say 'Our God' to the work of our hands.
> In you the orphan finds mercy.'

Hosea gives a prescription to the sick Israel. If followed, it will bring about the healing and salvation that God, in his compassionate character, stands ready to extend.

The final verse of the book, then, addresses the reader and speaks of a wisdom that is able to understand these things. The upright walk *in the ways of God*. Given the manner in which this theme is developed in the Book of the Twelve and elsewhere, these 'ways' are not ethical alternatives primarily, but rather bespeak a deportment of the wise in respect of God's revealed 'ways' – as the book of Exodus sets these forth.⁴ The 'ways' of God are what Moses asks to see within the context of his intercession and Israel's grave sin (33.13): so grave that God threatens to send a surrogate and to work with a fresh people. His glory betokens his ways and they cannot be looked on directly (33.17-23). Rather, one is brought into proper relation to them by

---

² Compare Joel 2.12 and 2.13. See also Hos. 12.7.
³ Jeremias, ATD, 169-70.
⁴ See again (note 14 of Chapter 5) the essay of R. van Leeuwen on this theme and its development in the first six books of the Twelve.

means of God's own sovereign address in his name. God's personal proclaiming of the name (34.6) is itself a penetration into God's very heart and character, as the compassionate/justice character of God is brought into full focus and proper balance (34.6-7). The response this kindles is worship (34.8).

The wise reader understands that the turning to God in the fullness of his 'ways' is the means whereby one may 'walk' with him and thereby find the invitation extended in Hosea fulfilled in fact. Hosea says what is to be done. Words of confession are to be taken up. The request is for the removal of iniquity. The true offering is the confession of the lips. 'Our salvation was wrongly invested in Assyria and in material strength and not in God alone. Mercy is for the orphan, whom we have indeed become' (14.5).

In our view, the Book of Joel has been composed to respond to the scenario set out at Hosea's conclusion. It consists of the opportunity of a later generation to walk in God's ways and to exhibit the wisdom that comes from knowing God's judgements in spirit and in truth. Hosea's pleas for the wise reader to understand the ways of God, can be put into clearer focus by attending to the (intercalated) confessions offered in Jeremiah, to which we have made reference above. They are useful for they show a later generation doing what the Book of Hosea has set out in the form of invitation. Jeremiah 3.24-5 presupposes a judgement that arose because Jeremiah's calls for repentance were not heeded. The prophets who declared that judgement would not come were false (4.9-10). Explanations are provided for why judgement indeed came (5.18-19). The culminating text in 9.12-16 speaks, as does Hosea 14.9, of wisdom. Wisdom is that endowment which enables Israel to bear up, under the confession that God was fully just in his destruction of his own people and to allow that verdict to be given fullest expression.[5]

---

[5] See the discussion in Seitz, 'The Place of the Reader' (note 19 Chapter 5).

What the Book of Joel does in its three-chapter 'liturgy' is give expression to the fullest possible account of God's righteous judgement over his people. He uses the traditional language of the Day of the LORD, as this is available to him in the prophetic tradition. By means of a combination of natural and national distress, he develops the theme of judgement on the terms that Hosea typically spoke of it: as a desolation of God's blessings in grain, wine and oil. The 'return to Egypt' theme (undoing the Exodus) occasions the curses of Deuteronomy (as that tradition will develop it). Yet, Hosea also spoke of Assyria and Egypt and false trust in worldly national power and the ensuing books of Amos, Obadiah, Micah and Zephaniah will major in this particular focus: Israel in the grip of the nations. Joel 3–4 focus on the national/martial imagery purposefully introduced in Joel 1–2. The introduction to the book (1.2-3), describes what will unfold in Joel (the multi-faced assault of the Day of the LORD) as without precedent. Here he picks up on the plague traditions, which also had used the incomparability motif and its educational purpose for the generations to come.[6] What Israel is to know in divine victory over Pharaoh, by means of the plagues, is in fact the LORD himself (Exod. 10.2).[7] Joel understands this in a different way, by speaking of the locust plague as God's judgement *against his own people*. The Day of the LORD in Isaiah 13 – explicitly cited by Joel in his description at 1.15 – moved in two stages in Isaiah's typical tableau. The nations are rallied for a massive battle and its effects are universal, but within that also comes the final destruction of the Babylonians – prefigured in Isaiah 1–12 by Assyria – by the Medes (Isa. 13.17). The plan of God and the outstretched arm, concerned in fact the whole earth and not just Israel and the Assyrian rod of fury (14.24-7 is the final

---

[6] Seitz, 'Divine Name'. Also, Wolff, Jeremias. Anna Karena Mueller, *Gottes Zukunft: Die Möglichkeit der Rettung am Tag YHWHs nach dem Joelbuch* (WMANT 119; Neukirchen: Neukirchener, 2008), 41–58.
[7] Joel's specific version of the recognition formula appears at the climax in 2.27.

text in the series begun in 5.25 and it now bookends the Day of the LORD in Chapters 13–14, which serve as the introduction to the 'Oracles against the Nations' to follow).[8] But now this Day is directed against God's own people. Little wonder that Joel speaks of this Day as without any precedent (1.2).

The purpose of the Book of Joel, is to offer a performance inside of that which Hosea has invited Israel to do – take words and repent – might take place, thereby displaying the wisdom achieved that chooses to walk 'in the ways of the LORD'. The Day of the LORD appears in Joel as the sum total of any and every indictment God has against sinful people and the pride of the nations, now focused in the dramatic context of his own people. It is the collective sum of all of God's righteous judgement against human sin, from the wilderness generation of Moses until the exile's repeat of that death in judgement, in spite of the warning of the prophets. These older prophetic words continue to sound forth from a living record of indictment. The Book of Joel allows that cumulative prophetic word to sound forth in all its cacophonic terror, the sin and judgement of the ages welling up in the onslaught of the Day of the LORD. Jeremias is correct to see this day as more than end-time and more than a single event.[9] Though the text of Joel has a final culminating Day in view, it is a Day already breaking in upon the people Israel, in every situation of distress the prophet can set forth. The words of the prophets must complete their accomplishing purpose. The prophet does not seek to help Israel avoid this Day, but to accept the verdict that the gravity of God's eternal judgement is having its way in the present time. This is why it is impossible to assign the depiction to any specific single historical moment. The only temporal fact is that the Day will at some time come to its final crescendo in time, but

---

[8] Seitz, *Isaiah* (Interpretation; Westminster John Knox, 1993).
[9] 'Joel is the first prophet who not only expects the Day of the Lord for the future, but who also detects its roots in the present' ('Function', 81).

at present it is simply a multi-faceted and unavoidable reality that those who are wise acknowledge. God's judgements as prophesied in former times were true and righteous altogether. Some of them arguably have come in time and space, but this coming is always only ever a foretaste of an ongoing and eternal state of affairs bound up with God's character as revealed to Israel.[10]

Joel's purpose in describing this Day as a present and unfolding reality – 'near' and 'coming' – is made clear by the opening charge (1.2-3) and its connection to the book's centre (2.18-19). That centre is introduced with the call for godly intercession in the midst of the Day (2.12-17) and culminates in the revelation that God *has acted* in mercy. The God of Hosea is the forbearing and merciful YHWH, who in Joel's reception and extension, in spite of a more dramatic and encompassing Day than Hosea or any single prophet in times past has declared, acts in mercy for his people. The position of Joel *before* the unfolding Day, as this will be set forth in the various witnesses of the Twelve, means there is no coming announcement or fulfilment which can outstrip or leave as un-encompassed what Joel declares here. In every episode of judgement to be played out in the 'history' of the Twelve, Joel stands in a position of anticipation and of possible, accessible intercession on behalf of the 'Israel' who now surveys that history and its scope and scale of judgement. The opening charge has as its purpose the resultant announcement to every generation to come that God can save and deliver within the most dramatic and catastrophic manifestations of his Day, for those who turn to him in penitence and in acknowledgement of the uprightness of his 'ways'. The intercession of Moses in his Day is forever available for each generation and available as well is the encounter with God's justice

---

[10] One thinks here of the decision of the Synoptics to place the end time scenario prior to the Cross (Matt. 24; Mark 13; Luke 21). The Cross becomes the end-time event, which nonetheless does not void that end-time, but offers a glimpse into judgement and mercy in its eternal dimension.

and mercy, which was his to know and to convey. Moses' concern was for the present generation and God's being with them and God's response was one of judgement and of mercy both, as a generation died in the wilderness and a new one was brought forth, forgiven and given new life, under the shadow of his divine name and ways. Joel sets forth that encounter for each generation who will heed his word of prophetic life.

It has been asked why, if the confession of sin was made such that God's positive response arose (2.18-19), it is merely presupposed and not made clearer in the book's present form – the alternative being that it did not occur and that forgiveness is only a future possibility somewhere in a time beyond the book's present address to a specific audience.[11] In our view, this reading cannot be justified because the verbs used in the central episode are clearly not future-oriented. Something *has happened* in the way of forgiveness and new life. What such an alternative reading may track correctly, inadvertently, is that the dynamic of the Book of Joel is precisely to underscore that the act of forgiveness is targeted to any and every coming generation.[12] That is precisely what the opening charge states. Only when one sees it as directed toward, not an unprecedented episode of judgement as such, but alongside that and critical to its significance, *the central episode of forgiveness and the revelation of God's self in manifesting that,* will the

---

[11] For a clear recent discussion of the issue, see R. Troxel, 'Time'.

[12] In my view, this explains the wrestling with verb tenses one can see in Calvin. He wants 2.18 to refer to a future divine response (will be jealous and will have mercy) because he knows that the book does not end at the end of Chapter 2, but presses on to extend its horizon into a future where Israel must make confession and so find God's mercy strong to save (3.1-5). Yet, because 2.19 speaks of a genuine answer, Calvin will have recourse to the idea that in God's time he has determined something whose future will nevertheless still require playing out. The editor of the volume, declares this too refined and prefers a consistently future portrayal. But the problem is not in verse 19 alone, but in verse 18 as well. One sees the matter still causing problems in the modern Twelve discussion, as Nogalski also wants the repentance and response at a future time. That is because of his singular view that what has not happened before in time (1.2-3) is the repentance of Hosea. Our view here is the precise opposite. We share with Calvin, however, the position that the Day of the LORD in Joel does indeed spill into the future and that this is precisely the generation-bridging effect of the book's total presentation.

point of the opening charge and its significance for the hermeneutical character of the book as such be properly grasped. What the book says has happened, has happened for all who are wise and who seek a similar encounter with the ways of YHWH.

So why is the confession not provided in specific form? If we are correct that a) the Day of the LORD scenario unfolding in the opening chapters – in the run-up to the assembling of the elders and the act of forgiveness – and again in the tableau of Chapters 3–4 is as intentionally comprehensive as it is; and b) the point of it is to encompass all that the prophetic word has said and will say on this theme; then Joel is intended to relate to *all encounters with the word of God in the Book of the Twelve* – in the judgement over all the generations to which it is addressed, original audiences and subsequent readers – and the precise confession of future generations will need to arise from that encounter itself. To offer a single confession in the context of Joel would threaten to historicize what Joel is seeking to release to the future generations (1.2-3). The prophet Hosea has at his conclusion offered a template of confession for his own generation and any ensuing one to follow. One can 'take words and return to the LORD' on the precise terms he offers and that certainly would be a sure start on what Hosea initiates and what he and Joel, as comprehensively as any prophet could state it, together intend. Joel pursues the invitation of Hosea 14 and presents the most drastic terms under which it may be found effective, for every generation to come. The temporal perspective of the Day of the LORD in the book of Joel – 'here', 'near', 'coming' and 'afterward' – is intentionally calibrated so as to encompass the rich history that follows in the Twelve and in the future generations' encounter with the prophetic word as a total canonical address.

The locust plague and its wider elaboration in the opening chapters belong together with the descriptions of the day of the LORD in Chapters 3 and 4, as the first stages of the Day of the LORD scenario. The locust plague serves as a present example of how God can save, in the midst of a dramatic assault at whose head he himself stands and also as he intends in the future to save, as the Day of the LORD continues to escalate in the portrayal of the final chapters. Here we see why the recognition formula in 2.27 has an obvious counterpart in 4.17. The Day of the LORD material in Chapter 1 leads into a modification and intensification in Chapter 2 and this in turn is followed by two further elaborations in the final chapters. The point of the positioning of the LORD's positive response is to show it as continuing to be on offer for all generations to come, who will endure a yet greater unfolding of the Day of the LORD. The version of Joel 3–4 is a shorthand for what the reader will see of this being played out in the 'history' represented by the Book of the Twelve as a whole.

Seen in this light, it is hard to imagine what the point of an 'original' Joel comprising only Chapters 1–2 would have accomplished hermeneutically, as prophecy. It would have consisted of an account of a locust plague (itself then complicated by Chapter 2's temporal perspective) from which Israel was delivered, due to intercession and an ensuing (but now missing) confession. This would indeed turn the 'historical Joel' into a kind of strange *Heilsprophet* (as Rudolph held) yet lacking any genuine future address in the manner we see for example in Hananiah (with whom he was unfavourably compared).[13] The 'eschatology' said to represent secondary supple-

---

[13] Rudolph's comparison of Joel with Hananiah was of course based on his reading of the book in its entirety and not on a theory of an 'original Joel'. That said, Rudolph based his view on the idea that Joel was primarily *functionally* addressing a fear of the Day of the LORD that needed correcting with his optimistic version and the grounds for that are found in the original Day of the LORD material in the first two chapters. As Childs puts it, 'It remains a puzzlement in Rudolph's interpretation how such an erroneous message was ever retained after the catastrophe of the exile and was heard by successive generations of Jews in such a different way from that outlined by this learned commentator (cf. Qumran, NT, midrashim)' (*Introduction to the Old Testament as Christian Scripture*, 389). Regarding the canonical form and the temporal movement already at work in the opening two chapters, he writes, 'The pattern of chs. 1 and 2 belongs to the integral shape of the canonical book and forms the basis for its subsequent expansion in chs. 3 and 4' (391). Though Childs will permit speculation regarding whether this is redactional or original, the book only makes its canonical sense when one comprehends the intention of the present shape and form.

mentation in the latter two chapters (in either one phase or two), in fact belongs to the original and only hermeneutical conception the book ever worked with and without it, Joel would be a prophetic text without OT analogy. As it stands, the first part of the book (Chapters 1–2) already begins the movement from present assault to yet further elaboration, so that the deliverance at the core of the book serves to anticipate and prepare one for a yet greater, future Day of the LORD.[14]

The Book of Malachi represents something of the same hermeneutical dynamic. The 'messenger' to come (3.1) who is to prepare Israel for the great and terrible Day of the LORD (4.5) has come in the 'Malachi' who is the present work's own prophetic voice. His vocation of warning and exhorting the present generation, is but a harbinger of that of the 'messenger' yet to come. In Joel, the single voice of the present text accomplishes that same dynamic. And the charge with which the book opens (1.2-3) makes clear that what Israel experiences in the Day of the LORD and God's salvation inside of it, is to be communicated to the coming generations, which will face the Day of the LORD on the terms the second half of the book describes it. In this way the hermeneutical purpose of Joel as a specific kind of 'learned prophecy' is accomplished. The coming generations are summoned by Joel, to the testimony that is to flow from his generation's report, which is his present book.

In his intriguing discussion of the Book of the Twelve and the use by Paul of Habakkuk 2.4, Francis Watson argues that the 'vision' the prophet sees is not Luther's cry at the reformation (2.4) written on tablets; nor is it something that a running person can make out, so clear is it; nor is it the oracles against Babylon that appear immediately following (2.6-19). He argues on the basis of Isaiah 40.31 and other texts, that the running (2.2) refers to encouragement and rejuvenation: it is what the vision *enables*. He sees the final refrain at

---

[14] See the quote from Childs in the previous note.

3.19 as the prophet's own depiction of this in his own rejuvenating by God. The vision (*ḥazôn*) to be written down, then, is the prophet's very book we are now reading, appropriately introduced as 'the oracle that the prophet Habakkuk saw (*ḥāzâ*)'. The historical dimension and the hermeneutical dimension, are simply too deeply single-purposed to imagine any other governing conception at the root of the book's very composition and development, as it now exists.[15] We believe the same is true of Joel. This may well have to do with the character of written prophecy and it surely has to do in Joel's case with the obvious debt the prophet has to earlier written prophecy. Joel's message and purpose are to be understood on the same plane of interpretation.

Joel's use of Day of the LORD material, or his awareness of it in textual form, is obvious in the case of Zephaniah and Amos particularly, with the compass of the Book of the Twelve. We have argued for his awareness of Isaiah 13 and Jeremiah 14 as well and of the generational appeal, such as we see it in Exodus 10 and the Psalms of recital. The editorial development of Jeremiah, such that later generations are brought within the historical context of the book and there offer confession and acknowledgement of the justice of God's actions in past judgement, match what we find at the heart of Joel's own portrayal.

The effect of reading the ensuing books in the 'Twelve' collection in the light of Joel, is to have Joel anticipating the depictions to follow. His intention is, in our view, to cooperate with them and to provide hermeneutical coordination, so that the generations he anticipates as hearers of his testimony might hear him alongside them. The Day of the LORD in Amos, becomes a tragic example of the generation

---

[15] Watson, *Paul and the Hermeneutics of Faith*, 142–8. He writes, 'To study this text with the primary aim of restoring it to a so-called "original historical context" is to refuse the role that the text itself assigns to its own reader' (145).

that prophet addresses failing to do what both Hosea and Joel hold out as the only way forward. Amos sought in vain to bring about the proper response in Israel, though he was diligent in his vocation of intercession and of warning. Amaziah the priest silenced him and so cut the lifeline that was Israel's only hope. Far from interceding in the manner Joel describes for the priests in 2.17, Amaziah, in effect, destroys his own generation.

The Day of the LORD depictions reach their zenith in Zephaniah. Standing before Haggai, it is reasonable to conclude that the Day of the LORD in Zephaniah has in view the destruction of Judah and Jerusalem and the Babylonian exile. And yet, they are sufficiently extreme in their tenor and description, that in the present book of the Twelve they cannot be contained within that historical moment, no matter how much it was a genuine death and return to chaos (the context assumed in Isaiah 40–55, Lamentations, Psalm 89). Reading them in the light of Joel, they now entail a horizon much wider than that of Israel, as indeed Zephaniah 3.8-20 makes clear. The promise of a humble and lowly remnant of survivors (3.12) now joins up with the whole generation Joel insists is delivered and will in future be saved by attention to his word.[16]

Unmistakable as well, is the relationship between Joel and Jonah. The 'perhaps' of Joel's hopefulness in YHWH's character (2.14) is mirrored in the King of Nineveh's own more distant grasp of the Elohim's possible 'Yes' (3.9). Jonah's privileged knowledge of God's character (4.2 and compare Joel 2.13), which for him has its own burden *vis-à-vis* his vocation to Nineveh, is of such a nature that it can also break forth for perception by the nations. Jonah is prophetic in spite of himself and in God's judgement of Israel in him, the sailors learn who God truly is, conduct themselves accordingly and indeed offer right worship (1.14-16) – an ironic enactment of Jonah's own

---

[16] Jeremias (BZAW 433).

vowed pledge (2.9), when in the belly of the fish God makes the one who knows him also the one who will worship him again. One kind of diachronic reading will insist that Jonah 'corrects' Joel and offers a more kindly view of God's attitude toward the nations.[17] Another will say, Jonah's account of God's freedom to forgive is itself an assault on the idea of repentance leading to or effecting God's reversals – God is gloriously capricious and simply does as he likes.[18] If Joel is later than Jonah, then perhaps he intends to narrow what the prophet had said *vis-à-vis* Nineveh and the nations.[19] On our view a more complicated diachronic account, is one that must allow for the possibility of intentional mutual enrichment and reciprocity. That is, Joel and Jonah 'know one another' and whichever is 'first' and whichever 'second', they assume that they will co-exist in a single, complicated portrayal – because such is the theological truth of the matter.

Jonah, therefore, insists that the privileged revelation to Israel entails the One God whose will it is to be known – via Israel, in positive proclamation and extension (Ruth and Naomi), or via Israel in disobedience and judgement (Isa. 52.13-15; Jonah). Elohim is YHWH and vice-versa. Joel insists that in the context of the nations' overpowering and sought-for extinction of Israel, the nations will themselves find they have entered into judgement with the One God. The violence and might of worldly power will implode on itself. Nineveh will be destroyed if the lesson of Jonah is not truly learned, as indeed it was not (Nahum). The same LORD who makes himself known via Jonah to the nations, will come as a 'jealous and avenging'

---

[17] Schart, 'Jonah-Narrative', 122.
[18] Cooper, 'In Praise of Divine Caprice'.
[19] Bergler (214). Spieckermann believes on literary grounds that the compassionate formula is more integrated in Jonah than Joel and that this shows the direction of dependence, the latter displaying a more polemical/nationalistic *Tendenz* over against Jonah ('Barmherzig', 15–16). Compare Müller, *Gottes Zukunft*, 128–34. There is an important difference between the *šûb ʿad* of Joel and the *šûb min* of Jonah, but the texts are meant to interpret one another by enlarging the frame of reference. This does not amount to harmonizing them, for it requires us to note differences alongside the similarities.

Elohim (Nah. 1.2). He is slow to anger, as Joel and Jonah insist, but he is also great – not in *ḥesed* alone, but also – in power (*kōaḥ*) and 'will by no means clear the guilty' (Nah. 1.3). In sum, one must read Jonah and Joel in the light of the widest rehearsal of the theme in the XII, as well as in response to the particularities given in the Exodus 32–4 textual foundation. We shall have more to say about that in the commentary proper. It is obvious, for example, that Joel's 'relents from punishing' is a critical formal ending in the context of his own use of the Exodus text, which continues in that original context 'yet by no means clears the guilt, visiting the iniquity of the parents upon the children and upon the children's children'. The opening *Höraufruf* of Joel (1.2) means to see that God's steadfast love and forgiveness is communicated across the generations: 'tell your children of it, and let your children tell their children, and their children another generation'. The means whereby this is possibility, is the reversal envisioned in 2.12-14, based upon the character of God as revealed at Sinai, in Joel's own specific expression of that.

8

The Day of the LORD in the Book of Joel

One of the most familiar texts related to the Day of the LORD (hereafter DOL) appears in the prophet following Joel, namely Amos.

'Alas for those who desire the *day of the LORD*! Why do you want the *day of the LORD*? It is darkness, not light; as if someone fled from a lion and met a bear; or went into the house and rested a hand against the wall, and was bitten by a snake. Is not the *day of the LORD* darkness, not light, and gloom with no brightness' (5.18-20).

Indeed, we have argued above that Joel is aware of Amos' statements concerning the DOL (see Joel 2.2), as well as other renditions of this available to him in the prophetic legacy. It is clear from Amos – or so it would seem – that the DOL was for his audience plausibly to be regarded as a day of deliverance by the LORD. Von Rad theorized that the Day hearkened back to the Holy War traditions in which YHWH delivered Israel. Mowinckel speculated in detailed terms on an annual enthronement festival, where the Messiah-King's enacted installation augured a coming season of blessing for Israel. The prophets presuppose this festival and its promises of bounty and so do not explain in any greater detail where the Day comes from or what it means. Rather, they counter this presupposition in the manner of Amos.

The idea of a day more generally where the LORD establishes his sovereignty can be seen, for example, in Isaiah's opening chapters.

The LORD of hosts 'has a day against all that is proud and lofty, against all that is lifted up and high' (2.12). Isaiah speaks of a day when the LORD alone – and not the nations – will be exalted. In the canonical flow of Isaiah's chapters Assyria is introduced as the agent of God's judgement ('Ah Assyria, rod of my fury'), though at first the nation is not named (5.26). What we know is that the LORD is unveiling a plan that involves his hand being stretched out against his own people (5.25) and that this plan will unfold in stages (5.25; 9.12, 17, 21; 10.4; 14.26-7), culminating finally in the bringing low of Assyria herself (14.24-7; cf. 10.12-19). Throughout this unfolding 'plan' we find sustained reference to the 'day' (2.11, 12, 17, 20; 3.18; 4.2, 5; 5.30; 7.18, 20, 21, 23; 10.20, 27; 11.10, 11; 12.1) culminating in the oracles against Babylon and Assyria (13.1–14.32) who are types in the Book of Isaiah's ambitious temporal scheme (13.6, 9, 13, 22).[1] We hold the view that the prophet Joel is aware of Isaiah 13 specifically, if not also this larger portrayal.[2] There may as well be mutual influencing in Isaiah's presentation, with Joel and other texts, though that is a topic beyond the scope of this section's discussion. Clearly Isaiah's text has found much narrative supplementation (including a massive extension in Chapters 40–66).[3]

In Isaiah, then, the Day is itself deeply paradoxical. It involves a plan. The plan admits the nations – in seeming abrogation of the Zion presentation of the royal psalms – to emerge as agents of

---

[1] See Seitz, *Isaiah 1–39*, 127–32.
[2] Jeremias, J., 'Der <<Tag Jahwes>> in Jes 13 und Joel 2', in *Schriftauslegung in der Schrift* (eds R. G. Kratz, T. Krüger and K. Schmid; Berlin/New York: Walter de Gruyter, 2000), 129–38.
[3] The literature here is enormous. See the foundational essays of Peter Ackroyd ('An Interpretation of the Babylonian Exile: A Study of 2 Kings 20; Isaiah 38–39', *SJT* 27 [1974], 329–52) and R. E. Clements ('Beyond Tradition-History: Deutero-Isaianic Development of First Isaiah's Themes', *JSOT* 31 [1985]: 95–113). A very thorough account of Isaiah research can now be seen in English in Ulrich Berges, *The Book of Isaiah: Its Composition and Final Form* (Sheffield: Sheffield Phoenix Press, 2012). My own contributions are in *Zion's Final Destiny* (1991), *The New Interpreter's Bible* (2001) and *JBL* 109 (1990), *JBL* 115 (1996) and the *ABD* (III.472–88).

judgement against King, Zion, people. They overflow and reach up to the neck, to use the language of Chapter 7. Yet, this onslaught becomes the occasion both for their overreach and their routing and judgement. Inside of this, Isaiah depicts a remnant and indeed is given time and space to prepare them for the dark days ahead. An obedient replacement for the refractory Ahaz is promised within the tableau of judgement he unrolls. His own prophetic speech – which God tells him will in fact close ears and shut up hardened wills, as in the days of Pharaoh – will be bound up and preserved, to be opened in the latter times and enabling new life. That latter 'day' will have to wait for Assyria to be replaced by Babylon, but it will come in its time. Hezekiah's deportment in Chapters 36–9 provides the pious counterpart of Ahaz and typifies the salvation that will come in its fullness when the days of Babylon are brought to an end. This will be a day when the quintessential expression of human pride and unchecked violence is defeated. It will be a day for wailing, destruction, dismay, agony and untold trembling, even in the heavens themselves (13.13).

'Wail for the Day of the LORD is near; it comes like destruction from the Almighty' (13.6) is repeated verbatim in Joel 1.15 and the descriptions of the Day in Joel, as we have already noted, find verbal correspondences with texts in the Twelve.[4] So any inquiry into the meaning of the Day of the LORD must operate at a twin level. We need to be clearer conceptually about the meaning of *yôm YHWH*, in the basic sense of the term. But we also must comprehend how Joel is using the term in his own dedicated portrayal. Additionally, as he is so clearly indebted to other texts' presentation, we will need to see what his adaptation of their presentation in his own looks like. And finally, we must account for what we assume is Joel's intention

---

[4] 'When one isolates the Day-of-YHWH virtually everyone has a close (if not verbatim) parallel in the Book of the Twelve' (*Reading*, 104–5).

vis-à-vis those same texts, which he has drawn on but which he will also be read alongside of. This is the theological task and it flows from Joel's own theological achievement.

Reading Joel carefully, we can note several distinctive features – there are five in total – that come alongside and are distinctive within his portrayal of the Day. The first is that in Joel the Day is intended to lead to a specific outcome. The fact that this outcome is twice repeated in the book, alerts us to its significance as such and also its role in Joel's depiction of the Day. Moreover, the pivotal location of the texts in question is a further significant signal. At the close of the first main section (2.27) we find the recognition formula familiar from its use elsewhere in the Old Testament (Exod. 3–15[5]; Ezekiel[6]), though here in Joel's particular expression.

> 'You shall know that I am in the midst of Israel, and that I, the LORD, am your God and there is no other.' (2.27)

The text comes at the culmination of the rhetorically purposeful first main section (and is so marked in the MT). Twice we are told that in consequence of this recognition, the promise, 'my people shall never again be put to shame' (2.26, 27), will be in force.

The second appearance comes at the conclusion of the two further DOL sections represented by 3.1-5 and 4.1-16 (MT).

> 'So you shall know that I, the LORD your God, dwell in Zion, my holy mountain. And Jerusalem shall be holy and strangers shall never pass through it again.' (4.17)

---

[5] C. Seitz, 'The Call of Moses and the "Revelation" of the Divine Name: Source-Critical Logic and Its Legacy', in *Theological Exegesis: Essays in Honor of Brevard S. Childs* (eds C. Seitz, K. Greene-McCreight; Grand Rapids: Eerdmans, 1998), 145–61.
[6] W. Zimmerli, *Erkenntnis Gottes nach dem Buche Ezekiel* (ATANT 27; Zürich: Zwingli, 1954).

The difference with 2.27 is, obviously enough, a function of its appearance following DOL passages concerning the nations. Moreover, its temporal fulfilment is projected out beyond the timeframe presupposed by the earlier text. The recognition in this second case entails not the revelation of God as such, but the revelation of his dwelling place as restored. It would have made little sense to simply repeat the earlier text given the elaboration – thematic and temporal – represented by the movement of the final two chapters. That said, the recognition theme is obvious and its significance must be evaluated in any account of Joel's distinctive presentation of the DOL.

The second distinctive feature is to be noted in the *inclusio* represented by 1.4 and 2.25. Both are obviously directly concerned with the locust motif. The first one dramatically (if not also abruptly and without much setting of the scene) introduces the locusts as the first example of unprecedented divine action in Israel's midst. But we learn this latter fact only by watching the locusts emerge as but one feature of a much wider tableau of DOL judgement, where YHWH's personal role is made clear. In the commentary proper, we will need to take up this admixture in more depth, especially as we observe the transition in Chapter 2 to scenes more obviously of warfare and national assault; How are these two aspects to be related? At this point, it is simply to be observed that the recognition formula does not appear, *until* the locust threat with which the book opens, has been fully eliminated. Indeed, the text speaks of not just halting the threat, but of recompensing for it in days to come. It is in this context that the praise of God (2.26) and the recognition of him, as 2.27 expresses this, is grounded. That is, however, we are to understand the elaboration of the locust threat in 1.5–2.24, its elimination at 2.25 reminds us of its initial – if abrupt and unclear – introductory appearance at 1.4 and significance as such. Only then does the critical recognition formula appear. The emphasis on the locust plague is dramatically undiminished by the ambitious associating of it with a wider DOL tableau. The inclusio, followed by the recognition formulas, assures this.

The third critical feature of the DOL motif in Joel has been underscored in assorted reflections from Jeremias. He sees the absence in Joel's depiction of the word for wrath as significant, *vis-à-vis* other DOL texts – where it is prominent and indeed where its presence explains why the DOL is unfolding (Nah. 1.6; Zeph. 1.16). But more significant, I believe, are his observations about this DOL *vis-à-vis* other renditions we are familiar with in Isaiah, Jeremiah, Amos, Zephaniah and elsewhere. As he puts it 'the Book of Joel (1–2) is the *only book in the Old Testament daring to speak of the survival of a whole generation in Israel in the context of the Day of the LORD.*'[7] Also, Joel is unique in that the DOL is a present reality '*embedded already in any extreme distress* like in the drought and in the locusts of his own time.'[8] This second remark, requires further amplification if we are to understand its implications. The way I would put it is that the DOL is not just being presently experienced – other prophets can speak this way, though his distinction is sound enough. What Joel does is describe something that *has already transpired* as part of a DOL still to come. He has protracted the usual DOL conception. There is still a DOL yet to come (Chapters 3 and 4) and in that sense Joel's presentation there finds ample attestation elsewhere in the OT. Rather, what Joel has done is 'back-date' the DOL so as to enclose realities already unfolding around him into its grip.

What this enables him to do, then, is to speak of an unprecedented DOL, introduced as such in 1.2-3, as already underway in full and

---

[7] Emphasis in Jeremias ('Function', 78). He notes that while Zephaniah can speak of survivors, it is a small remnant and notable for that distinction. Compare the ironic comment of Amos 3.12 as well.
[8] Jeremias, 'Function', 81.

dramatic expression – here he uses language from prophetic texts regarding the terrible DOL to point to this fact – and yet deliverance is not only possible but will be enacted within the book's own present unfolding. Survival of the DOL in the future already has a harbinger in the present time and indeed it is this enacted survival that allows one to see the DOL in the future for what it is and also to see it in hope. The incomparability motif, then, is a crucial feature in Joel's presentation precisely because he associates it with an already present/yet still coming DOL, on the one hand (there has never been a DOL with these two dimensions integrally combined), while, on the other hand, the incomparability dimension – given this already-but-not-completed feature – pertains as well to the emergence of an enactment of deliverance in the present time. Nothing like this has happened before. The generation who experiences this must tell it to future generations.

And, finally, the way this particular DOL rendition in Joel is possible is due to an encounter with God as he revealed himself at Sinai, in mercy and in forgiveness, in Joel's presentation of the compassionate formula at the pivotal location in 2.12-14. It is here, then, that the various threads in Joel's depiction find the centre that allows them all to be pulled together. The (1) locusts/plague motif; (2) the recognition formula; (3) the generational deliverance; (4) the incomparability theme, and (5) the compassion declaration all direct us to the book of Exodus, where these various themes are interwoven in the presentation of that dramatic work. The repeated appearance of the latter feature in the book of the Twelve has been the subject of much dedicated reflection.[9] In Joel, it is the crucial feature that allows his particular presentation of a protracted DOL – already-and-yet-to-come – and salvation for God's people within this unfolding, to take

---

[9] Denten, Dozeman, Van Leeuwen, Seitz and most recently (and, in my view, with less illumination) in Wöhrle's redactional model.

place in an incomparable way. That is, incomparable for its own sake in Joel and for the sake of the generations who will be recipients of their report (1.3), via the present Book of Joel as it sits before us.[10]

In Exodus 10 we find the locust texts, the incomparability motif, the recognition formula and the promise of a generation to be delivered, which will give report to future generations. More broadly, the recognition formula is connected to the revelation of the divine name to Moses in Chapters 3 and 6. In my account of it, the only way to make full sense of Moses' concern about telling a people who are imagined as asking him for it (3.13) – if they do not know it, how could his reproduction of it confirm anything he worries they may rightfully ask to know – is to conclude that he is the one without knowledge of the name, while they do. Yet, this becomes the occasion for God to reveal the name to Moses as such (3.14), but also to reveal more fully his own character, now to be known in the events about to be experienced by Moses and the people both. God will be known in his name – I will be as I will be – in the context of Moses' and Israel's obedient walking with God in the demonstration of his sovereignty *vis-à-vis* Pharaoh.[11] This explains the refrain as it is solemnly introduced at 6.7:

> 'I will take you as my people, and I will be your God. You shall know that I am the LORD your God, who has freed you from the burdens of the Egyptians.' (6.7)

The recognition formula is repeated as we watch Moses in his encounters with Pharaoh. Pharaoh (7.17; 8.10, 22; 9.29), his people (7.5; 10.7; 14.18), all generations in Israel (10.2) and all creation will

---

[10] Here the similarity to the hermeneutical function of Habakkuk's vision is striking. See the discussion above. See also the fruitful hermeneutical observations of R. Scolarick, 'Auch jetzt noch (Joel 1.2, 12a)': Zur Eigenart der Joelschrift und ihrer Funktion im Kotext des Zwölfprophetenbuches', in *'Wort JHWHs, das geschah ...' (Hos. 1,1) Studien zum Zwoelfprophetenbuch* (HBS 35; ed. Erich Zenger; Freiburg et al., 2002), 47–69.
[11] 'Who is the LORD? I do not know the LORD and I will not let Israel go' (5.2).

come to know the LORD precisely by virtue of the protracted contest and repeated dissembling of Pharaoh (11.9). Finally, at the Sea, in judgement and in deliverance, the LORD is all that he has promised to be in his seemingly elliptical response to Moses: 'I will be as I will be.' Far from elliptical, 'to be as he is' (the third person YHWH of *ʾehĕyeh ʾăšer ʾehĕyeh*) is to be faithful through time with his people, to the degree they remain alongside and obedient to his speaking to them, such they witness him in the events of the Exodus.

In these narrative texts from Exodus, however, we never see anything like a technical application of DOL language to what Israel (and Pharaoh) experiences. Given the preponderance of associations with Exodus traditions in Joel especially, what is one to make of this? Is it a bit too constraining to ask that Exodus traditions use the DOL language of the prophetic tradition, if that in turn is to be the warrant for our seeing significance in relation to these foundational texts (in whatever form they may exist at Joel's time)? We shall need to return to this question shortly. What we do see in Exodus is ample use of the language of 'day' and other temporal markers ('this month shall be for you the first of months' – Exod. 12.2) in the context of Israel's (to be expected and carefully regulated) later remembrance ('this day shall be a day of remembrance for you' – Exod. 12.14). 'Moses said to the people, "Remember this day on which you came out of Egypt … because the LORD brought you out"' (13.3). What this language seeks to underscore is that a definite day in historical time was the DOL's acting and that in consequence Israel's mighty deliverance was accomplished. The signs that are done among them before Pharaoh will culminate in a final deliverance and that will be the means by which, as Exodus 10.2 puts it, the Egyptians will be made fools of once and for all. However much the contest is protracted – Pharaoh decides to let them go in 10.8 only to renege in 10.11 – the point of the plagues' remembrance is always their pointing to the final defeat rendered in Passover and at the Sea. When the language of incomparability is used in connection with the locust plagues and their subsequent reporting to all generations (10.6 and 10.2), it is obvious that the locusts themselves are but a part of the fuller remembrance entailed by the denouement of Chapters 10–15 as a whole, which will be cultically recalled and celebrated for all time subsequently, in the feasts of Passover and Unleavened Bread, on fixed calendar 'days'.

In my view, it would be wrong to look for precise DOL in Exodus as the warrant for how and why Joel proceeds as he does in his presentation. The unprecedented events of the Exodus are the grounds for subsequent 'day' celebrations of remembrance and praise. The events in Exodus are not analogy-congenial happenings, but are foundational in every sense of that word. They themselves are capable of 'creating days' of remembrance, much as once God created the days that constitute his foundational acts in time (Gen. 1). What the prophet Joel does do is survey the language of DOL as it exists in the prophetic record and then fills it with content based upon recourse to the primal events of Israel's deliverance in Egypt and the subsequent retelling of that. His DOL, like the foundational divine action in judgement and mercy in the exodus, exists to generate a telling and retelling, now for a different though kindred purpose as those first events.[12] He takes the DOL tableau as the prophets render it and applies it to the locust plague of his own time and place and then he expands this enormously to correlate it with the accumulated witness of the DOL, as it exists in the prophetic record, because he believes this witness presses ahead for its final denouement, for Israel and for the nations.

What he sees in Exodus is the full display of God's character in

---

[12] So the obvious parallel between Joel 1.2-3 and Exodus 10.2. Theodoret of Cyr also draws attention to the similarity of Joel 1.2-3 to Psalm 78.6-7, both linguistically as well as in intent ('that they should set their hope on God') thus anticipating recent scholarship on this matter.

time. The recognition formula of those primary events retains its force in the context of the DOL. God made himself known in the judgement over Pharaoh and in the deliverance at the Sea and in that once-and-forever happening he revealed himself as his Name. Moses was introduced to God at the bush and on the basis of that initial encounter, he and Israel both come to know him as YHWH, as he makes himself known in the acts of deliverance. Joel believes that same divine revelation is happening in the DOL. It is happening in judgement over all that is proud and haughty, as Isaiah has it and it is happening *vis-à-vis* his own people, as the prophets had described that. But as in the original revelation, God is making himself known in judgement and in mercy both. In the original revelation, God was known in judgement over Pharaoh and in mercy over his people. But that was not the whole story by any means. We were put on notice about that much earlier, when God was described as dangerous *vis-à-vis* his own people.[13] And that character and reality become real in force as soon as Israel enters the wilderness and begins to complain and long to return. This initial resistance to God, in the form of undoing the deliverance and so undoing his character as such, takes a particular form in the chapters that lead up to Exodus 32. But at that point, with the wholesale rebellion of all the people, Moses alone is absent; he is alone with God on the mountain – we are poised to understand the revelation of God in his name (in Exodus 3 and in imparting the knowledge of himself in those episodes right through to the deliverance at the Sea in Exodus 15) now in a kindred but more darkened way. That is, the wholesale disobedience of the people – anticipated in the murmuring stories between Sea and Sinai – occasions the critical narratives in Chapters 33–4. Here the question is YHWH's continued presence with Israel. Will he now

---

[13] 'The God of the Hebrews has revealed himself to us; let us go a three days' journey into the wilderness or he will fall upon us with pestilence or sword' (5.3). Compare 4.24-6 as well.

send a surrogate? Will he cast his people off and work with Moses alone (33.1-2)?

In securing God's 'No' in response to these fateful questions concerning his presence, Moses seeks reassurance from YHWH. It sounds like he is given this (33.14), but oddly enough the text preserves Moses' ongoing questioning (33.15-16). At issue, then, is his presence with Moses and the people *both*.[14] In the context of this exchange YHWH reveals himself to Moses in such a way as to allay this double concern. As is congruent with this request, as far as he is able, YHWH reveals himself to Moses: in his Name and his 'ways'. Here we find the solemn presentation of the Name ('The LORD, the LORD') and alongside it the compassion formula as such (34.5ff.). There can be no doubt that this is presented as a solemn encounter of the most intimate kind. Yet, inside of it we also are given to see the character of God in relation to human affrontery and sin. This YHWH is both for and against his people whom he has taken to himself, for the sake of his Name.

What Hosea describes in his own inimitable way, in the closing chapters of his book (11-14), is this YHWH struggling with the divine character that is inextricably his own, such as it has been revealed in Exodus 33-4. 'Merciful and gracious' – 'yet by no means clearing the guilty' (34.6, 7). Luther spoke of fleeing to the God of mercy who is also the God of righteous judgement, as itself the basis of any hope of new life. This is the God before whom Moses bows in worship. The YHWH he is concerned with will divide himself and only partially accompany Israel – in whatever way we might imagine that (33.2); it does not transpire – remains the YHWH he most essentially is, whose character we are given to see here in the narrative theology of Exodus 33-4. The further, dramatic dealing with a sinful people in Numbers 14 can only take its bearings from this pivotal text, which

---

[14] 'Do not carry *us* up'; 'I *and your people*' (33.15-16).

Moses repeats in YHWH's presence (14.18). YHWH remains true to his own character with his people, though the judgement over his people must in consequence fall in some measure. 'I do forgive, just as you have asked; nevertheless – as I live, and as the whole earth shall be filled with the glory of LORD – none of these …' – and here the solemn verdict is given. Striking in this text is the mention of the 'whole earth'. However much the solemn revelation of God's most personal character is the possession of his own people, God declares to them and through them that his character entails a filling of the whole earth with his glory.

When we turn now to the DOL in the prophetic legacy, we can *in a manner of speaking* see in the DOL texts that the 'Day' is in fact an encounter with God himself.[15] The various ways in which this is asserted, however, justifies our caution in qualifying this. Amos tells those who desire the DOL, 'prepare to meet your God'.[16] Isaiah is clear that YHWH himself is the agent of the Day.[17] So too Zephaniah.[18] But because the DOL texts refer to the DOL not as a present but as a pending reality, in differing rhetorical forms of expression, the realistic, present 'knowing' of YHWH is framed in a manner distinctive over Israel's knowledge of God in the events of Exodus,

---

[15] Müller will therefore refer to the Day as a 'Chiffre' for YHWH himself (*Gottes Zukunft*, 99). In this context, she is referring to Joel 2.11 ('who can endure it'). This is true enough of the Day in its final denouement, but Joel is of course 'back dating' the DOL for a particular encounter in his present time. See also Spieckermann on Amos 5.18-20 (Dies irae, 198). He regards the '*licht*' and '*glanz*' to be concrete *Präsenzangeigen*. But of course, then, what Israel would be encountering would be the non-presence of God (*Finsternis* and *Dunkelheit*).

[16] 'Therefore this is what I will do to you, Israel, and because I will do this to you, Israel, prepare to meet your God' (Amos 4.12). The plague tradition is referenced in 4.10 (as not engendering repentance in Amos' day). A theophany (in literary description) follows (4.13).

[17] '… the LORD and the weapons of his wrath – to destroy the whole country. Wail, for the day of the LORD is near; it will come like destruction from the Almighty' (Isa. 13.5b-6).

[18] Typical of his rendition is the steady first-person drumbeat. 1.7 introduces a liturgical context (Be silent before the Sovereign LORD, for the day of the LORD is near. The LORD has prepared a sacrifice; he has consecrated those he has invited) which may be close to what Joel seeks to achieve in his portrayal. That is, the encounter with YHWH is cultically intimated.

where the recognition formula is so central. Again, this underscores the foundational character of that once-for-all encounter, as well as its acknowledgement in the distinctive way the DOL texts do their work.

Joel, by means of the performance of his work, retains the final DOL language as related to a horizon in the future (3.1, 'then afterward'; 4.1, 'in those days and at that time'). This pushes the DOL into a place of final denouement, thus bringing it in line with other prophetic texts whilst altering the rhetorical effect of urgency in those same texts, which have only one plane of encounter in view. But the urgency is retained by Joel *for the very present time he is addressing* as this unfolds in 1.2–2.27. The already of the locust plague (1.3ff.) spills into the 'coming and near' of Chapter 2's presentation. *Joel's audience is inside the DOL.* Inside the DOL the urgent appeal is made in 2.12-14, perfectly introduced temporally with the 'yet even now' (*wĕgam 'attâ*) of YHWH's own direct address. As has been noted, the 'with all your heart' (*bĕkol-lĕbabkem*) language closely tracks the direct appeal to Israel made – likewise in the midst of judgement – in Deuteronomy 30. There too we have the *šûbû 'ad* of Joel 2.12 (*wĕšabtā 'ad YHWH*).[19] Joel, however, proceeds to introduce the language of Exodus 34 in his distinctive portrayal (vv. 13-14), thus clearly evoking the foundational encounter of Israel in the wilderness.

It is in this way that Joel opens up the DOL tableau known to him from other prophetic texts and with which he situates his own portrayal. Inside of the DOL, it is possible to encounter YHWH as he has made himself known at Sinai. This is the point of the clear allusion to Exodus 34. Now not Moses but rather the priests are called forward for the task of intercession. The answer to the question of 2.11

> 'Truly the day of the LORD is great;
> terrible indeed – who can endure it?'

---

[19] Jeremias, et al.

is answered directly and without pause. Israel can. Because God is himself in inside his own Day, the compassionate and merciful YHWH. Unmistakable is Joel's own version of the foundation text of Exodus 34.6-7. The references to 'who by no means will clear the guilty' and the visitation of sin on coming generations are absent and instead we find 'he relents from sending calamity' (2.13). Joel's adaptation here matches similar counterparts elsewhere in the Twelve (Hosea, Obadiah, Jonah, Micah, Nahum). Further, Jeremias and other have carefully evaluated the 'Who knows?' language of 2.14. This does not represent, as he puts it, 'nobody knows for sure'.[20] Instead, it is a strong confession that YHWH's character, at its very essence, is such that room is always left for God's freedom to act in mercy. It is the prophet's sharp 'No' to the verdict being already final. The priestly intercession to follow is indeed efficacious. YHWH has pity on his people.

The commentary proper will give us occasion to trace more fully the precise achievement of Joel in this significant, indeed central, panel of his work. Our point here is to explore how Joel has taken up the DOL and reframed it for the purpose of 1) setting forth a present encounter with the LORD of Sinai for Joel's generation, 2) emphasizing the possibility of forgiveness inside the DOL and 3) indeed enacting that. This enactment prepares, in turn, the generation he addresses and those who will be the recipients of their report to face the DOL as this is depicted in the final two chapters of the book. Joel creatively merges the original Sinai narrative theology (past) with the DOL language of the prophets still pressing for fulfilment (future) and does this to open up an encounter with the God of Sinai in all his forgiving and merciful plenitude.

To conclude this section on the Day of the LORD, it is necessary to return to our starting place. We spoke there of needing conceptual

---

[20] "Function", 82.

clarity on *yôm YHWH* though our attention thus far has been on how the Day might plausibly be understood to have emerged in Joel's portrayal, as a melding of Sinai and prophetic DOL material. But what about the quest for basic conceptual clarity? Why a 'day' of the LORD?

Several things require to be noted here. First, the liturgical remembrance of Sinai spoke of a 'day' even though the plagues and the final defeat are not co-terminus; they represent a series of happenings in the final drama between YHWH and Pharaoh. Yet the point surely is that any subsequent calendar re-enactment and remembrance must be riveted to fixed moments in time. The remembrance *yôm* seeks to gather to itself a specific event in past time and encapsulate it in some concrete way. This gets at the core fact that something once happened in time that is not vague ('a week of the LORD' or a 'time of the LORD') but is representative of a unique decision to act. The fact that the action only makes sense as a divine action because it has been so promised beforehand in speech, only underscores this definitive quality. As Barr once laboured to remind us, the 'acts of God' are not his footprints in sand, but his making good on what he had said in speech, as he had promised.[21] No less the 'act of God' is what continues to be recalled in specific calendar remembrances.

Second, the basic sense of the word *yôm* in the OT surely devolves from creation itself. God acted via speech to create and this happened in 'days'. Even the decision to rest and not act entails a fixed period of

---

[21] '... we shall not succeed if we try to formulate the centre of the tradition as an "event" or series of events, which can then be talked about as "acts of God in history". This will not work either descriptively or historically ... If we, first of all, take the actual form of the documents, the way in which they express themselves as they stand, it is clear that an important place belongs to the acts narrated; and some of these seem to be miraculous divine interventions at a past historical point, such as the deliverance of Israel from Egypt. If we speak on this level, however, i.e. descriptively of the actual form of the tradition, *we have to give space to all sorts of elements other than these "acts". Particular emphasis would have to be given to the speaking of God, to his communications in which he makes known his will and his intentions to the men whom he designates to hear this and communicate it to the people*' (emphasis mine; *Old and New in Interpretation: A Study of the Two Testaments* [London: SCM Press, 1966], 16).

time: the seventh *yôm*. To speak of the *yôm* of YHWH is minimally, then, to evoke the activity of God in primordial time: the foundational activity of God is his daily speech-creating work. A 'day of the LORD' by extension, in the present or future, would be a resumption of that basic acting, but now in the context of his deployment of time for his purposes. In Exodus 3 the name of God is explained to Moses as entailing his 'being' through time ('I am in my I am-ing'). YHWH's being through time, in revelation of his name, is a disclosure of his ways with Israel and as he himself put in Numbers 14, with the whole of creation that is his own.[22] To speak of the DOL is fundamentally to describe an action in time, after creation, that is an action on analogy with the fundamental creative daily acting: it is God on his 'eighth' day, as it were. He breaks through the temporal categories of day-to-day – itself his own creation, over which he is LORD – to speak again and do undertake the divine fiat, 'let there be', in accordance with his sovereign designs for Israel and all of the world.

Joel's DOL participates in this conceptual framework, which he shares with the wider prophetic legacy. God has a Day. YHWH is lord over time, beginning through to the end. In Joel, the end time day opens onto a generation whose is addressed by God in his ways of compassion and forgiveness. He proposes a 'day' on which a generation might return to the LORD, inside the end time Day of judgement and in the light of God's own self-revelation, might have new life.

---

[22] 'nevertheless – as I live, and as the whole earth shall be filled with the glory of the LORD'.

9

The Living God of Joel in the Lived Life of the Church

Based as it is on the events of the Cross and Resurrection, Easter emerges from the earliest moment as what will be the fixed point – the Day of the LORD – in a developing (more comprehensive, cyclical) Church Year. That it is itself a replication of Passover – now in a New Day – only underscores the point. Alongside this commemoration of the Cross and Empty Tomb, we know that from the earliest times a period of fasting was set aside to prepare for (what will come to be known as) Holy Week: Passion and Good Friday. The forty days of Christ in the wilderness, figurally present in Israel's life in the wilderness sojourns of Moses and Elijah, are now enacted by the Church to prepare spiritually for Christ's once-for-all sacrifice. Leo the Great's (b. 400) Sermon 88 ('On the fasts of the seventh month') writes the following after this introductory rubric, 'The Fasts, which the ancient prophets proclaimed, are still necessary':

> Of what avail, dearly-beloved, are religious fasts in winning the mercy of GOD, and in renewing the fortunes of human frailty, we know from the statements of the holy Prophets, who proclaim that justice of GOD, Whose vengeance the people of Israel had again and again incurred through their iniquities, cannot be appeased save by fasting. Thus it is that the Prophet Joel warns them, saying, 'thus saith the LORD your GOD, turn ye to Me with all your heart, with fasting and weeping and mourning, and rend your hearts and not your garments, and turn ye to the LORD your GOD, for He is merciful and patient,

and of great kindness, and very merciful,' and again, 'sanctify a fast, proclaim a healing, assemble the people, sanctify the church.' And this exhortation must in our days also be obeyed, because these healing remedies must of necessity be proclaimed by us too, in order that in the observance of the ancient sanctification Christian devotion may gain what Jewish transgression lost.

I want to return to the concluding comment of Gregory below. For now my point is only to observe the reference to Joel 2.17 and the connection of Joel to the tradition of fasting in the Church.

The council at Nicaea (325), we know, presupposes a Lenten period of fasting called Quadrigesima. It was Gregory I (590–604) who fixed the Wednesday of the sixth Sunday before Easter as the fast's beginning and it would come to be called 'Ash Wednesday'. On this day, the priests and people both sprinkled dust and ashes on themselves, declaring, 'Remember, O man, that dust thou art, and unto dust thou must return; repent, that thou mayest inherit eternal life.'

The Book of Common Prayer prepared in the sixteenth century by Thomas Cranmer, gives clear evidence of the persistence of Ash Wednesday also within those churches that would part from the Roman Church. In 1549 the service is referred to as 'The Firste Date of Lente, Commonly Called Ashe-Wednisdaye' and it is to follow immediately after Matins on that day.[1] In subsequent editions (including the 1662) the service will be referred to as 'A Commination Against Sinners'. There are no fixed readings assigned. In part, this is to be explained by the simple fact that the service is itself already comprehensively scriptural. It begins, following the Litany (so the rubric) and the priest's introduction from the pulpit, with a solemn recitation of the curses found in Deuteronomy 27.

---

[1] No trumpet is sounded (Joel 2.1) – instead we have 'the people beeyng called together by the ryngyng of a bel, and assembled in the churche'.

The Living God of Joel in the Lived Life of the Church

This is all undertaken so that the congregation might have before them 'the dredefull judgement hanging over our heades, and beyng alwayes at hande' and in the light of that might:

> 'returne unto our lorde God, with all contricion and mekenes of heart, bewailing and lamenting our sinful life, knowlaging and confessing our offences, and seekyng to bring furth worthie fruites of penance.'

The priest's address continues for some length (the text is marked with the scriptural references; '7' from the Old Testament and '12' from the New Testament). It is worth citing in full to give a sense of proportion.

> For even now is the axe put unto the roote of the trees, so that every tree whiche bryngeth not furth good fruite, is hewen downe and cast into the fyer. It is a fearefull thing to fall into the handes of the living God: he shal powre downe rayne upon the sinners, snares, fyer and brimstone, storme and tempest: this shalbe theyr porcion to drynke. For loe, the lorde is cummen out of his place, to visite the wickednes of such as dwell upon the earth. But who may abyde the daye of his cumming? Who shalbe hable to endure whan he appeareth? His fanne is in his hande, and he wil pourge his floore, and gather his wheate into the barne, but he will burne the chaffe with unquencheable fier. The day of the lorde cummeth as a thiefe upon the night, and when men shall say peace, and all thynges are safe, then shall sodayne destruccion come upon them, as sorowe cometh upon a woman travaylyng with chylde, and they shall not escape: then shall appeare the wrathe of God in the daye of vengeaunce, whiche obstinate synners, through the stubbernes of theyr hearte, have heaped unto themselfe, which despised the goodnesse, pacience an long-sufferaunce of god, when he called them continually to repentaunce. Then shall they cal upon me (sayth the lorde), but I wil not heare: they shal seke me early, but thei shal not finde me, and that because they hated knowlage, and received not the feare of the lord, but abhorred my counsell and despised my correccion: then shal it be to late to knocke, when the doore shalbe shut, and to late to cry for mercy, when it is the tyme of justice. O terrible voice of most just judgement, which shalbe pronounced upon

them when it shalbe sayde unto them. Go ye cursed into the fyer everlasting, which is prepared for the devil and his angels. Therfore brethren, take we hede by time, while the day of salvacion lasteth, for the night cometh when none can worke: but let us while we have the light, beleve in the light, and walke as the children of the light, that we be not cast into the utter derkenes, where is weping and gnashing of teeth. Let us not abuse the goodnes of god, whiche calleth us mercifully to amendement, and of his endlesse pitie, promiseth us forgevenes of that which is past: if (with a whole mind and a true hert) we returne unto him: for though our sinnes be red as scarlet, they shalbe as white as snowe, and though they be lyke purple, yet shall they be as whyte as woolle. Turne you cleane (sayth ye lord) from all your wickednes, and your synne shall not be your destruccion Cast away from you all your ungodlines that ye have doen, make you new hertes, and a new spirite: wherfore will ye dye, O ye house of Israel? seing I have no pleasure in the death of him that dieth (sayth the Lord God). Turne you then, and you shall lyve. Although we have sinned yet have we an advocate with the father Jesus Christ the righteous, and he it is that obteyneth grace for our sinnes; for he was wounded for our offences, arid smitten for our wickednes: let us therfore returne unto him, who is the merciful receiver of al true penitent sinners, assuring ourselfe that he is ready to receive us, and most willing to pardon us, if we come to him with faithful repentaunce: if we wil submit ourselves unto him, and from heceforth walke in hys waies: if we wil take his easy yoke and light burden upon us to folowe hym in lowlynesse, pacience, and charitie, and bee ordred by the governaunce of his holy spirite, seking alwayes his glorye, and serving him duely in our vocacion with thankesgevyng. This yf we doe, Christe wil deliver us from the curse of the law, and from the extreme malediccion whiche shall lyght upon them that shalbee set on the left hand: and he wyl set us on his right hand, and geve us the blessed benediccion of hys father, commaundyng us to take possessions of hys glorious kyngdome, unto the whiche he vouchsafe to bryng us al, for hys infinite mercye. Amen.

Following this exhortation, Psalm 51 is read aloud corporately, all kneeling. Following this, we have Suffrages (priest and congregation) and two prayers. The second will come to be known as the 'Collect for Ash Wednesday' and it can be found in the present Book of Common Prayer (USA). It is one of Cranmer's finest compositions.[2] Note, then, how the service ends.

> Then shal this antheme be sayed or song. TURNE thou us, good Lord, and so shall we be turned: bee favourable (O Lorde) be favourable to thy people, which turne to thee in wepyng, fasting and praying; for thou are a mercifull God, full of compassion, long suffering, and of great pietie. Thou sparest when we deserve punishment, and in thy wrathe thynkest upon mercy. Spare thy people, good Lorde, spare them, and lette not thy heritage bee brought to confusion: Heare us (O Lorde) for thy mercy is great, and after the multitude of thy mercyes looke upon us.

Striking is that the service ends solemnly with scripture (in the form of prayer) and that the text is largely from Joel. The priest's final prayer takes the form of what Joel scripted for the priests of his own day.

> Between the vestibule and the altar
>   let the priests, the ministers of the LORD, weep.
> Let them say, 'Spare your people, O LORD,
>   and do not make your heritage a mockery,
>   a byword among the nations.
> Why should it be said among the peoples,
>   'Where is their God?' (2.17)

In modern versions of Cranmer's Book of Common Prayer, where lessons are indeed read (alongside corporate recitation of Psalm 51), the first lesson provided is from Joel (2.1-2, 12-17).[3] The lesson ends

---

[2] 'Almighty and everlasting God, you hate nothing you have made and forgive the sins of all who are penitent: Create and make in us new and contrite hearts, that we, worthily lamenting our sins and acknowledging our wretchedness, may obtain of you, the God of all mercy, perfect remission and forgiveness; through Jesus Christ our Lord, who lives and reigns with you and the Holy Spirit, one God, for ever and ever. Amen.'

[3] The present lectionary goes back to the fine work of Vatican Two scholarship.

at the same place Cranmer originally allowed his final prayer to end (see above). The opening two verses of Joel, Chapter 2 serve the now (greatly reduced) purpose of setting the day of the LORD before the congregation, such as the litany, commination and address originally did in 1549 and subsequently (through 1662, the legally authorized Prayer Book in England).

What is retained in the service Cranmer constructed is the clear sense from Joel that the DOL is a day of God's judgement, without any lessening whatsoever. Recent scholarship has likewise made this clear. The full force of Joel 1–2 is retained, which from the perspective of Cranmer's liturgical time is the final judgement of God, that is, the temporal perspective of Joel's final two chapters. Yet Cranmer is quick to add in the context of his own temporal perspective, that this judgement retains the force of 'beyng always at hande'.

In the quote from Gregory the Great above, we see the continuity between Christian fasts and those 'which the ancient prophets proclaimed'. Joel serves to guide the present life of the church, Gregory avers, so 'that in the observance of the ancient sanctification Christian devotion may gain what Jewish transgression lost'. Here he represents a common theme in the history of Christian reception of the Old Testament. The ongoing life of Judaism is set in contrast with that of the Church and in the case of the Old Testament, its urgent applicability turns on a forfeit the Church believes mars that present life. In other words, Gregory is not interested in Joel bearing witness to a successful 'sanctification' at some point in Israel's own life. Presumably that is neither here nor there. Rather, he believes that Jewish 'transgression' means only that the chance is present now for Christians to heed Joel more urgently.

Cranmer's own example of Joel in the Christian assembly is rather different at this point. There is no repentance at the human level, which is not at once occasioned by the sovereign God himself.

'Turn thou us, good Lord, and so shall we be turned'. The turning in weeping the service is meant to engender ('which turn to thee in weeping, fasting and praying') is itself God's quickening, out of spiritual generosity and love. It flows from his own divine character and *in the light of that* it reaches into the darkened heart and will so that repentance might occur and the sanctification of God find root via his forgiveness. This is not something one sets in contrast with something else at the human level. God is the source of the repentance and new life he occasions in sinful men and women. Our eyes are to remain on him. Joel bears witness to this Christian truth.

Michael Fishbane has published a fine volume on the *Haftarot* of present Jewish lectionary use.[4] When one searches for the presentation of Joel in the liturgical life of Judaism, what does one find?

Perhaps, unsurprisingly, the core of Joel (2.15-27), given its description of the compassionate and merciful YHWH, is also present in Jewish lectionary texts. What is extremely interesting, given the place of Joel in the Twelve as presently under discussion, is a) where Joel exists alongside other OT testimony, and b) in just what place in the liturgical time of Jewish observance. Joel 2.15-27 is appointed to be read on Shabbat Shuvah ('Turn Sabbath'), the Sabbath before Yom Kippur ('The Day of Atonement'). But it is the second lesson appointed. The first lesson to be read is Hosea 14.2-10. This is fully consistent with critical observations about Joel and the Twelve above. Fishbane's own summary takes this form:

> 'The Prophet [Hosea] urges the nation to return to the LORD and provides a statement of confession and supplication the people should recite (vv. 3b–4). Israel should appeal to divine mercy and stress their

---

[4] *The JPS Bible Commentary: Haftarot* (English and Hebrew Edition) (Philadelphia, PA: Jewish Publication Society, 2002). The word *haptarôt* refers to a series of selections from the 'Prophets' division of the *Tanak* that is publicly read, following the main (Torah) reading, in Synagogue worship.

trust in God's power and salvation. In response the Lord promises to "heal" the people's affliction.'

As he puts it later, Hosea's final appeal 'sets the context for Joel's call to "solemnize a fast" for all the nation and have the priests beseech God for mercy in the temple court (Joel 2.15-17)' (177). This Hosea–Joel pairing is found in the Ashkenazim tradition. The Sephardim pairing is equally compelling. The same use is made of Hosea as here described, but the text to follow is now Micah 7.18-20. Both the Joel and Micah texts contain references to the foundational Sinai disclosure, in their own creative presentations. The Sephardim pairing allows the focus to remain on that. The confession that arises in Micah 7 is 'who is a God like you forgiving iniquity and remitting sin' (7.18) picking up from Hosea 14.4 but now from the standpoint of a completed act. His turning back in love (7.19) also echoes Hosea 14's use of *šûb*.

It belongs to the core Christian confession that God himself bears the judgement he righteously executes over sin, in his Son. 'For our sake he made him to be sin who knew no sin, so that in him we might become the righteousness of God' (2 Cor. 5.21). In Hosea, we see God's 'fierce anger' over sin and the decision of God himself to forebear (11.9). The text gives clear testimony to the anguish of God in withholding this judgement out of love. But he does so, as the final chapter makes clear, so that his love might lead to repentance and in so doing give new life. Joel shows the righteous judgement of God unleashed in full force, as his unwavering verdict over human sin, as the prophets as a whole had proclaimed this. Yet, inside of this judgement God himself provides, out of his own righteousness, the means for Israel's rescue. He makes himself known for the purpose of raising Israel from the dead.

The compassionate formula from Exodus, tells of a God who countenanced a way to let his transcendent righteousness and holiness stand aloof from sin, else the only recourse was destruction. In the dialogue with Moses that ensues, God forebears – for the sake of his Name. He will not 'divide himself'. He will not detach himself from his people and start again. He will indeed accompany Moses and the people because his character – merciful but by no means clearing the guilty – cannot do else but carry on in love. Perhaps, even more so, in the movement from Hosea to Joel and the DOL presentation of the latter, we see Israel brought into the vortex of judgement and a way found forward. This way will become a surety, an earnest of forgiveness and new life, through all that God's judgements in time will wreck.

Surely the point of Cranmer's work and that of the *Haftarot* is to bring the sinful human soul straight into the vortex of judgement – the confrontation with God's righteousness through all time – and plot the course of forgiveness and new life. Not just describe it, but enact it. This is what Joel accomplishes in its own literal sense presentation. And in its place in the Twelve, the reader confronted with his testimony (1.2-3), in whatever generation to come he or she find themselves, is made able to move through the history represented by its past unfolding in the Twelve and find new life for the future, through repentance and new grace extended. That generational out-reaching continues to this day and is born witness to in Joel's reception history in church and synagogue.

Bibliography

Allen, Leslie. *The Books of Joel, Obadiah, Jonah, and Micah*. NICOT; Grand Rapids, MI: Eerdmans, 1976.

Assis, E. *The Book of Joel: A Prophet Between Calamity and Hope*. New York: Bloomsbury, 2013.

Barton, J. *Joel and Obadiah: A Commentary*. OTL; Louisville, KT: Westminster John Knox, 2001.

Beck, M. *Der 'Tag YHWHs' in Dodekapropheten: Studien im Spannungsfeld von Traditions- und Redaktionsgeschichte*. BZAW 356; New York and Berlin: Walter de Gruyter, 2005.

Beck, M. 'Die Dodekapropheten als Anthologie', *ZAW* 118 (2005): 558–81.

Ben Zvi, E. 'Twelve Prophetic Books or "The Twelve": A Few Preliminary Considerations', in J. W. Watts and P. R. House, eds, *Forming Prophetic Literature*, 125–56. Sheffield: Sheffield Academic Press, 1996.

Bergler, S. *Joel als Schriftinterpret*. Frankfurt: Peter Lang, 1988.

Bewer, Julius A. *A Critical and Exegetical Commentary on Micah, Zephaniah, Nahum, Habakkuk, Obadiah and Joel*. ICC; New York: Charles Scribner's Sons, 1911.

Bosshard-Nepustil, E. *Rezeptionen von Jesaja 1–39 im Zwölfprophetenbuch*. Göttingen: Vandenhoeck und Ruprecht, 1997.

Coggins, R. 'Interbiblical Quotations in Joel', in J. Barton and D. J. Reimer, eds, *After the Exile: Essays in Honor of Rex Mason*. Macon: Mercer University Press, 1996, 75–84.

Coggins, R. 'Joel', *CBR* 2: 85–103.

Crenshaw, J. *Joel*. Anchor Bible; New York: Doubleday, 1995.

Deissler, Alfons. *Zwölf Propheten. Hosea, Joel, Amos*. Würtzburg: Echter, 1992.

Hagedorn, A.C. *Die anderen im Spiegel: Israels Auseinandersetzung mit den Völkern in den Büchern Nahum, Zefania, Obadja und Joel*. BZAW; Berlin and Boston: Walter de Gruyter, 2011.

House, P. R. *The Unity of the Book of the Twelve*. Sheffield: Sheffield Academic Press, 1997.

Jeremias, J. 'The Interrelationship between Amos and Hosea', in *Forming Prophetic Literature: Essays on Isaiah and the Twelve in Honor of John D. W. Watts*, 171–86, eds, James W. Watts, Paul House; *JSOTS* 235; Sheffield: Sheffield Academic Press, 1996.

Jeremias, J. ' "Denn auf dem Berge Zion und in Jerusalem wird Rettung sein" (Joel 3,5): Zur Heilswartung des Joelsbuches', in F. Hahn, F.-L. Hossfeld, H. Jorissen u. A. Neuwirth, eds, *Zion – Ort der Begegnung: Festschrift für Laurentius Klein*, 35–45. Bodenheim: Athenaeum Hain Hanstein, 1993.

Jeremias, J. 'Joel/Joelbuch' in *TRE* XVII (1988): 91–7.

Jeremias, J. 'Neueren Tendenzen der Forschung an den kleinen Propheten', in F. G. Martinez/E. Noort, eds, *Perspectives in the Study of the Old Testament and Early Judaism*, 122–36. FS A. S. van der Woude, VTS 73; Leiden: Brill, 1998.

Jeremias, J. 'Der <<Tag Jahwes>> in Jes 13 und Joel 2', in R. G. Kratz, T. Krueger and K. Schmid, eds, *Schriftauslegung in der Schrift*, 129–38. Berlin and New York: Walter de Gruyter, 2000.

Jeremias, J. *Die Propheten Joel, Obadja, Jona, Micha*. ATD; Göttingen: Vandenhoeck und Ruprecht, 2007.

Jeremias, J. 'The Function of the Book of Joel for Reading the Twelve', in Rainer Albertz, James D. Nogalski, Jakob Wöhrle, eds, *Perspectives on the Formation of the Book of the Twelve*, 21–34. BZAW 433; Berlin and Boston: Walter de Gruyter, 2012.

Jeremias, J. 'Gelehrte Prophetie: Beobachtungen zu Joel und Deuterosacharja', in *Vergegenwärtigung des Alten Testaments: Beiträge zur biblischen Hermeneutik* (Festschrift für Rudolph Smend zum 70. Geburtstag; eds, Christoph Bultmann, Walter Dietrich, Christoph Levin), 97–111. Göttingen: Vandenhoeck & Ruprecht, 2002.

Müller, A. K. *Gottes Zukunft: Die Möglichkeit der Rettung am Tag YHWHs nach dem Joelbuch*. WMANT; Neukirchen-Vluyn: Neukirchener Verlag, 2008.

Nogalski, J. *Literary Precursors to the Book of the Twelve*. BZAW 217; Berlin: Walter de Gruyter, 1993.

Nogalski, J. *Redactional Processes in the Book of the Twelve*. BZAW 218; Berlin: Walter de Gruyter, 1993.

Nogalski, J. *The Book of the Twelve: Hosea-Jonah*. Smith and Helwys Bible Commentary; Macon, GA: Smith and Helwys Publishing, 2011.

Plöger, O. *Theocracy and Eschatology*. S. Rudman, trans.; Richmond, VA: John Knox Press, 1968.

Redditt, Paul L. and Aaron Schart, eds, *Thematic Threads in the Book of the Twelve*. BZAW 325; Berlin: Walter de Gruyter, 2003.

Robinson, T. H. and F. Horst. *Die zwölf kleinen Propheten*. HAT 14; Tübingen, 1964.

Rudolph, Wilhelm. *Joel, Amos, Obadja, Jona*. KAT XIII.2; Gütersloh: Gütersloher, 1971.

Schart, Aaron. *Die Entstehung des Zwölfprophetenbuches*. BZAW 260; Berlin: Walter de Gruyter, 1998. Schwesig, Paul-Gerhard. *Die Rolle der Tag-JHWHs-Dichtungen im Dodekapropheten*. BZAW 366; Berlin: Walter de Gruyter, 2006.

Scolarick, Ruth, ' "Auch jetzt noch (Joel 1:2,12a": Zur Eigenart der Joelschrift und ihrer Funktion im Kontext des Zwölfprophetenbuches', in Erich Zenger, ed., *'Wort JHWHs, das geschah ...' (Hos. 1,1) Studien zum Zwölfprophetenbuch*, 47–69. HBS 35; Freiburg et al., 2002.

Seitz, Christopher R. 'Prophecy and Tradition-History: The Achievement of Gerhard von Rad and Beyond', in *Prophetie in Israel: Beiträge des Symposiums >>Das Alte Testament und die Kultur der Moderne<< anlässlich des 100.Geburtstags Gerhard von Rads (1901–1971) Heidelberg, 18.-21. Oktober 2001*, 30–51. I. Fischer, K. Schmid, H. G. M. Williamson, eds, Münster: Lit-Verlag, 2003.

Seitz, Christopher R., 'The Book of the Twelve: New Horizons for Canonical Reading, with Hermeneutical Reflections', *Scottish Bulletin of Evangelical Theology* 22 (2004): 151–72.

Seitz, Christopher R. *Prophecy and Hermeneutics*. STI; Grand Rapids, MI: Baker Academic, 2007.

Seitz, Christopher R. *The Goodly Fellowship of the Prophets: The Achievement of Association in Canon Formation*. Grand Rapids, MI: Baker Academic, 2009.

Smith, George Adam. *Expositor's Bible: The Book of the Twelve Prophets, Vol. 1*. London: Hodder and Stoughton, 1906

Spieckermann, H., 'Dies irae: der alttestamentliche Befund und seine Vorgeschichte', *Vetus Testamentum* 39 (1989): 194–208.

Spronk, K. 'Jonah, Nahum and the Book of the Twelve: A Response to Jakob Wöhrle', *JHS* 9 (2009): 2–9.

Sweeney, M. 'Sequence and Interpretation in the Book of the Twelve', in Nogalski, ed., *Reading and Hearing the Book of the Twelve*, 49–64. Atlanta, GA: Society of Biblical Literature, 2000.

Sweeney, M. *The Twelve Prophets, Volume 1: Hosea, Joel, Amos, Obadiah, Jonah*. Berit Olam; Collegeville, MN: Liturgical Press / Michael Glazer, 2000.

Troxel, Ron. *Prophetic Literature: From Oracles to Books*. Chichester: Wiley-Blackwell, 2012.

Troxel, Ron. 'The Problem of Time in Joel', *JBL* 132 (2013): 77–95.

Weiser, Artur. *Das Buch des zwölf kleinen Propheten*. ATD 24; Göttingen: Vandenhoeck & Ruprecht, 1949.

Wöhrle, Jakob. *Die frühen Sammlungen des Zwölfprophetenbuches*. BZAW 360; Walter de Gruyter, 2006.

Wöhrle, Jakob. *Der Abschluss des Zwölfprophetenbuches*. BZAW 389; Berlin: Walter de Gruyter, 2008.

Wöhrle, Jakob. 'Joel and the Formation of the Book of the Twelve', *BTB* 40 (2010): 127–37.

Wolff, H. W. *Joel, Amos*. BK XIV.2; Neukirchen-Vluyn: Neukirchener, 1969.

Wolff, H. W. *Joel and Amos*. Hermeneia; Philadelphia, PA: Fortress, 1997.

The Book of the Prophet Joel

Note: The English translation of Joel which appears below is the New Revised Standard Version. It is reproduced for easy reference based upon a commonly available Bible translation. The rubrics (in bold) introduce sub-sections of the Hebrew text, which in turn correspond to divisions of the text as they are treated in the commentary to follow. The NRSV translation will be supplied in the commentary, along with notes detailing text-critical issues where necessary. The rubric headings provided below will give the reader a good overview of the approach taken in the commentary (where the canonical Joel in its entirety is treated as a dramatic unity). Because the Book of Joel is relatively short (73 verses), and because we believe the final form of the text is intended to be read as a comprehensive whole, it has been judged useful to have an accessible English translation available at this juncture in the overall treatment. This also provides us a baseline from which to discuss translation and text-critical issues. Fortunately, in Joel these are minor compared with other Old Testament books.

The verse enumeration below follows the customary translation practice in English versions. The Masoretic Text has a brief five-verse Chapter 3 at 2.28-32. The final Chapter 3 below corresponds to MT 4.1-21. This minor divergence affects the sub-section commentary evaluation very little.

NRSV follows a practice of distinguishing prose from poetic lines (at 2.30–3.8). We reproduce this below, as it will be subject to the commentary evaluation *ad loc*. Frequently the implication of this practice is that we are encountering secondary additions, or some kind of supplementation over and above the main poetic/prophetic original. Because we judge the 'original Joel' already to be a mature witness, indebted to prior prophecy and from its inception rhetorical literature, the usual distinctions between primary text and secondary elaboration require a different conception. The Introduction has discussed this topic and it will be handled in the Commentary proper.

Superscription (1.1)

The word of the LORD that came to Joel son of Pethuel:

Joel's Hermeneutical Introduction (1.2-3)

> ² Hear this, O elders,
>   give ear, all inhabitants of the land!
> Has such a thing happened in your days,
>   or in the days of your ancestors?
> ³ Tell your children of it,
>   and let your children tell their children,
>   and their children another generation.

The Crisis Described (1.4)

> ⁴ What the cutting locust left,
>   the swarming locust has eaten.
> What the swarming locust left,
>   the hopping locust has eaten,
> and what the hopping locust left,
>   the destroying locust has eaten.

Elaboration and Charge I (1.5-7)

> ⁵ Wake up, you drunkards, and weep;
>   and wail, all you wine-drinkers,

over the sweet wine,
> for it is cut off from your mouth.
⁶ For a nation has invaded my land,
> powerful and innumerable;

its teeth are lions' teeth,
> and it has the fangs of a lioness.
⁷ It has laid waste my vines,
> and splintered my fig trees;

it has stripped off their bark and thrown it down;
> their branches have turned white.

Elaboration and Charge II (1.8-10)

⁸ Lament like a virgin dressed in sackcloth
> for the husband of her youth.
⁹ The grain offering and the drink offering are cut off
> from the house of the LORD.

The priests mourn,
> the ministers of the LORD.
¹⁰ The fields are devastated,
> the ground mourns;

for the grain is destroyed,
> the wine dries up,
> the oil fails.

Elaboration and Charge III (1.11-12)

¹¹ Be dismayed, you farmers,
> wail, you vinedressers,

over the wheat and the barley;
> for the crops of the field are ruined.
¹² The vine withers,
> the fig tree droops.

Pomegranate, palm, and apple—
> all the trees of the field are dried up;

surely, joy withers away
> among the people.

A Call to Lamentation (1.13-14)

¹³ Put on sackcloth and lament, you priests;
  wail, you ministers of the altar.
Come, pass the night in sackcloth,
  you ministers of my God!
Grain offering and drink offering
  are withheld from the house of your God.

¹⁴ Sanctify a fast,
  call a solemn assembly.
Gather the elders
  and all the inhabitants of the land
to the house of the LORD your God,
  and cry out to the LORD.

The Day of the LORD (1.15-18)

¹⁵ Alas for the day!
For the day of the LORD is near,
  and as destruction from the Almighty it comes.
¹⁶ Is not the food cut off
  before our eyes,
joy and gladness
  from the house of our God?

¹⁷ The seed shrivels under the clods,
  the storehouses are desolate;
the granaries are ruined
  because the grain has failed.
¹⁸ How the animals groan!
  The herds of cattle wander about
because there is no pasture for them;
  even the flocks of sheep are dazed.

Closing Personal Appeal (1.19-20)

[19] To you, O Lord, I cry.
For fire has devoured
    the pastures of the wilderness,
and flames have burned
    all the trees of the field.
[20] Even the wild animals cry to you
    because the watercourses are dried up,
and fire has devoured
    the pastures of the wilderness.

The Unfolding Day of the LORD (2.1-11)

[2] Blow the trumpet in Zion;
    sound the alarm on my holy mountain!
Let all the inhabitants of the land tremble,
    for the day of the Lord is coming, it is near—
[2] a day of darkness and gloom,
    a day of clouds and thick darkness!
Like blackness spread upon the mountains
    a great and powerful army comes;
their like has never been from of old,
    nor will be again after them
    in ages to come.

[3] Fire devours in front of them,
    and behind them a flame burns.
Before them the land is like the garden of Eden,
    but after them a desolate wilderness,
    and nothing escapes them.

[4] They have the appearance of horses,
    and like war-horses they charge.
[5] As with the rumbling of chariots,
    they leap on the tops of the mountains,
like the crackling of a flame of fire
    devouring the stubble,

like a powerful army
  drawn up for battle.

⁶ Before them peoples are in anguish,
  all faces grow pale.
⁷ Like warriors they charge,
  like soldiers they scale the wall.
Each keeps to its own course,
  they do not swerve from their paths.
⁸ They do not jostle one another,
  each keeps to its own track;
they burst through the weapons
  and are not halted.
⁹ They leap upon the city,
  they run upon the walls;
they climb up into the houses,
  they enter through the windows like a thief.

¹⁰ The earth quakes before them,
  the heavens tremble.
The sun and the moon are darkened,
  and the stars withdraw their shining.
¹¹ The Lord utters his voice
  at the head of his army;
how vast is his host!
  Numberless are those who obey his command.
Truly the day of the Lord is great;
  terrible indeed—who can endure it?

Direct Call to Return and Elaboration (2.12-17)

¹² Yet even now, says the Lord,
  return to me with all your heart,
with fasting, with weeping, and with mourning;
¹³ rend your hearts and not your clothing.
Return to the Lord, your God,
  for he is gracious and merciful,

slow to anger, and abounding in steadfast love,
and relents from punishing.
¹⁴ Who knows whether he will not turn and relent,
and leave a blessing behind him,
a grain offering and a drink offering
for the Lord, your God?

¹⁵ Blow the trumpet in Zion;
sanctify a fast;
call a solemn assembly;
¹⁶ gather the people.
Sanctify the congregation;
assemble the aged;
gather the children,
even infants at the breast.
Let the bridegroom leave his room,
and the bride her canopy.

¹⁷ Between the vestibule and the altar
let the priests, the ministers of the Lord, weep.
Let them say, 'Spare your people, O Lord,
and do not make your heritage a mockery,
a byword among the nations.
Why should it be said among the peoples,
"Where is their God?"'

The Lord's Response and Promises (2.18-20)

¹⁸ Then the Lord became jealous for his land,
and had pity on his people.
¹⁹ In response to his people the Lord said:
I am sending you
grain, wine, and oil,
and you will be satisfied;
and I will no more make you
a mockery among the nations.

²⁰ I will remove the northern army far from you,
    and drive it into a parched and desolate land,
its front into the eastern sea,
    and its rear into the western sea;
its stench and foul smell will rise up.

    Surely he has done great things!

Response to God's Verdict (2.21-4)

²¹ Do not fear, O soil;
    be glad and rejoice,
    for the LORD has done great things!
²² Do not fear, you animals of the field,
    for the pastures of the wilderness are green;
the tree bears its fruit,
    the fig tree and vine give their full yield.

²³ O children of Zion, be glad
    and rejoice in the LORD your God;
for he has given the early rain for your vindication,
    he has poured down for you abundant rain,
    the early and the later rain, as before.
²⁴ The threshing floors shall be full of grain,
    the vats shall overflow with wine and oil.

Divine Reply for the Present (2.25-7)

²⁵ I will repay you for the years
    that the swarming locust has eaten,
the hopper, the destroyer, and the cutter,
    my great army, which I sent against you.

²⁶ You shall eat in plenty and be satisfied,
    and praise the name of the LORD your God,
    who has dealt wondrously with you.
And my people shall never again be put to shame.
²⁷ You shall know that I am in the midst of Israel,

and that I, the LORD, am your God and there is no other.
And my people shall never again be put to shame.

The Great Day of the LORD to Come (2.28-32 = MT 3.1-5)

²⁸ Then afterward
I will pour out my spirit on all flesh;
your sons and your daughters shall prophesy,
your old men shall dream dreams,
and your young men shall see visions.
²⁹ Even on the male and female slaves,
in those days, I will pour out my spirit.

³⁰ I will show portents in the heavens and on the earth, blood and fire and columns of smoke. ³¹ The sun shall be turned to darkness, and the moon to blood, before the great and terrible day of the LORD comes. ³² Then everyone who calls on the name of the LORD shall be saved; for in Mount Zion and in Jerusalem there shall be those who escape, as the LORD has said, and among the survivors shall be those whom the LORD calls.

The Great Day Elaborated (3.1-3 = MT 4.1-3)

³ For then, in those days and at that time, when I restore the fortunes of Judah and Jerusalem, ² I will gather all the nations and bring them down to the valley of Jehoshaphat, and I will enter into judgement with them there, on account of my people and my heritage Israel, because they have scattered them among the nations. They have divided my land, ³ and cast lots for my people, and traded boys for prostitutes, and sold girls for wine, and drunk it down.

Internal Footnote (3.4-8 = MT 4.4-8)

⁴ What are you to me, O Tyre and Sidon, and all the regions of Philistia? Are you paying me back for something? If you are paying me back, I will turn your deeds back upon your own heads swiftly and speedily. ⁵ For you have taken my silver and my gold, and have

carried my rich treasures into your temples. ⁶ You have sold the people of Judah and Jerusalem to the Greeks, removing them far from their own border. ⁷ But now I will rouse them to leave the places to which you have sold them, and I will turn your deeds back upon your own heads. ⁸ I will sell your sons and your daughters into the hand of the people of Judah, and they will sell them to the Sabeans, to a nation far away; for the LORD has spoken.

The Coming Day Dramatically Depicted (3.9-17 = MT 4.9-17)

⁹ Proclaim this among the nations:
Prepare war,
    stir up the warriors.
Let all the soldiers draw near,
    let them come up.
¹⁰ Beat your plowshares into swords,
    and your pruning hooks into spears;
    let the weakling say, 'I am a warrior'.

¹¹ Come quickly,
    all you nations all around,
    gather yourselves there.
Bring down your warriors, O LORD.
¹² Let the nations rouse themselves,
    and come up to the valley of Jehoshaphat;
for there I will sit to judge
    all the neighbouring nations.

¹³ Put in the sickle,
    for the harvest is ripe.
Go in, tread,
    for the wine press is full.
The vats overflow,
    for their wickedness is great.

¹⁴ Multitudes, multitudes,
    in the valley of decision!
For the day of the LORD is near

in the valley of decision.
¹⁵ The sun and the moon are darkened,
 and the stars withdraw their shining.

¹⁶ The LORD roars from Zion,
 and utters his voice from Jerusalem,
 and the heavens and the earth shake.
But the LORD is a refuge for his people,
 a stronghold for the people of Israel.

¹⁷ So you shall know that I, the LORD your God,
 dwell in Zion, my holy mountain.
And Jerusalem shall be holy,
 and strangers shall never again pass through it.

Finale and Transition to the Twelve (3.18-21 = MT 4.18-21)

¹⁸ In that day
the mountains shall drip sweet wine,
 the hills shall flow with milk,
and all the stream beds of Judah
 shall flow with water;
a fountain shall come forth from the house of the LORD
 and water the Wadi Shittim.

¹⁹ Egypt shall become a desolation
 and Edom a desolate wilderness,
because of the violence done to the people of Judah,
 in whose land they have shed innocent blood.
²⁰ But Judah shall be inhabited forever,
 and Jerusalem to all generations.
²¹ I will avenge their blood, and I will not clear the guilty,
 for the LORD dwells in Zion.

Solemn Opening (1.1-4)

Superscription (1.1)

1 The word of the Lord that came to Joel son of Pethuel.

The prophet Joel is introduced with a notice only of his patronymic, presumably to distinguish him from others with the same name. He is the son of Pethuel. That is all the biography we are given and the name Pethuel tells us nothing more on this score.[1]

Like the prophets who are his neighbours in the Twelve, we are told that the 'word of YHWH' came to him (cf. Hosea, Micah, Zephaniah). Unlike them, it came in a distinctive and characteristic way: he is a prophet indebted to other prophets (see Introduction above). The phrase refers to the way the Word of the LORD encounters him and inspires him to produce the work before us. At the same time, it is important to note that the same language is used of Joel as of those earlier prophets, however we might measure what is distinctive about him. The word of YHWH came to him.[2] As with them, we are given no detailed account of how this happened and just what the phrase

---

[1] The name Pethuel is unknown apart from the reference here. Some manuscripts read the more frequently appearing 'Bethuel' (as, e.g., the father of Rebecca as in Gen. 22.22-3).
[2] *dĕbar-YHWH ʾăšer hāyāh ʾel yôʾēl*

means in history-of-religions terms. In the case of Joel we are arguing that the literary deposit of the prophet is itself the inspiration. This is all the more true in Joel where we have no 'call narrative' as such and no vestige of the 'historical' prophetic at work in past time, but rather a book which is from its inception designed to address the future generations to come (1.2-3).

I hold the view, with Rendtorff, that a decision to provide detailed superscriptions (historically coordinated with the Kings of Israel and Judah) for books in the Twelve (e.g., Hosea, Amos, Micah, Zephaniah) concomitantly means that a decision has been made in other cases precisely not to do so.[3] That is, the superscripting of the individual works in the Minor Prophets is an external act whose editorial origins are difficult to determine. It could well be that the earliest prophets are those for whom coordination with the events of the Deuteronomistic History is simply a most obvious desideratum. That is, the four prophets Hosea, Amos, Micah and Zephaniah are genuinely the first four to be active in Israel's history, however we are to judge the subsequent growth of their respective books. They are all 'pre-exilic prophets' whose oral speech to contemporaries warned the generations they addressed of the judgement of God at the hands of the nations.[4] They prophesised in the period from Uzziah/Jeroboam (Hos. 1.1), through the time of Jotham, Ahaz and Hezekiah (Mic. 1.1; also Hos. 1.1) until the reign of Josiah (Zeph. 1.1). Left to our own devices we would then judge Amos and Hosea as contemporaries, with the latter having a longer career as befits the range of his literary legacy. Jeremias has conjectured that the students of Hosea had a greater influence on the editing of Amos than

---

[3] 'Theological Unity', 76-7. It is not the position of this commentary that there was something like a four-book or deuteronomistic 'precursor' (so Nogalski, Schart, Wöhrle and others) to be identified due to a common superscripting pattern. Though Rendtorff's observation was not made to contest this, it does in some measure follow from it. See also the recent critique of C. Levin, 'Das "Vierpropheten Buch": Ein exegetischer Nachruf', *ZAW* 123 (2011): 221-35.

[4] It does not follow from this that they together circulated as the earliest precursor of the Twelve. That is speculation of a different order.

the obverse, as their respective works were coming to form collaboratively. The fall of the Northern Kingdom brought the tradents of Hosea to Judah where the addressees of Amos were seen as seconding their prophetic leader in what he had himself said. The Hosea editors of Amos helpfully clarified how and why Amos' sentence of judgement was fulfilled and answered key questions about the divine decision no longer to respond positively to Amos' intercession. Amaziah silenced him and so wrote the death sentence over Israel.[5]

The point here is not to unroll the details of Jeremias's proposal, but only to say that the position of Hosea is understandable from the standpoint of what he has offered. We are to read Amos through the lens of Hosea and as we have seen, in time, through the lens of Joel as well. Hosea's witness is the more substantial literarily and its scope reaches further into the future than does Amos' ('two years before the earthquake, in the days of Uzziah and Jotham'). Such is the editorial notice which locates his basic achievement.[6]

One commentator has sought to bring Joel into coordination with these four early prophetic works, by noting the similarity of their superscriptions. He has an earlier Joel circulating with Amos, Micah and Zephaniah, having successfully – so the theory runs – displaced Hosea from initial position (for the purpose of the theory, which requires Joel to be 'first').[7] This would, however, require the

---

[5] J. Jeremias, 'Interrelationship', 171–86.
[6] Is the original superscription of Amos the trigger for the development of a more standardized deuteronomic form applied subsequently to the other three pre-exilic witnesses? That is surely possible and it would oppose the idea of a four-book precursor as the starting point for the development of the Twelve. See the classic treatment of Gene Tucker, 'Prophetic Superscriptions and the Growth of a Canon', in *Canon and Authority: Essays in Old Testament Religion and Theology* (eds George W. Coats and Burke O. Long; Philadelphia, PA: Fortress, 1979), 56–70.
[7] Wöhrle has adopted this account of the matter: 'It is thus reasonable to suppose that the Book of Hosea was part of the exilic book of the Four, that it was replaced by the primary layer of the Book of Joel when the Joel-Corpus was edited, and that it was reintegrated into the Book of the Twelve not until a very late stage' ('Joel and the Formation', 134). One supposes this conclusion is necessary to hold together disparate bits of the larger conception, including both an original Four Book idea and also the complex redaction history of Joel being put forward, with five redactional levels.

deuteronomistic chronological material to be elided so that the superscriptions match, which is the most obviously distinctive feature of them. The more salient point of the comparison of Joel with these four superscriptions, is in fact that his provides no chronological cross-reference and we believe that is purposeful. Joel is located where he is for thematic reasons and not for historical reasons.[8] The purpose of indicating no historical setting, is so that the Book of Joel can function in a hermeneutically significant way. The discussion above has sought to establish this point carefully.

In the earliest history of interpretation, the view assumed by Jerome, that the undated prophetic books are to be situated historically in the period of their neighbours, seems in a low-flying way to be operative more broadly. We can see it in Theodore of Mopsuestia and in the next Antiochene generation, in Theodoret of Cyrus. Cyril also holds this view even, as has been held, his text follows a different order in which Joel follows Micah. Calvin's cautions are still relevant today: let the text tell us what it does and also does not prioritize.[9]

---

[8] See the discussion in Seitz, *Prophecy and Hermeneutics*, 234–8; *Goodly Fellowship*, 86–7. The theory of Watson, which sees the undated books as subsumed into the past is required for his understanding of Habakkuk. This allows Habakkuk, on his view, to release the alleged past witness of the prophets into a future with hermeneutical purpose. See Francis Watson, *Paul and the Hermeneutics of Faith* (London: T.&T. Clark, 2004), 129–38. But that is Joel's only purpose as it now stands and the same can be argued for Obadiah and Jonah (the other 'undated books'). See my evaluation of Watson's approach in *Prophecy and Hermeneutics*, 118 n. 8.

[9] 'The time in which he prophesied is uncertain. Some of the Jews imagine that he exercised his office in the time of Joram, king of Israel, because a dreadful famine then prevailed through the whole land, as it appears evident from sacred history; and as the Prophet records a famine, they suppose that his ministry must be referred to that time. Some think, that he taught under Manasseh, but they bring no reason for this opinion; it is, therefore, a mere conjecture. Others think that he performed his office as a teacher not only under one king, but that he taught, at the same time with Isaiah, under several kings. But as there is no certainty, it is better to leave the time in which he taught undecided; and, as we shall see, this is of no great importance. Not to know the time of Hosea would be to readers a great loss for there are many parts which could not be explained without a knowledge of history; but as to Joel there is, as I have said, less need of this; for the import of his doctrine is evident, though his time be obscure and uncertain. But we may conclude that he taught at Jerusalem, or at least in the kingdom of Judah. As Hosea was appointed a Prophet to the kingdom of Israel, so Joel had another appointment; for he was to labour especially among the Jews and not among the Ten Tribes: this deserves to be particularly noticed.'

He concludes that unlike Hosea, we really are unhindered by not knowing the historical context of Joel.

Joel's Hermeneutical Introduction (1.2-3)

> ² Hear this, O elders,
>   give ear, all inhabitants of the land!
> Has such a thing¹⁰ happened in your days,
>   or in the days of your ancestors?
> ³ Tell your children of it,
>   and let your children tell their children,
>   and their children another generation.

We are confronted right away with a question of the literary structure of Joel. Incumbent upon a commentary is the provision of units for discussion, which requires one to say where they begin and end and why and how these decisions are to be reached. One older view was that the units went back to the oral ('live') speech of the historical prophet. This in turn offered the possibility, that stylistic and metrical explanations were to hand to argue for a unit's length and integrity and also that supplemental additions could be identified.[11]

With Joel, we are not operating with this same presupposition, that is, of being able to reach back into the oral phases of the historical prophet's once-upon-a-time. The next step – showing the movement of the historical material into a redactional presentation for an anticipated readership – was also required in this model. But on our view these two phases – however much one could trust previously that they were present and that they could be tidily extricated – are one

---

[10] The Hebrew simply repeats 'this' (*zōt*) here. Compare NIV translation where the double 'this' appears.
[11] The presupposition goes back to Gunkel and Gressmann and one can see it operative even in later prophetic texts like Isaiah 40–55. The latter material has shown itself far more amenable to a rhetorical analysis and it likely imitates earlier oral prophetic forms. For a full evaluation with reference to the work of Gunkel, Gressmann, Begrich and others, see R. Melugin, *The Formation of Isaiah 40–55* (BZAW 141; Berlin and New York: Walter de Gruyter, 1976). I have my own evaluation in 'Isaiah 40–66' (NIB).

and the same phase in Joel. Indeed, our view is that the first verses as we see them above *seek to make this very point*. For this reason, among others to be referred to below, we do not want to move too quickly to attach them to what follows (1.5-7). One often speaks of the 'motto' of Amos as 'The Lord roars from Zion, and utters his voice from Jerusalem', because the single verse (1.2) stands out and seems to epitomize the prophet's larger message, or certainly the opening two chapters. Joel's motto is 1.2-3. The same is true in our view of Joel 1.2-3. Correctly appreciating this is critical to reading all that follows.

Fortunately, the significance of these opening verses is now widely acknowledged.[12] Nogalski held that they pointed back to Hosea's ending and described what was not happening in Joel's day, namely the unprecedented repentance called for at Hosea 14.1-3. This seems unlikely for a number of reasons. The first 'this', only with difficulty, could make sense as a call for the elders to read the last chapter of Hosea or somehow otherwise have it in view; after all, they – not redactors or their presumed audience – are the ones being realistically addressed by the opening exhortation. Form-critically, the imperatives describe something they presently are to do *within their own real/envisioned frame of reference*. Further, the idea that the prophet wants generation after generation to hear of a failure, strikes one as a strange use of the common motif of educating the generations, such as we see it elsewhere in the Old Testament. This is, of course, why virtually all interpreters – I am unaware of any exceptions in the history of interpretation, ancient or modern – take 'this' (*zō't*) in 1.2 and its counterpart in verse 3 (*'ālêhā*) as references to one and the same thing. The elders and those who live in the land are being called to attend to something that is happening before them. For most interpreters the natural referent is the unprecedented locust

---

[12] See especially Jeremias. His teacher Wolff referred to the opening two verses as 'gewichtige[n] Introitus' (22) and classified the unit as a *Lehreröffnungsruf* (*Joel*, 22).

plague about to be reported in 1.4. Alternatively, it is that but also the entire scenario of judgement about to unroll in the opening chapters. Its position is therefore precisely as we find it elsewhere. It *proceeds* what is to be described and sets up a dramatic tension by asking us to hold on and hear what is about to be said; it never is used to point backwards, as it were (to Hosea's last words).

Above all it is to the credit of Jeremias to turn our attention to the wider import of this opening unit for the interpretation of Joel as a whole.[13] He notes first that those addressed in 1.2 ('elders and inhabitants of the land') are the same as those who are assembled in 1.14 for a fast and it is their cry to the LORD, along with other developments in the intervening depiction, which occasions the dramatic denouement in 2.15-17. Their 'telling' pertains to that climax as well as to what leads up to it.[14] Second, a comparison of the motif identified in 1.2-3 ('call to tell future generations'), with similar passages in the OT, shows that a consistent element is seeking to reassure the future recipients of the report by means of testifying to God's past favour. This is very evident in Exodus 10, which we have discussed in detail above (see Introduction, section 5). But it is a major theme in the Psalter as well. It is in initial position and what follows is a report of God's reversal of fortune and/or marvellous act.

---

[13] See ATD 24/3, 11. His focus is on Chapters 1–2 in this regard. We, however, believe the verses serve to introduce the entire portrayal of Joel, including the final chapters. To speak of a late creative work, written in character and hermeneutically crafted for future generations, *which is then in turn* secondarily supplemented burdens overmuch what we might mean by 'successive phases' of editing so closely related to one another – a point Jeremias otherwise accepts even as he departs from his teacher Wolff on the more specific question of 'original author'. Beyond registering the details of a theory, it is unclear what it actually means to produce a text in ATD and set a major part of it off in italics. See the longer discussion of Jeremias and the unity of the book below.

[14] '... not only a hint at the unusual need of the drought and locusts is the focus of the urgent call, but the whole horizon of the imminent threat of the Day of the LORD and its final avoidance' (Jörg Jeremias, 'The Function of the Book of Joel for Reading the Twelve', in *Perspectives on the Formation of the Book of the Twelve* [eds Rainer Albertz, James D. Nogalski, Jakob Wöhrle; Berlin:Walter de Guyter, 2012], 83).

> 'I will tell (*spr*) of all your wonderful deeds.' (Ps. 9.1)
>
> 'The heavens are telling (*spr*) the glory of God.' (Ps. 19.1)
>
> 'We have heard with our ears, O God, our ancestors have told (*spr*) us, what deeds you performed in their days.' (Ps. 44.1)
>
> 'We will not hide them from their children; we will tell (*spr*) to the coming generation the glorious deeds of the LORD, and his might, and the wonders he has done.' (Ps. 78.4)
>
> '... he commanded our ancestors to teach to their children; that the next generation might know them, the children yet unborn, and rise up and tell (*spr*) them to their children, so that they should set their hope on God.' (Ps. 78.5)

The motif is used flexibly of various forms of transmission as the above examples indicate. The motif occurs also in the middle of psalms to the same effect, with the key verb being *spr* (26.7; 40.6) as well as at the end (48.13; 79.13). As the motif is introduced at the very beginning of Joel, we should expect the referent to follow and so must wait for what is said. For this reason it has been assumed that the following verse (1.4) supplies the referent of *zō't* – not least because verse 4 stands out from the following, imperative-laden, rhetorical structure (1.5-7; 1.8-10; 1.11-12). This in turn culminates in the repeated imperatives of verses 13-14 ('put on', 'mourn', 'wail', 'come', 'lodge', 'declare', 'call', 'summon', 'cry out'). What the elders are to tell is that a four-series assault of locusts has invaded. The verse is odd enough in its clipped form that it has served the purpose nicely of an unprecedented occurrence ('Has this ever happened?' [NIV]; 'Has such a thing happened?' [NRSV]). But the other passages noted above make clear that we should be on the lookout for a longer recital and one that may use dramatic judgement to underscore God's favour in the midst of this, so as to exhort future generations. This transpires in Joel at 2.18-19.

Implications for reading Joel

We have argued above for the integrity of a single conceptual portrayal that includes the present work in its entirety (Introduction, sections 5 and 8). The dramatic deliverance at 2.18-19 is intentionally positioned, so that future generations can take heed of the enacted compassion of YHWH and face with confidence the future unfolding day of the LORD. The subject of the latter two chapters is equally the subject of the ensuing books of the Twelve and has been intentionally so designed.

A knock-on effect of seeing 1.2-3 as anticipating a wider frame of reference than 1.4 alone or 1.4-20, as has been persuasively argued by Jeremias, is that it makes it difficult to restrict the report to future generations to just the opening two chapters of Joel and to them alone. To be sure, a lesson can be learned from the dramatic deliverance that concludes these two chapters (2.20-9). But the final two chapters (MT 3.1–4.21), put this lesson into play, as it were. If a supplementor is responsible for adding them, was this done in such a way that 1.2-3 would be viewed as only reaching to 2.18-27 and no farther? On our view, this is the difficulty of trying to describe two levels of text and also make sense of them hermeneutically as distinctive, given the shape of the final book itself. A reading in which Joel is allowed to maintain its own distinctive portrayal *vis-à-vis* the Twelve, and also in relation to them, works best when the book in its entirety is allowed to function at the same hermeneutical level.[15]

---

[15] On this point, note the congruence between the recognition formula in 2.27 and its appearance again at the end of the book (3.17). The knowledge of YHWH is to be gained via both halves of the presentation. That is in turn what shall be passed onto coming generations.

Introitus: The Crisis Described (1.4)

⁴ What the cutting locust¹⁶ left,
    the swarming locust has eaten.
What the swarming locust left,
    the hopping locust has eaten,
and what the hopping locust left,
    the destroying locust has eaten.

This is an extremely important text for the interpretation of Joel. It has been so as well in the history of interpretation. Our decision to separate it from what precedes and what follows means to emphasize this.¹⁷ It cannot be denied that the unprecedented events the elders are to report are properly/chiefly to be viewed through the lens of 1.4, which follows hard upon it.¹⁸ The four-phased description of the locust plague is arresting and means to be so.

At the same time, it is crucial to attend to the structural implications of this signal verse. References to locusts in what follows are unmistakable. Yet, mixed into the descriptions of a locust plague are military (1.6; 2.1, 4-5), drought (1.10, 12, 17) and fire (1.19; 2.3, 5b) themes, whose relationship to one another and to locusts is not always clear. Are locusts like a military invasion? This is certain. But equally a military invasion is like a locust plague. Do locusts crackle and destroy like fire, leaving drought-like conditions? Certainly. To have an unprecedented event intimated (1.2-3) and then a dramatic notice of four phases of consumption follow hard upon it (1.4), in turn invites the reader to see what is coming in the depiction to follow. What is coming is comprehensive in the fullest sense of the

---

¹⁶ NRSV follows the translational tradition of rendering these as four distinct kinds of insects/locusts (the English translation of Wolff [Hermeneia, 17] gives 'biter', 'locust', 'hopper' and 'jumper'; Crenshaw [AB, 82] has 'chewer', 'swarming locust', 'jumper', and 'finisher'). See the discussion below.

¹⁷ The obvious structural motif uniting 1.5-14 is the imperatival form, superbly rendered to indicate urgency.

¹⁸ So, for example, the commentary of Theodore (105).

word. It is difficult to describe properly without extensions of various kinds, such as are carefully deployed by Joel.[19]

When one does look ahead, what is unmistakable is that this wide-ranging invasion/s, presaged with the locust text of 1.4, eventually is halted, summarily and dramatically. This is obvious at the concluding unit of the opening two chapters, where the recognition formula appears (2.26-7). The verdict over the four-phase locust assault is clear just before the conclusive formula is introduced.

> I will repay you for the years
>   that the swarming locust has eaten,
> the hopper, the destroyer, and the cutter,
>   my great army, which I sent against you. (2.25)

The metaphorical extension ('my great army') is also recalled, picking up the admixture evidenced in 1.5–2.17. The point here is just as we must be careful to allow the report-to-generations theme to extend to its proper conclusion in 2.18-19, so too Joel's stunning introduction of the four-phase locust assault means to awaken us to a drama we must carefully watch unfold and then conclude in the elimination of

---

[19] The fecundity is routinely noted in the history of interpretation, where in consequence the realistic and the metaphorical often vie for due emphasis. See the insightful essay of Lossl ('When is a Locust Just a Locust?'). This is surely a proper implication of the literal sense's own richness. Theodoret and others also allow the text's richness and ambition to invite reflections on spiritual phases of deterioration. This is triggered, one suspects, by the reference in 1.5 to drunkenness and to signs of moral decline, elsewhere assumed in Joel's exhortations to follow. He writes, 'If on the other hand, you wanted to take them spiritually as well you could in turn apply such things to sinful people. Into their mind and heart, in the manner of a locust and a young locust as well as the cutting locust, evil demons are constantly entering along with passions of many kinds and forms …' (267–8). The intermixture of realistic and metaphorical in Joel's depiction is an achievement that gives rise to these homiletical reflections and may properly grasp an intentional element in Joel's discourse by not dividing them into redactional levels or otherwise cancelling them out. In pre-modern interpretation this narrowing can also happen when the locusts are taken *only* as references to phases of military assault (Assyria, Babylonia, Media, Persian, Roman, Hellenistic – depending upon the temporal location deemed appropriate for Joel).

the threat in 2.25. The repaying theme of 2.25 winds back and retracts what was unwound in 1.4 and in the presentation that follows.

One theme I am not aware is typically highlighted, is the correspondence between phases of locust assault (the four-fold series) and the phases of retelling Joel exhorts in 1.2-3. In the one case, we have a positive report that is to extend over four generations (from 'your children' to theirs, and theirs, and to the generation after that), while in the latter we have four phases of consumption, for which the author has had to seek out strange synonyms. The refrains of Amos 1–2 also come to mind (1.3, 6, 9, 11; 2.1, 4, 6). The 'three yea four' motif means to evoke an overloading, that has in consequence demanded God's justice.[20] God will not relent (*šûb*) because the fourth repetition of sin amounts to an inuring or searing of conscience that must be punished if health is to be restored. Four phases of locusts, by extension, represents a thoroughgoing assault, beyond which there can be no further iteration.[21]

If this is so, then the emphasis of the text is on the exhaustion of an assault. This in turn means that our ability to describe the difference between various kinds of locusts in ancient Israel, may run up against the limits built into the motif itself. It would then not be the case – as with 'Eskimos and words for snow' – that Israel had a rich vocabulary for locusts due to close familiarity with them, or that what we have here are quasi-scientific phases in the maturation of a genus. Rather, the author tries as best he can to supply four different words for 'locust' so that he can accomplish his main purpose in emphasizing: nothing will be left. The repetition of *yeter* ('what x left') would then be the key item in the refrain. By the time we get to phase four, the point would be: nothing can remain after a four-fold assault.

---

[20] Wisdom literature presents the same basic idea (Prov. 30.15, 18, 21, 29; Job 33.14-18).
[21] Duane Garrett has suggested that Amos' use of 3+4 may point to the number 7 and its evocation of completeness. That would be consistent with the interpretation here. See Duane A. Garrett, *Amos: A Handbook on the Hebrew Text* (Baylor Handbook on the Hebrew Bible; Waco, TX: Baylor University Press, 2008).

Of course, the idea of a tetrad representing *totality* is also close to hand and is frequently noted by ancient commentators. Jerome notes four horns, four chariots, four winds in Zechariah 1.19 and 6.1-5. As indicated above, many ancient commentators eschew inquiry into etymology – Jerome's learned temperament inclines toward this, even when it will cause him trouble (the *qîqāyôn* in Jonah) – not because it is difficult business in the case of *gāzām*, *'arbeh*, *yeleq* and *ḥāsîl*, which it most assuredly is.[22] Rather, they see the tetrad as *literally related to nations*. That is, the literal sense of 1.4 deploys the metaphor of locusts to speak of a series of national invasions of Israel. So clarifying them and distinguishing them in a realistic, natural sense would be like asking how big were the wings of the eagle in Ezekiel 17.7.[23] A few modern interpreters adopt something of the same position.[24]

Another position regarding the tetrad has emerged in the more recent research into Joel and the intertextuality that is his trademark.[25] The locust hoard (*gāzām*) is an agent of judgement in Amos (4.9) – where they also appear in the same context as blight (*šiddāpôn*) and other kindred descriptors. The generation of Amos failed to repent

---

[22] Augustine reports that a fistfight broke out in Tripoli upon hearing the new Latin rendering by Jerome of the tree God raised up to provide shade for Jonah (4.6).

[23] Theodoret works with the idea that prophetic speech is never primarily focused on the local details of history, whose descriptions would in consequence look very different in their writings. Joel wants to make a larger point than a once-upon-a-time locust plague, that concerned the activity of God with Israel through a very broad historical period (Jerome's tetrad of nations is different though the basic point remains). The locusts, like the animals in Ezekiel, are intended to be metaphors. The local point for him is a spiritual application. Incidentally, the idea that Joel prophesies the tetrad assault of nations, is yet another reason the idea developed that he was an early prophet, to be dated with reference to his contemporaries Hosea and Amos. That is, the entire unfolding of national assaults in judgement on Israel/Judah needs to lie in the distant future. That is our view as well, though we distinguish between the actual historical location of Joel and the one the book asks us to assume in respect of the Twelve as a whole. This is why Joel is and remains undated.

[24] Crenshaw, AB, 88-9.

[25] See, especially, the recent monograph of A. K. Müller and her exhaustive analysis of the locust references in Exodus 10 (the word *'arbeh* appears there seven times); in the Psalms, with reference to the Egyptian plagues (*ḥāsîl* in Ps. 78.46 and *yeleq* in Ps. 105.34, in both cases in parallel to *'arbeh*); and in Amos. Of course, the motif of generational remembering and reporting also links the Exodus and Psalm texts. See *Gottes Zukunft*, 41-3.

(4.12), tragically (the repentance theme is central in Joel).[26] Pestilence (*deber*), like the pestilence of Egypt, is directed by God against his own people (Amos 4.10). Locusts (*gōbay*) appear as well in Amos' first vision of judgement (7.1), alongside fire (7.4) and destroyed fruit (8.1). In the locust plague in Egypt, the term consistently used in Exodus 10 – a clear reference text for Joel – is *'arbeh* (Joel's locust #2). The other two terms (*ḥāsîl* and *yeleq*) appear in Ps. 78.46 and Ps. 105.34, with reference to the Egyptian plagues.[27] So alongside the totality motif betokened by the tetrad in 1.4, there may also be the totality of locust references as they now exist in the plague traditions in the OT. By juxtaposition, Amos has already closely associated" his *gāzām* judgement on Israel with the plagues-like-Egypt (*deber*) visited on his generation (4.10). The locust judgement of 7.1 is joined by three further visions vouchsafed to the prophet Amos, which show the relenting of God being brought to an end.

It is hardly a stretch to think of locusts in relation to a more general picture of drought and crop devastation, such as this unfolds in the verses to follow.[28] That the images swim in and out of one another may also be explicable if Joel wants to relate the ecological judgement of

---

[26] Rendtorff holds that the frequent reference to *šûb* in the refrains of 1.3, 6, 9, 11, 13; 2.1, 4, 6 is based upon the motif such as we find it in Joel. He writes regarding Amos 1, 'This time we read "I will not turn (it) back"' (1.3, 6, 9, etc.). What does 'it' refer to? In the context of Joel, the reader thinks of the announcement of the '"Day of YHWH", which will come inexplicably upon the nations' (The Canonical Hebrew Bible: A Theology of the Old Testament [Leiden: Deo, 2005], 279). He leaves unclear what the earlier witness (Amos) might have meant by the phrase 'Day of YHWH', without Joel there to provide a strong association ('Theological Unity', 81). See my discussion in 'Scriptural Author and Canonical Prophet: The Theological Implications of Literary Association in the Canon', in *Biblical Method and Interpretation: Essays in Honour of John Barton* (eds K. Dell and P. Joyce; Oxford: Oxford University Press, 2013), 176–88. The essay interacts with J. Barton ('The Day of Yahweh in the Minor Prophets', in *The Old Testament: Canon, Literature and Theology* [Aldershot: Ashgate, 2007], 279–88) over how the Day of the Lord functions in Amos and in subsequent renditions in the Twelve, while retaining its own particular character.

[27] *'arbeh* accompanies *yelek* in Ps. 105.34.

[28] See Jeremias, ATD 24/3, 13; 'Gelehrte', 105. 'Die Joelschrift entfaltet in ihrem ersten Kapital eine mehrdimensionale Katastrophenwelt, die sich nicht auf eine Linie reduzieren lässt. Die Sphären von Militär und Landwirtschaft überlagen einander' (Scolarick, 'Auch jetzt noch', 64).

Hosea, as the judgement of God over his people in that work (2.8-9, 22 [Eng]; 4.3; 5.12; 6.3, 11; 7.14; 8.7; 9.2, 16; 13.15; 14.5-8), with the DOL in his own work. And the obvious extension to the nations we witness in the unfolding portrayal, was not wrongly held by the history of interpretation to be a major, if not the major, point of reference for the locusts as metaphors. Four locusts in a series mean four waves of national, total judgement. In this, Joel anticipates the judgement of the nations, as this will unfold in Amos and the books to follow.

> We hold the view that the natural–realistic dimension is always the ground-floor upon which the extensional senses operates, not least because of the intertextual linkages put in the foreground in recent research. The locusts, in fourfold form, are the plagues of Egypt par excellence. Moreover, because the way Israel will be judged by God in time, in the long prophetic view, is by Assyria and Babylon and other ensuing powers (see Daniel), Joel uses the potential in the overwhelming locust plague engulfing his generation to bespeak a Day of the LORD with wider, anticipatory significance.[29]

Locust Plagues Today

In the appendix, I have lodged a 6 March 2013 report from the *New York Times* with the title 'A Locust Plague, Shy of Biblical Proportions, in Israel', written by Isabel Kershner. We know from modern accounts of locust plagues just how dreadful and devastating they could be, especially in Saharan Africa, India, Egypt and the Sinai Peninsula. 'Locusts eat their own weight in green food each day. An invasion of Somaliland in 1957 was estimated to include 1.6×10 (to 10th power) locusts and weighed 50,000 tons' (ABD 3, 867). The *New York Times* report concerns a recent episode of locust infestation, in 2013, from Egypt into Israel, 'like a vivid enactment of the eighth plague

---

[29] For Aquinas on the literal sense, see Don Collett, 'Reading Forward: The Old Testament and Retrospective Stance', in *Pro Ecclesia: A Journal of Catholic and Evangelical Theology*, XXIV:2 (2015), 182, citing Thomas Aquinas, *Summa Theologicae*, I.1.10.

visited upon the obdurate Pharaoh'. Israel went on the alert after large swarms were spotted in the Cairo region, leading to worries – given wind and climate conditions – of an 'entomological cross-border invasion'. A hot line was set up to report swarm sightings.

> 'By Tuesday, grasshoppers the size of small birds were reported on balconies and in gardens in central and northern Israel. But the largest concentration and ominous black cloud of millions, settled for the night near the tiny rural village of Kmehin in Israel's southern Negev desert, not far from the border of Egypt.
>
> 'Potato farmers in the area complained that their fields were being ruined. Drivers said they could not see through their windshields for all the bugs flying in their direction.'

Note, how in the telling of this story we have all the main ingredients in Joel's description: different kinds of locusts ('grasshoppers the size of small birds'); military language ('a cross-border invasion'); reference to the original plagues, now visited on Israel ('like a vivid re-enactment of the eighth plague visited upon Pharaoh'); crop devastation ('their fields were being ruined'); swarms producing darkness ('an ominous black cloud of millions'); and the necessity of reporting the affair.

What we do not have is any understanding of what this plague means in God's larger time and purpose. For that we needed 'the word of the LORD coming to' someone like the prophet Joel, whose understanding of the significance of this event in God's time and purpose constituted his inspired achievement.

Early Christian Interpretation

In the useful survey of early Christian interpretation of Joel 1.4 ('When is a Locust just a Locust?')[30] J. Lossl organizes the naturalistic interpre-

---

[30] 'Patristic Exegesis of Joel 1.4 in the Light of Ancient Literary Theory', *JTS* 55 (2004): 575–99.

tation popular in the modern period in this way: 'Presumably each word *somehow* refers to locusts. But how? Does it mean four different species, four stages in the ontogenesis of one species, or regionally varying expressions for species or ontogenetical stages?' (585). By contrast, the ancient interpreters typically prefer the metaphorical/ tropological interpretation of a tetrad of nations or stages of moral decline, or both. Even Theodore, known for his rejection of allegory and preference for literal/historical senses, sees in Joel 1.4 a figurative sense (Greek is on Lossl, 591). The four types of locusts are Tiglathpilesar, Salmanassar, Sennacherib and Nebukadnezzar; his Assyrian–Babylonian series is typical for him in its historically limited (only the OT) range. He judges the Persians in a positive light in his historical conception and so they are not locust-represented. Jerome does not pursue with his typical diligence a fresh Latin rendering from the Hebrew via etymology/lexicography, because he also opts for the figural tetrad (his Latin *bruchus* merely reproduces the LXX βροῦχος). Joel is speaking of historical events by means of a figure and his sequence of nations is: locust 1) Assyrians, Babylonians, Chaldeans; 2) Medes and Persians; 3) the Macedonians; and 4) the Romans – the *rubigo* of imperial red.[31] The prophets speak of historical events such as we see in Kings and Chronicles. Locust plagues are universal natural phenomena. Cyril of Alexandria and Julian of Aeclanum have the same national series as Jerome, with slight variations if individual kings are mentioned. Cyril reckons that Joel does not name the nations directly, as we might expect of Israel's prophets, as this would be too bold for his audience and so he deploys instead figurative language. The natural disaster language allows him to ease his audience into the historical reality he intends. Theodoret alone is uncertain we should flee too quickly to the figurative meaning, since locust plagues are

---

[31] *Rubigo* can have the association of lewdness as well (so Seneca). This may also partly trigger the association of the tetrad with stages of moral decline notable in Jerome and Julian.

not unusual in Joel's context. This may be an instance, to be noted elsewhere, of the more mature and careful Theodoret simply wanting to get some distance on his predecessor Theodore.[32]

In our view, the significance for Joel lies not at the level of natural descriptions of locust species or some precise understanding of how these four terms differ from one another or otherwise describe a sequence. His concern with thoroughness and the four-fold form assures that note is sounded. He may also know of the four words used to describe locusts, plagues or divine judgement elsewhere (Exodus, Amos, Psalms) and decides the cumulative effect is best registered *vis-à-vis* this tradition, by enclosing them all in 1.4. The natural realm corresponds with Hosea's horizon and also with the plague event itself that Joel and his generation are experiencing. But it is also, in addition, a harbinger for the DOL in its larger sense, as this will involve the sequence of nations dispatched to render judgement over Israel. That various possibilities exist for fleshing this out, is a function of reading the four locusts as sequential national assaults and plenty are the candidates for this subsequent alignment. We doubt that Joel is thinking in these more precise terms and instead has the totality motif in view. Theodoret offers a careful appraisal from the ancient commentators.

---

[32] Note the reference to Amos and Jeremiah. '... I also suspect the events, to be taken at face value, happened in reality; blessed Amos also mentions locust, young locust, scorching, mildew and the spoiling of figs, olives and vines by the cutting locusts and in addition to these parching and drought ... And the divinely-inspired Jeremiah also made clear mention of this'). Note the careful way the extensional sense ('attacking enemy') remains grounded in the natural sense ('chastisement imposed from heaven'). He continues, 'It is therefore necessary to take the statements not only figuratively, since the sacred prophets are in accord in stating, that what was prophesied also happened in reality; in fact, for them to learn that in being given up to the attacking enemy they were paying for lawlessness and impiety, they were rightly exposed to the chastisement imposed from heaven, learning through them that for being neglected God punished them in one form and another' (86–7).

Part One

The Day of the LORD Upon Israel (1.5-20)

On our view, the Book of Joel is conceptually designed as a dramatic portrayal of the Day of the LORD in three parts. The first part (1.5-10) describes a present assault resulting in the devastation of Israel in a locust plague and its aftermath. It is a DOL *upon* Israel in the sense that it is being presently, dramatically experienced within Joel's temporal logic. The comprehensive DOL scenario familiar from the prophetic literature as a whole has been 'back-dated', as it were, so as to enclose events of judgement Israel is depicted as experiencing *in her present tense and not as an end-time anticipation only, out in the temporally distant*. Jeremias has properly underscored this dimension of creative adaptation of the DOL by Joel.[1] In Part One, we see the day described and we also witness an exhortation for formal lamentation to the priests and summoned elders (1.13-14), that we will argue is then taken up by them in 1.15-19. The prophet Joel personally responds with his own cry to God in 1.20.

Part Two (2.1-27) consists of the DOL as yet more fully *unfolding* for the same generation. This heightening is purposeful. The *upon*

---

[1] 'Joel opens the eyes of his contemporaries to the possibility that *the Day of the Lord is imbedded already in any extreme distress* like in the drought and in the locusts of his own time. He is the first and only prophet that not only warns his own generation of the coming Day of the Lord, but claims they are already experiencing the dreaded effects of this day, though the day is only beginning and has not reached its full power' ('Function', 81).

DOL moves resolutely forward into an *unfolding* DOL, so as to occasion a yet fuller exhortation (2.12-17). The DOL theme is more clearly indicated in Part Two (2.1 and 2.11). Here God responds in favour (2.18-19) and a new day of bounty and the knowledge of God is described as a reality unfolding for the same generation (2.20-7). This is followed by Part Three (2.28–3.21) where the DOL constitutes a *Finale* involving the nations formerly sent in judgement (likened in Parts One and Two to a locust plague). Simply organized, we see the following structure:

OPENING (1.1-4)

PART ONE: Upon (1.5-20)

PART TWO: Unfolding (2.1-27)

PART THREE: Finale (2.28–3.19)

CLOSING: Transition to Amos and Obadiah (4.20-1)

We begin our commentary on the first main section of Joel as follows. The dramatic opening section picks up from 1.4 and is marked by a tone of urgency.

Charge I and Elaboration (1.5-7)

> ⁵ Wake up, you drunkards,[2] and weep;
>   and wail, all you wine-drinkers,
> over the sweet wine,
>   for it is cut off from your mouth.
> ⁶ For a nation has invaded my land,
>   powerful and innumerable;

---

[2] G provides the explanatory gloss 'from their wine' (*ex oinon auton*).

its teeth are lions' teeth,
   and it has the fangs of a lioness.
⁷ It has laid waste my vines,
   and splintered my fig trees;
it has stripped off their bark and thrown it down;[3]
   their branches have turned white.

This portion of text (1.5-7) is but the first section of a longer rhetorical unit, composed of three parts (1.5-7; 1.8-10; 1.11-12) culminating in 1.13-14 and the cry of 1.15. Each of the units is introduced with imperatives. The final unit (vv. 13-14) itself contains nine imperatives in two brief verses. The effect of this is to underscore an atmosphere of great urgency, in the light of 1.4 and the ensuing descriptions of a natural assault. The tendency to remove 1.15 was predicated on the idea that the theme of the DOL belonged to secondary redaction, an overlay on the original natural disaster theme proper.[4] Jeremias is representative of a newer trend which sees in 1.15 a carefully placed anticipation of Chapter 2's DOL material (1.1 and 2.11) and which regards the first two chapters as a literary unit.[5] A bit less clear is whether 1.15 constitutes the cry referred to in 1.14 and whether it stands more closely with what follows (1.15-18). We will take the issue up below.[6]

---

[3] BHS proposes a change in word order of the Hebrew of no exegetical consequence (or versional support).
[4] On the background of this tendency, see Introduction Chapter 4. It goes back to B. Duhm, 'Anmerkungen zu den Zwölf Propheten', ZAW 31 (1911): 1–43; 81–110; 161–204 and is reproduced, e.g., in the ICC commentary of Bewer.
[5] 'Gelenk zwischen ihnen stellt 1,15 dar, ein Vers, in dem der Prophet schlagartig in die Klage des Volkes über furchtbare Naturerfahrungen hinein die Perspektive des endzeitlichen "Tages Jahwes" eröffnet, die 2,1-11 dan näher ausführt' (3).
[6] Wolff allows the verse to remain the subject of individual comment, though the link with 1.14 is unmistakable in his treatment. He concludes his treatment of v. 14: '… the great call to communal lamentation only prepares the way for recognition of the significance of the extraordinary hour' (Hermeneia, 33). Jeremias says we must wait patiently for the execution of 1.14 until 2.15 (ATD 24/3,17). Rudolph likewise does not see a direct continuation of v. 14 in v. 15, even as he refuses to regard it as a secondary addition as in the original work of Duhm. Barton writes, 'The approach adopted here is that in these verses [15-16] we have the words of the lamentation that the priests and people are exhorted to make in vv. 13 and 14' (OTL, 58).

The first urgent address is to those who enjoy drink to excess (1.5). It is similar one supposes to the first woe oracle of Isaiah, following the Song of the Vineyard (5.11-12).

> Ah, you who rise early in the morning
>   in pursuit of strong drink,
> who linger in the evening
>   to be inflamed by wine,
> [12] whose feasts consist of lyre and harp,
>   tambourine and flute and wine,
> but who do not regard the deeds of the LORD,
>   or see the work of his hands!

In our context, however, the oracle of Joel is not an indictment in the manner of Isaiah, but an ironic summoning of those who enjoy wine – because they are about to enter a period of forced detox. The vineyards have been devastated.[7] The locust plague of 1.4, described in the figure of national assault, is responsible. Verse seven summarizes:

> It has laid waste my vines,
>   and splintered my fig trees.

The late-sleeping (one supposes) wine enthusiasts are awakened with bad news and are instructed because of it to wail. The wine/new wine which is their sought-after daily bread is no more. The locusts' anatomical prowess is fully on display. They can easily eat their own body weight daily. The metaphors enrich the description. Their teeth are like lion's teeth; their fangs those of a lioness. They are indeed like a mighty nation in thunderous assault, one unable to be numbered. Such is the scale and force of the locusts as they embroil and devour all in their path. This is not a cry to repent or an indictment that might lead to that (so Isaiah) but rather a statement

---

[7] Barton is correct to distinguish Joel 1.5ff. from Isaiah 5.1-13, 28.1-8; Amos 6.6; Prov. 20.1, 23.29-35) where the emphasis is on drunkenness as such (*Joel*, 50).

of fact that underscores the reality described in 1.4. Joel's people are witnessing an unparalleled natural disaster as the locust hoards cut down all in their path. The 'vine and fig tree' devastation and judgement of Hosea is here in full swing. The metaphorical resemblance to national attack is Joel's touch, designed to underscore the severity of the attack and to anticipate the unfolding DOL in Chapters 2–4.

Charge II and Elaboration (1.8-10)

> [8] Lament like a virgin dressed in sackcloth
> for the husband of her youth.[8]
> [9] The grain offering and the drink offering are cut off
> from the house of the LORD.
> The priests mourn,
> the ministers of the LORD.
> [10] The fields are devastated,
> the ground mourns;
> for the grain is destroyed,
> the wine dries up,
> the oil fails.

Here the addressees are not as obvious as in the first unit. But the context soon clarifies who is central in the address. This is not wine 'snatched from the lip' of drunkards, but a cutting off whose consequence is a different kind of deprivation. Not the loss of drink for those excessively thirsty (who are overdue for a respite), but loss leading to mourning because the priests and ministers are unable to exercise their proper, temperate and holy vocation. This pairing finds correlates in 1.13 and 2.17 and as such deserves to be considered as significant, given the brevity of Joel and also the paucity of specific, identifiable referents.

---

[8] Greek has *ton andra autes ton parthevikon* ('the husband of her maidenhood').

In Hosea, with the prophet's emphasis on cultic apostasy, it is not surprising that the priests are often the object of specific rebuke, as in 4, 6-9.

> ⁶ My people are destroyed for lack of knowledge;
>   because you have rejected knowledge,
>   I reject you from being a priest to me.
> And since you have forgotten the law of your God,
>   I also will forget your children.
>
> ⁷ The more they increased,
>   the more they sinned against me;
>   they changed their glory into shame.
> ⁸ They feed on the sin of my people;
>   they are greedy for their iniquity.
> ⁹ And it shall be like people, like priest;
>   I will punish them for their ways,
>   and repay them for their deeds.

In Amos, the priest Amaziah is singled out and mentioned by name. It is he who severs the intercessory life-line of Amos and dooms the nation and his own house (7.10-17). The first vision of judgement in Amos is surprisingly similar to that of Joel:

> 7 This is what the Lord God showed me: he was forming locusts at the time the latter growth began to sprout (it was the latter growth after the king's mowings). ² When they had finished eating the grass of the land, I said,
>
> "O Lord God, forgive, I beg you!
>   How can Jacob stand?
>   He is so small!"

Amos' personal intercession and plea – thwarted by the priest at Bethel – has its counterpart in Hosea's poignant address to his own people, the priestly failure of his day notwithstanding:

> Come, let us return to the Lord;
>   for it is he who has torn, and he will heal us;

he has struck down, and he will bind us up.
² After two days he will revive us;
on the third day he will raise us up,
that we may live before him. (6.1-2)

The similarity with Joel 2.12 is unmistakable. It is the priests who are set forth as the primary agents of prayer and appeal in 2.17, which in turn brings forth the verdict of forgiveness in 2.18.

The priesthood in Joel is without personal name or further specification, which may serve to make the text available to future generations as well (see Introduction of Chapter 9).[9] The priests/ministers, unlike in Hosea and Amos, both stand in a position of responsibility and are expected by the text in fact to discharge that vocation positively. The priests are here depicted as mourning – appropriately, because what they wish to do they are hindered by God's judgement and not faults assigned to them, from doing. The drought-like conditions the prophet describes are not a theme redactionally supplemented (v. 10), unrelated to the locust devastation, but simply describe the conditions that obtain that prevent offerings from being made to YHWH.[10] Joel here shows us a priesthood ready and able to exercise the vocation God has given them, who are instead in mourning because they are prevented from that sacred duty. It may be his purpose to offer a strong contrast to the depiction of the priesthood elsewhere in the XII and so to model a reliable 'second-chance' deportment. This need not exclude the fact that he means what he says and expects the priesthood of his address to respond properly, which they will in fact do as we read on.

---

[9] The jussives in 2.17, for example, allow for this.
[10] Wöhrle has here revived the multiple-redactional-layering refined analysis of R. E. Wolff and earlier Joel interpreters. Theodoret, who assumes a natural referent for the devastation (unlike his contemporaries) writes, 'He describes also what will be the effect of them, giving a glimpse of vines destroyed, their branches bleached, and fig trees stripped of their foliage, as normally happens in a locust plague' (87). See the recent evaluation of Wöhrle's approach by Spronk in *JHS* 9 (2009): 2-9.

As noted in the Introduction (Chapter 5), the concept of a 'second chance' acknowledgment of wrong doing and the appropriateness of God's judgement in the past, one can see in the final chapters of Deuteronomy (see 30.1-20) and in the opening chapters of Jeremiah.[11] This constitutes the conduct and bearing that is to characterize the 'wise' (so the final refrain of Hosea that opens onto Joel and the Twelve as a whole).

Charge III and Elaboration (1.11-12)

> [11] Be dismayed, you farmers,
>   wail, you vinedressers,
> over the wheat and the barley;
>   for the crops of the field are ruined.
> [12] The vine withers,
>   the fig tree droops.
> Pomegranate, palm, and apple—
>   all the trees of the field are dried up;
> surely, joy withers away
>   among the people.

If Charge I represents an exhortation to those who have exploited and misused God's blessings and so immediately feel the pain of the locust plague; and Charge II is directed to those who are deprived from doing what is their sacred obligation (whose point and purpose is to maintain and uphold the healthy relationship with YHWH); then Charge III focuses on those most immediately affected: the farmers and vine growers who now have lost everything and have nothing to harvest. The vine and fig destruction – a familiar theme in Hosea, alongside grain, new wine, oil – is but a small part of the locust diet Joel describes. Wheat, barley, pomegranate, palm, apple tree – all the trees – are dried up. And so is the people's joy (v. 12).

---

[11] See Dennis Olsen, *Deuteronomy and the Death of Moses: A Theological Reading* (OBT; Minneapolis, MN: Fortress Press, 1994).

This last note is significant in that it does not suggest that the locust plague is being depicted as a clear, unilateral judgement on sin. The three units now discussed focus on the locust plague as a fact, a reality that has encompassed all the people; even the drunkards are not condemned for their drunkenness (as in Isaiah 5), but are told to mourn because they are soon to be deprived of their daily fix. Jeremias has noted that the motif word 'wrath' is absent in these opening two chapters.[12] Whatever else that might mean in precise terms, it appears that the locust plague is a more generalized example of God's judgement presently engulfing a generation. Absent are indictments for sinful conduct deserving punishment, such as we find it elsewhere (especially Zephaniah). Joel sees in the terrible locust plague a generalized divine judgement, like gravity or what Christian theology might register as the effects of 'original sin'. The 'people's joy' is erased as the locust plague renders its own stalking judgement. One thinks of the destruction of the plant at the end of Jonah. This happens not in direct relationship to sin – the text nowhere says that – but instead for pedagogical purposes as such. The pedagogical intention is also central in Joel (1.2-3). Joel sees in the locust plague an example of the final DOL presently spilling into time and bringing destruction in its generalized wake. The question Joel poses is not unlike that posed at the end of Jonah. Will Israel learn? Will Israel allow herself to be taught by God in these dramatic events? With these questions now sharply and urgently posed by the locust plague, the prophet moves to his next 'teaching moment'.

---

[12] '... the reader should note that *one of the most important ideas of Isa. 13 and Zeph. 1 is missing: the wrath of YHWH* ('Function', 80). Jeremias goes on to discuss this in the light of the offer 'yet even now' invitation of YHWH (2.12), which is the signature feature of Joel. On our view it is difficult to assess the avoidance of the term as such, but easier to conclude that the 'back-dating' motif of Joel's DOL in Chapters 1–2 intends to see the DOL more generally at work in the events of the locust plague and its effects, quite apart from a focus on sin and its consequences.

Final Charge: Call to Lamentation (1.13-14)

> ¹³ Put on sackcloth and lament, you priests;
>   wail, you ministers of the altar.
> Come, pass at the night in sackcloth,
>   you ministers of my God!¹³
> Grain offering and drink offering
>   are withheld from the house of your God.
>
> ¹⁴ Sanctify a fast,
>   call a solemn assembly.
> Gather the elders
>   and all the inhabitants of the land
> to the house of the LORD your God,¹⁴
>   and cry out to the LORD.¹⁵

The prophet backs up and addresses the priests/ministers again. They stand in a unique position and can be effective agents in the cause of YHWH. To repeat, nothing suggests that they are the occasion of the plague unfolding before the people, such as we view their negative depiction elsewhere in the Twelve.¹⁶ They are rather in the position of Moses in the foundational Sinai intercession.¹⁷ They are in the position of the prophetic intercessor Ezekiel, who will also lie down and bear the judgement of God though he is himself

---

¹³ All major Greek witnesses have 'God' without the first-person suffix. See discussion below on the transition of MT from 'my' to 'your' (pl.) in verse 13. V (*ministri dei mei*) confirms MT.

¹⁴ BHS annotates the Göttingen LXX (what they call *textus Graecus originalis*) as lacking the Tetragrammaton.

¹⁵ Syriac presupposes *le'mor*, thus interpreting the following verses (vv. 15-20) as a quotation of the lament itself. On this, see the discussion below.

¹⁶ See Hos. 3.9; 5.1; Amos 7.10-17; Mic. 3.11; Zeph. 3.4; Mal. 2.1; 3.3-4. See Wolff's passing comments in support of our position here (38).

¹⁷ It may be noted that Cyril also drew the parallel with Moses. He speaks of the priests 'grieving exceedingly for the people in their care and being assigned to the sacred and commendable liturgy, the purpose being that they would give their attention to the God of all before everything else and imitate Moses the revealer himself, leader of Israel, who says to God, "I ask you, Lord, this people has committed a grave sin; if you forgive them the sin, forgive it, but if not blot me also out of this book you have written." The office of priesthood acts as mediator between God and the people ...' (270).

cleansed and inoculated (Ezek. 4.1-17). They are not Moses and they are not prophets and their vocation is as it is in God's ordaining. They are to exercise their vocation by putting on sackcloth and by mourning and wailing, because they are not able positively to bring the 'wonted offerings' to God, but have a vocation all the same. When in the fifth book of the XII the King of Nineveh and all his people (and beasts) conduct themselves as the priests are here charged by Joel (Jonah 3.5-10), it is most likely that we witness an intentional cross-association, meant to fill out the characterization of YHWH as compassionate and merciful – even toward those who do not know him or their right hand from their left (Jonah 4.11), but are coming to know him through his servants the prophets, including the reluctant and tardy Jonah. The moaning cattle in Joel (1.18) become sackcloth-laden beasts in Jonah's depiction. But in the case of Joel the theme of sinfulness – indeed of an extreme nature[18] – is not developed in anything like the same manner. Israel is engulfed in a locust plague of enormous scale. Rather than seeking to assign sin and guilt, the prophet instead urges wholesale and dedicated lamentation. The nine imperatives in this brief unit are all focused on acts of mortification and solemn assembling. It is not that sin or guilt is denied, but that the focus is elsewhere. Later when the call to 'return' is sounded, it takes the form not of 'repent from' but 'turn to' (Joel 2.12; cf. Hos. 6.1; 14.1).

The elders who were introduced at the solemn opening of Joel (1.2) are again addressed here. The priests are to be joined by the summoned elders and indeed by 'all who live in the land' (1.14). The LORD they are to cry out to is YHWH *'ĕlōhêkem*, 'your (pl.) God'. The prophet Joel speaks first of 'my God' (*'ĕlōhāy*) in 1.13 in his charge to the priests, but follows this with reference to 'the house of *your God*'. Is this a flirtation with the distancing of God *vis-à-vis* his people such

---

[18] So, God's clear verdict (1.1) and also the acknowledgement of the King of Nineveh (3.8). In Joel, this theme is not highlighted in the same way.

as we see it introduced in Exodus 33.1-3[19] and the wider depiction of this chapter (see 33.12-16), with Moses in the middle position as intercessor? That is not said plainly. What we do note is that if there is any space for this conception, it is firmly closed at the end of the chapter, where the first-person voice of the prophet (1.19-20) follows hard on the cry of the people to God in 1.15-18. More on this shortly. The unit in question now follows.

The Cry of All: The Day of the LORD (1.15-18)

[15] Alas for the day!
For the day of the LORD is near,
    and as destruction from the Almighty it comes.[20]
[16] Is not the food cut off
    before our eyes,
joy and gladness
    from the house of our God?

[17] The seed shrivels under the clods,[21]
    the storehouses are desolate;
the granaries are ruined
    because the grain has failed.
[18] How the animals groan!
    The herds of cattle wander about
because there is no pasture for them;
    even the flocks of sheep are dazed.[22]

---

[19] 'Go, leave this place, you and the people you have brought up from the land of Egypt ... I will not go up with you' (33.1-3). 'Consider, too, that this nation is your people' (33.13).

[20] See the discussion below on the proper very tense rendering here. 'Almighty' renders Hebrew Shadday. Wolff tries to recreate the consonance he believes is at work and the English translation also makes the effort, 'like might from the Mighty One it comes' (Hermeneia, 19). Crenshaw offers 'dawning like destruction from the Destroyer' (AB, 84) which he calls 'a pun on the divine name El Shaddai' (106). It is doubtful Shaddai should here be translated 'Destroyer' to make this point.

[21] An old crux; MT has *taḥat megredotehem*. G rendered 'the cows stomp by their manger' doubtless influenced by the text to follow (vv. 17-18).

[22] NIV renders the final verb *ne'esmu* as 'suffering'. NRSV seeks to follow the versions with 'dazed' (for which BHS conjectures *nasammu*; G has 'obliterated' [reading *smm* instead of *'sm*]).

The Day of the LORD Upon Israel (1.5-20) 141

As noted above, two issues have dominated the interpretation of this unit and particularly 1.15. Earlier interpreters (Duhm, Bewer, Plöger) saw the DOL reference as an eschatological addition made by the same hand that supplemented Joel's original locust material with the final two chapters.[23] More recent commentators (Wolff, Jeremias, Barton) dispute this view. We have already emphasized that Joel is nuancing the final eschatological Day scenario and seeing it at work already in the present. So the distinction between an eschatological 'final day' and a natural disaster in the present *is precisely what Joel is conjoining. That is his theological achievement.* To posit a redactional seam is precisely to fail to recognize this achievement.

The second issue has to do with the relation of this unit to what precedes (and follows). Some take it as the actual cry of those addressed by Joel in 1.13-14. It shows what the prophet had exhorted being put into action.[24] The transition to the first-person singular of 1.19-20 must then be explained.[25] Rudolph rejects any continuation of 1.13-14 on the grounds that 1.15-18 is not a prayer but rather 'die Begründung dafür, warum Fasten und Beten unerlässerlich sind'.[26]

There can be little doubt that 1.15 sounds a critical if not also central note and it needs to be allowed to register its full force. No

---

[23] See the longer discussion in Introduction, Chapter 4.
[24] Barton (OTL, 58). Nogalski sees the 'our' references are bringing the prophet together with the people to offer intercessory prayer (223). Achtemeier (NIB) construes the unit for interpretation 1.13-16. Deissler sees in 1.15-20 'in prophetischem Geist das dieser Situation entsprenchende und nun fällige exemplarishe Wort'. The purpose of the triple 'alas' of LXX is likely to represent an enacted cry following on 1.14. Cyril therefore reproduces this text for his commentary: 'Sanctify a fast, proclaim worship, assemble the elders, all the dwellers of the land in the house of our God. Cry aloud to the Lord at length, Alas, alas, for the day' (274; cf Theodore, 'Alas, alas, alas for the day, because the day of the Lord is near', 108). Cyril writes in his comment, 'Once again he indicates the way in which they should manifest grief, presents himself to them as a wise commentator on the way of repentance, and clearly demonstrates what it is that makes the God of all gentle and benevolent' (274). He shares the view of his contemporaries that great sin is presupposed by the prophet.
[25] Theodoret (and Cyril) assume the first-person voice is the prophet's (89). In the recent period, the liturgical theory of Kapelrud evaluated 1.19-20 as 'the prophet's person address to Yahweh in the style of an individual psalm of lamentation' (*Studies*, 5).
[26] HAT, 47.

mention of what is Joel's central theme (the Day of YHWH) has been made until now.[27] Now dramatically the prophet lets arise the recognition that the natural assault all are experiencing, lies within the horizon of the great DOL itself. This is what the people are experiencing, nothing less. The verb tenses need some attention. The Day is 'near' (*qārôb*) – that is, within immediate 'woe range' (*ăhāh layyôm*). The second temporal reference uses the prefixed form *yābô'*. In the context of the verse, the prefixed verb following the participle of the first expression probably means 'near and dawning/coming' rather than a simple future (as NIV) 'will come'. This better captures the present and unfolding reality as Chapters 1–2 seek to depict it.

We find no good reason for distancing 1.15ff. from the preceding unit/s. 'House of our God' (1.16) is anticipated in 1.14. 'Joy and gladness' at 1.16 (*śimḥâ wāgîl*) find their counterpart in the joy of 1.12 (*śāśôn*). The collocation of joy and food both cut off (*nikrāt*) is familiar to us (1.12 uses *yābēšû* and *hōbîš*). Are those addressed and summoned the speakers at this point? The first-person plural references certainly accommodate that interpretation ('our eyes' and 'our God') if not also the voice of the prophet joining them.

One main question arising in 1.15 (and in connection with the material following) has to do with intertextuality and Joel's awareness of and use of previous prophetic texts; we have discussed this crucial aspect of the Book of Joel in the Introduction (Chapter 3). At Joel 1.15 we see arise the dramatic acknowledgement, that in the locust plague presently experienced, nothing less than the Day of the LORD is making itself felt and this is done using the exact same language as Isaiah 13.6. Some commentators take this as the utilization by Joel of a common expression. This would make sense if it were not for

---

[27] Wolff captures this well (Hermeneia, 33).

a pattern of what appear to be direct referencing of prophetic texts across the chapters of Joel.

The other issue that is relevant here, is the curious reference to fire in the unit to follow. In what sense is a locust plague capable of being described as fire? Not 'like fire' – so 2.5, where logically enough the swift consumption by locusts is likened to engulfing flames in a wildfire:

> like the crackling of a flame of fire devouring the stubble,
> like a powerful army drawn up for battle.

Instead, the first-person voice at 1.19 describes the plight being experienced in a (seemingly) non-metaphorical/realistic way:

> for fire has devoured the pastures of the wilderness
> and flames have burned all the trees of the field.

We have argued above that the drought references are not at all inconsistent with the after-effects of a realistically depicted (and experienced) locust plague. Modern locust plagues are chronicled in precisely this way.[28] But what of fire?

Jeremias has offered the view that here the prophet is making use of the traditions of Amos where a great locust plague (the first dramatic vision of judgement in 7.1-2) has been conjoined with a fire of cosmic scale (the second vision on judgement in 7.3-4).[29] As he describes the Day of the LORD, then, the prophet Joel taps into the judgement against the nations tableau of Isaiah 13–14 and merges it with the judgement descriptions against Israel from the prophet Amos. The locust plague tradition from Exodus, in addition, is also clearly on display in Amos 4, where drought and blight and fire

---

[28] See 'locust plague' discussion in the appendix.
[29] ATD, 19-20. See also the compact discussion of A. Deissler (*Zwölf Propheten. Hosea, Joel Amos* [4th edn; Würtzburg: Echter, 1992], 72–3. He counts a litany of texts influencing Joel in his descriptions (Ezek. 30.2; Isa. 13.6; Amos 5.18-20; Isa. 2.12; Zeph. 1.7,14; Amos 7.1-3. Malachi is certainly relevant here as well (3.2 and 4.1 [Eng.]) where fire and the Day of YHWH are linked.

are also collated.[30] The view taken here is that it is very difficult to determine the various influences at work when it comes to fire references in 1.19-20 and that likely a number of factors are at work at the same time. It is certainly to be noted that *we only have these more extended descriptions once the Day of the LORD is actually referred to in 1.15*. In other words, when the devastating locust plague is brought within the ambit of the DOL traditions in 1.15 and declared to be such a Day now unfolding, that is the point when the prophet begins to introduce the sorts of extended descriptions that more directly entail the judgement of God in other prophetic contexts – not to mention the theophany encounters of fire and flame, familiar in the exodus texts and in the Psalms.[31] At the same time, it must be stressed that the realistic dimension is never out of sight. Locusts as they consume like a mighty army are like flames and fire as they consume, driven by wind and drought conditions. The fact that 1.19-20 does not exist in isolation but is followed by the metaphorical descriptions of locusts as like fire and like a mighty nation (2.5) means that references like those that conclude the opening chapter sit firmly on the boundary of realistic-metaphorical, releasing neither side of the balance. The reason this is so, we believe, involves the fact that the prophet is thinking about the devastating locust plague in relation

---

[30] 4.9-12: 'I struck you with blight and mildew; I laid waste your gardens and your vineyards; the locust devoured your fig trees and your olive trees; yet you did not return to me, says the LORD. I sent among you a pestilence after the manner of Egypt; I killed your young men with the sword; I carried away your horses; and I made the stench of your camp go up into your nostrils; yet you did not return to me, says the LORD. I overthrew some of you, as when God overthrew Sodom and Gomorrah, and you were like a brand snatched from the fire; yet you did not return to me,' says the LORD. In the locust plague of Joel the possibility of return – refused in Amos' day – is extended within the context of locust plague, drought, and fire – all present in Amos 4.9-12.

[31] Jeremias ATD 24/3, 17-19. He cites in this regard v. 3 of the chapter to follow. Fire and flame appear *in extenso* as descriptors related to the DOL (2.1-3). 'Das Feuer ist Vorbote und Begleitung des zum Gericht nahenden Gottes (2,3)' (ATD 24/3, 19). Theophany texts referred to are, among others, Ps. 29.7; 50.3; 97.3. Rudolph also has theophany material in mind at 1.19, in order to strengthen the DOL associations (HAT, 49, citing Wolff). Wolff's discussion is on Hermeneia, 35.

to scenes of judgement elsewhere in the prophetic tradition and especially in explicit Day of the LORD texts.[32]

We have noted the first-person plural language in this unit ('our eyes' and 'our God') and have taken it as indicating a connection with the preceding call to lament (1.13-14). The priests, summoned elders and 'all the inhabitants of the land' who are to gather at 'the house of the LORD your God' and cry, here do just that. The prophet scripts their cry as an acknowledgement of nothing less than an unfolding Day of the LORD. The descriptions of food cut off and alongside that joy and gladness as well, match the earlier portrayal (especially vv. 11-12). Verse 17 is notoriously difficult (especially given the otherwise clear and unconfused text of Joel in general). We should nevertheless expect the first half of the verse to match the less difficult depiction of the second half: 'the granaries have been broken down, for the grain has dried up'. This is an elaboration of 1.16 and leads naturally to the final images of dazed and famished cattle and flocks.

In conclusion, our take on this unit is also influenced by the one to follow. The prophet scripts a plural lamentation that we can imagine represents the 'cry to the LORD' of 1.14. To this he then adds his own individual cry. With this the chapter and its theme 'The Day of the LORD upon Israel', comes to a close. Features of the final verses also serve to anticipate the next Day of the LORD portrayal that is the subject of Chapter 2.

---

[32] The ancient commentators are not much bothered by the verse. Cyril passes over it without comment beyond 'locust and blight devastated them in the manner of fire, as it were' (278). Theodore paraphrases, 'with all the troubles gripping us, we shall all in common beg you relief from such awful troubles, because like fire all the place is devastated along with the trees in it (109; he shares with Cyril the unusual rendering, 'charming things of the wilderness'). Theodoret, who holds to a natural referent, here comments, 'By fire one can understand the enemy, devastating all the country like fire, as well as the locust, the blight and what went with them, these things being by nature no less destructive of the crops of the earth' (89).

The Prophet's Own Final Stamp (1.19-20)

> ¹⁹ To you, O LORD, I cry.
> For fire has devoured
>   the pastures of the wilderness,
> and flames have burned
>   all the trees of the field.
> ²⁰ Even the wild animals cry to you
>   because the watercourses are dried up,
> and fire has devoured
>   the pastures of the wilderness.

One question to be posed at this point is whether the prophet means to describe a communal lament, that begins to loosen the traditional boundaries of prophetic/elder/priest/all inhabitants distinctions. By joining his own cry to that of the gathered assembly, he commits himself to the cause of faithful intercessor, in the manner of Moses, Amos (7.1-6), Samuel and the early Jeremiah. But he also comes alongside the gathered assembly of 1.15-19, whose words he has, as it were, scripted for them.[33] The taking of words to the LORD was the final exhortation of Hosea (14.2). If we are correct in seeing this being realistically deployed in Joel – though for its mature and climactic rendition we must wait until the central panel of the next chapter – what we find in 1.15-20 is the initial approach to God. It is an approach leaving no one out. It is an approach that includes the voice of the prophet himself in his distinctive role, but it may also presage the new prophetic conception the prophet will set forth in 2.28-9. That dramatic denouement proclaims that the spirit of God will be poured out on all flesh so that young and old, servant and master, women and men may altogether give voice as does the singular prophet under God's inspiration.

---

[33] Somewhat related, Deissler comments on how the unit 1.15-18 '... führt zum Hilfruf, den der Prophet im Ich-Stil – er macht sich damit entweder selbst zum repräsentativen Sprecher der Gemeinde oder legt inh ihr in den Mund (auch ein kolletives >>Ich<< ist denkbar) – formuliert nach der Weise der Psalmisten (vgl. Ps. 28.1, 30.9, 86.3 u.a.) und lenkt dabei zugleich Jahwes Augenmerk auf eine Not, welche die ganze Natur einem qualvollen Tod ausliefert' (72).

Part Two

The Unfolding Day of the LORD (2.1-27)

Part Two in Joel's portrayal is a continuation of the Day of the Lord tableau as this was dramatically introduced at 1.15 and anticipated by means of three urgent exhortations from the prophet culminating in the final unit at 1.13-14. The prophet then scripted the initial lamentation for the assembled Israel, followed by his own personal appeal (1.19-20). Now the DOL is front and centre. We find ourselves on the same urgent landscape. The achievement of Part Two is to ramp up the description of the locust plague, imbue it with the metaphorical clarity of national assault and put before Israel the possibility of a final reversal of fortune. But the central significance of this unfolding of Chapter 1 is the clarity regarding the agent of judgement. The LORD himself is at work in the locust plague and intends by means of it to do something unprecedented, that will stand the test of time and serve to teach future generations (1.2-3). Chapter 1 sets the stage. Chapter 2 has the main actor step into dramatic view.[1]

The opening verse (2.1) finds its *inclusio* at 2.15. In between, the unexpected possibility of a turn of affairs is dramatically heralded ('yet even now' – 2.12), opening us unto an entirely different plane of divine action. The Day of the LORD unfolding upon Israel (2.1

---

[1] For a nicely formulated summary of the relation of Chapters 1 and 2, see R. Scolarick, 'Joel 2.12a', 64–5.

and 2.11) holds within its compass the possibility of a DOL in compassionate forgiveness and restoration. This is the only reason we have chosen to separate 2.1-2 from what follows for discussion. In this way the important links to 2.15 and 2.11, set up by 2.1 and 2.1-2 respectively, are better on display.

> ² Blow the trumpet in Zion;
>   sound the alarm on my holy mountain!
> Let all the inhabitants of the land tremble,
>   for the day of the LORD is coming,² it is near—³
> ² a day of darkness and gloom,
>   a day of clouds and thick darkness!
> Like blackness spread upon the mountains
>   a great and powerful army comes;
> their like has never been from of old,
>   nor will be again after them
>   in ages to come.

The imperatives of 2.1 remind us of the basic structure of Chapter 1, where they served to reinforce the mood of urgency and a comprehensive appeal, culminating in 1.15-20. That mood is maintained here and is about to accelerate. Unmistakable as well, is the continuity of setting implied in that final culminating assembly, at whose head stands the prophet himself. Zion, the holy hill, is the place of the present unfolding drama (1.13, 14, 16).

Unmistakable as well, is the link back to 1.15. What was there suddenly and perhaps unexpectedly introduced – the Day of the LORD – is here the sustained theme of Chapter 2, in clearer unfolding. The language forms a proper continuation, but with a slight variation.

אֲהָהּ לַיּוֹם כִּי קָרוֹב יוֹם יְהוָה וּכְשֹׁד מִשַּׁדַּי יָבוֹא
כִּי בָא יוֹם יְהוָה כִּי קָרוֹב

---

² For a proper apprehension of the temporal implications here, see the discussion to follow.
³ Syriac conjoins this last phrase with the next verse.

In 2.1 we have a reversed word order, with the (same as in 1.15) adjective *qārôb* now at the conclusion of the line. Instead of the concluding prefixed form of *bô'* we have either a participle or a suffix form. If the link is unmistakable the interpretation is less so. Why the variation? Does it signal anything or is it simply a variation for stylistic reasons?

On our view, the first reference to the DOL speaks of its incipient but undeniable present introduction, in the unprecedented locust being portrayed. The suffix forms of Chapter 1 and the entire flow of the opening chapter are very clear that the prophet speaks of a present reality: a literal fact on the ground, for which the imperatives are designed to call Israel's attention in no uncertain terms.[4] It is a Day already upon Israel. It has drawn near and it is also at the same time unfolding (*yābô'*). That is the force of the collocation in 1.15. The use of the prefixed form, then, serves the purpose of saying, 'there is more to come of this Day yet to be experienced'.[5]

In 2.1 the perspective of 1.15ff. is assumed. We remain in the context of Zion. The solemn trumpet blast serves to underscore that what has begun in the events of Chapter 1 is gathering strength. If there is genuine variation in 2.1 over against 1.15, as against repetition and continuation, the prophet's point could be to alter the finite verb form

---

[4] *Pace* Barton. 'Perhaps the entire description of the invasion by locusts in both chapters is a prediction of an imminent disaster rather than a description of it once it has happened. I do not see how we are to tell' (47). Compare his reference to 'prophetic perfect' on p. 47.

[5] One could argue that a suffixed form would better serve this purpose in 1.15. The problem with introducing this form in Chapter 1 is a) it could confuse the reader/hearer into thinking the final Day has come *altogether and without anything remaining*. As it stands, the presently experienced locust plague is a clear enough marker of the actual reality on the ground. Also b) it misses the point that 1.15 is only introductory to the wider DOL portrayal of Joel, and so is only ever to work in tandem with 2.1 and its ensuing description. The prophet's real achievement is in insisting that the dramatic final Day of the LORD announced by the prophets is already at work in the present locust plague. He does not need a suffixed form in 1.15 for that point to be registered; indeed it could mar the wider flow of the book that is his genuine achievement.

by making it a participle to match the temporally flexible *qārôb* – the difficulty here being that Hebrew uses the same form for the present participle of *bô'* as for the suffixed form. The alternative would be that at issue is the clear statement that the Day of Chapter 1 has fully arrived. It *has come*. The point of the final (repeated) *qārôb* would be the maintenance of the sense of 1.15, *viz., that when we speak of the Day of the LORD in Joel 1–2 we are speaking of a unique characterization that the prophet has been given to understand is unfolding in his present time.*

In either case, then, what we are prepared for is the Day introduced already (1.15) *to continue declaring its present and unfolding sense.* This is what the repetition/variation of 2.1 achieves. The further evidence for this is the movement from suffixed to prefixed forms now to be seen in the next phase of the portrayal (2.3-11). However, we are to understand this in precise syntactical terms, the overall effect has been properly seen by Wolff, Jeremias, Müller, Beck, Scolarick and others.[6] It allows the present reality of the locust plague – captured by the general use of suffixed forms which maintain the continuity with what precedes – to open onto a fuller elaboration. This is the genuine achievement of Joel, the theological prising open of the Day accomplished syntactically by the use of prefixed forms. The best way to render these into English (in 2.3-11) is present tense or present perfect. As for the line in question, we would incline toward:

For the Day is come and indeed is (still) nearing.

---

[6] The technical discussion of Troxel ('Time in Joel') is not always evenly illuminating. He appears to hold that the Day of Chapter 1 is a reality in place (*pace* Barton) dealing with a locust plague. The Day of Chapter 2 is to be distinguished from that. He is not confident that the aspectual arguments for the suffix/prefix alteration in Chapter 2 go far enough. Less clear is whether his own analysis is an improvement, especially as its effect – so far as I can see – is to separate the Day of Chapter 1 from the Day of Chapter 2.

That is, the use of the final *qārôb* urges us to read on to see what this nearness means concretely.

The comprehensive 'all who live in the land' is also significant for it maintains the emphasis we have argued is in place in 1.15-20. It continues the action of Chapter 1 even as it suggests much more is nearing in God's present undertaking.[7] Verse 2 makes this immediately clear, as now the Day is given further colouration. This DOL, if there had been any doubt, is the same Day spoken of by the former prophets (e.g. Amos, Zephaniah, Isaiah). The images all stress the absence of light, which is of course the well-spring creative action of God. The 'un-creation-Day' we might well gloss it. The undoing of creative beneficence is the content of this 'eighth' Day of darkness (*ḥōšek*), gloom (*ăpēlâ*), clouds (*'ānān*) and blackness (*ărāpel*). In addition to whatever might be reproduced here from other prophetic sources (Zeph. 1.15 is virtually identical; see also Amos 5.18),[8] not to be missed is the familiar tetrad series whose significance as indicating totality was noted in the Introduction of Chapter 4.[9]

The plague traditions of Exodus are also not far from view. The land is described in Exodus Chapter 10 as black with locusts (10.15). The locusts, upon leaving, are followed by three days of dense darkness (10.22ff.; *ḥōšek-ăpēlâ*). The destruction of the first-born is at midnight (11.4). Again, within the ambit of the plagues and the exodus this too is an obvious un-creation motif.[10]

---

[7] The criticism of Jeremias by Troxel on this point is well founded. Jeremias does not see the response to the imperatives to the priests in Chapter 1 (v. 14) fulfilled until 2.15ff. ('Time', 85, n. 43)

[8] Zephaniah even has the trumpet blast (*yôm šôpār*) following in 1.16.

[9] This interpretation is preferable in our view to one limiting the description to basic theophany language (Barton, 72). The Genesis creation context may also be supported by reference to Eden in 2.3. Jeremias correctly speaks of 'Revokation der Schöpfung' (ATD 24/3, 24).

[10] T. Fretheim, *Exodus* (Interpretation: A Bible Commentary for Teaching and Preaching; Louisville, KT: Westminster John Knox, 1991).

As the blackness motif is extended (*kĕšaḥar*) in 2.2ff. we get a further glimpse of the prophet's impressive metaphorical range. The locust swarm is likened to blackness spreading on the mountains and like an army amassed – an evocation of the proverbial foe from the north (see Joel 2.20). The LORD himself appears in his Day (2.11) in the form of a devastation like no other. The language of 2.20cd both picks up the theme of unprecedented divine encounter from 1.2-3 but also seeks to trump what was said about the plagues of Egypt, as 10.14 had related it: 'such a dense swarm of locusts as had never been before, nor ever shall be again'. Something greater than that is now indeed being manifested and the DOL motif is brought into its fullest possible frame.

This is not a discrete Day over against one already described in Chapter 1. The motif of national military assault is metaphorical. The locusts are 'like warhorses' (2.4), 'like the crackling of flame' (2.5) and 'like a powerful army' (2.5) – an army, warhorse, or flame cannot be like themselves or together like one another. What we were given to see in Chapter 1 as a present reality we are given to see from the standpoint of the LORD's own 'nearing action' in Chapter 2. In Chapter 1 we saw the outer lineaments. In Chapter 2 we see the inner nerve, which can only be described by means of metaphor and intertextual association. How else can the dramatic activity of God himself be described? In his time, in his Day, metaphors are necessary to convey the divine meaning and purpose. Indeed, this is what it means to speak of something genuinely without any temporal analogy (2:2), including events which claimed that quite properly on their own 'day' of divine action (Exod. 10.14).

But there is a separate and obvious reason for the particular metaphor here deployed. The use of the metaphor of military assault is specific and intentional. It means to evoke the *topos* of the DOL in the prophetic literature as that so frequently *does* focus on God's deployment of the nations to render judgement (e.g. Isa. 13). The prophet means thereby to keep the national/military dimension of the DOL firmly in view and at the ready. He sees the inside the unparalleled natural assault the God of Creation and the God of History as one and the same LORD. As he sends the locust plague as one manifestation of his character ('his ways'), he likewise sends the nations from that selfsame divine life. Joel's location in the Twelve – following Hosea and anticipating the Books to follow – is mirrored in his own portrayal of the DOL. The description of the natural form of his manifestation – Day and ways – cannot be severed from the description of the historical/temporal manifestation – Day and ways – for they are united in one selfsame purpose in his soon to be revealed character (2.12-14). In this way the Third Section of the book (2.28–3.19) is anticipated as the national/military portrayal takes up where the natural/creation portrayal concludes.

Locusts on the March (2.3-11)

> ³ Fire devours in front of them,
>   and behind them a flame burns.
> Before them the land is like the garden of Eden,
>   but after them a desolate wilderness,
>   and nothing escapes them.[11]
>
> ⁴ They have the appearance of horses,
>   and like war-horses they charge.
> ⁵ As with the rumbling of chariots,[12]
>   they leap on the tops of the mountains,
> like the crackling of a flame of fire
>   devouring the stubble,
> like a powerful army
>   drawn up for battle.

---

[11] BHS wonders if this might be an addition. This is a critical speculation (that is, without attestation in reception history).
[12] BHS thinks an addition is in order, giving us 'as the rumbling of chariots *is their voice*'.

⁶ Before them peoples are in anguish,
  all faces grow pale.[13]
⁷ Like warriors they charge,
  like soldiers they scale the wall.
Each keeps to its own course,
  they do not swerve from their paths.
⁸ They do not jostle one another,
  each keeps to its own track;
they burst through the weapons[14]
  and are not halted.
⁹ They leap upon the city,
  they run upon the walls;
they climb up into the houses,
  they enter through the windows like a thief.
¹⁰ The earth quakes before them,
  the heavens tremble.
The sun and the moon are darkened,
  and the stars withdraw their shining.
¹¹ The LORD utters his voice
  at the head of his army;
how vast is his host!
  Numberless are those who obey his command.
Truly the day of the LORD is great;
  terrible indeed—who can endure it?

Stylistically and rhetorically these nine verses stand out as compared with the descriptions and style of Chapter 1. Indeed, one of the incidental arguments against dividing Joel into two sections and declaring the latter a secondary eschatological supplement to the former, was that this overstated the temporal complexity of Chapters 1–2 taken unto themselves. In the space of these nine verses we have sixteen prefixed (*yiqtōl*) verb forms. The perfective atmosphere of

---

[13] Wolff prefers 'all faces are aglow' (Hermeneia, 38) based upon the Versions' reference to heat.
[14] The line is difficult, but most agree with the NRSV effort at translation here.

Chapter 1 – the locust invasion as a fact on the ground – here gives way to a different aspect or tense sensation. Efforts to distil and skim off a supplemental editorial layer by attending to this difference has been a messy and unsuccessful affair, whether at the service of the two-editions theory (see Introduction, Chapter 4) or as part of a larger concern with redactional levels right across the Twelve as a whole.[15] We provide in an appendix a Hebrew text with translation to show the distribution of *qāṭal* and *yiqṭōl* forms and one can see almost immediately how difficult it would be to see any redactional level to be sustained on the basis of this distinction. The picture is simply too untidy for a consistent redactional supplement (the addition of 'future' tense perspective, for example).

It is our position that this untidiness for redactional purposes belongs to the actual genius of the depiction and in that we share the conviction of most modern commentators. The 'perfective' reality of a locust plague is here being opened up dramatically so as to continue the urgent description of Chapter 1 in service for the climatic turn of events which is in evidence at the next unit, which opens with the promise of 'yet even now' (2.12). Here we find as well the reason for the length and metaphorical richness of the unit – as long a piece of sustained depiction as we have in the entire book (nine verses in length). This sets up perfectly the dramatic possibility of reversal as that will arise in the context of the book's central panel (2.12-18).

Naturally, one way to understand the verb interchange in this section – for those who do not entertain redactional theories – is to have recourse to the explanation that prophetic and poetic texts simply maintain no standard practice when it comes to prefixed and suffixed forms (indeed, many poetic texts even seem to prefer the alteration within the space of the same repeated line). Barton has

---

[15] A handy discussion is now available in Troxel, 'The Problem of Time in Joel', *JBL* 2013.

taken this position in his OTL commentary.[16] The problem here is that a) there is a difference between the practice in Chapter 1 (which uses suffix forms) and Chapter 2, especially in 2.3-11 and 2) the recourse on Barton's part appears to be motivated by his desire to have Chapter 1 be predictive in character. This is manifestly a difficult position to hold when the verbs in Chapter 1 are all perfect and are so obviously different to what we find in this unit, where we have sixteen prefixed forms and nine suffixed forms in a single unit of text (along with participial and nominal sentences).[17]

The most convincing way of assessing the interchange in 2.3-11 is along the lines we have adopted here. That is, the 'imperfective' dimension serves to bring alive the ongoing character of the DOL. As Beck puts it, the *yiqtōl* forms infuse the locust plague of Chapter 1 with 'einem iterative-durative Aspekt'. The seemingly local and specific character of the locust plague is here opened up and shown to be something much grander.[18] The 'aspectual' argument – if that is a proper way to describe it – is also made by Wolff and Jeremias.[19]

If there is any pattern to be observed in these nine verses it is that, as the action mounts, when we arrive at verses 7-9, we find only prefixed forms. This gives one a sense of lively, frenzied movement. The NRSV translation we are using captures this without difficulty, using the present tense.

---

[16] 'The distinction in tense forms used is not a very powerful argument, given the way the two non-consecutive forms (*qatal* and *yiqtol*) oscillate in Hebrew verse and especially in the Prophets. As we have seen, Chapter 1 may in any case be a prediction, not a description of a past state of affairs, despite the use of perfect forms' (69).

[17] To call them 'prophetic perfect' would not explain why the practice ceases when we come to Chapter 2.

[18] Beck, 'Der Tag YHWHs', 166.

[19] Troxel wants to find inconsistencies in the German translations of Wolff and Jeremias when it comes to their use of present and future renderings, which he believes he can find in verses 3 and 6 (where suffix and prefix forms are in the same verse, see appendix). This is of limited value in challenging the larger argument since it is a basic difficulty of translation as such and also because, as the appendix shows, the one pattern that does emerge is a density of one form or the other in the central five verses (7, 8, 9, 10, 11).

> ⁷ Like warriors they charge,
>   like soldiers they scale the wall.
> Each keeps to its own course,
>   they do not swerve from their paths.
> ⁸ They do not jostle one another,
>   each keeps to its own track;
> they burst through the weapons
>   and are not halted.
> ⁹ They leap upon the city,
>   they run upon the walls;
> they climb up into the houses,
>   they enter through the windows like a thief.

The last two verses of the unit change tack and show us a string of suffixed forms. It is not impossible to render these into decent English, though the effect being sought may not come through. The point must surely be that this active movement (vv. 7-9) has been correlated with God's own perfected purpose. One could modify the NRSV accordingly.

> ¹⁰ The earth quaked before them,
>   the heavens trembled.
> The sun and the moon darkened,
>   and the stars withdrew their shining.
> ¹¹ The LORD has uttered his voice
>   at the head of his army;
> how vast is his host!
>   Numberless are those who obey his command.
> Truly the day of the LORD is great;
>   terrible indeed—who can endure it?

The challenge otherwise is how to render verses which alternate prefixed and suffixed forms into an English that is not woodenly rendered (and which may not be up to distinctions that obtain in Hebrew). Just for comparison sake, the appendix text tries to do that.

In this dramatic unit, the locust plague of Chapter 1 is fitted out in military garb and deportment. That we have not shifted ground from that original context – as some have argued – is made quite clear when we arrive at the denouement at the chapter's close.

> [25] I will repay you for the years
>   that the swarming locust has eaten,
> the hopper, the destroyer, and the cutter,
>   my great army, which I sent against you.

If the point was to replace the locusts with a different, military assault (or to show that Chapter 1 was always metaphorical only), the most obvious way to accomplish that would be to cut loose the locust theme altogether, showing it then to be a mere cipher for the real referent. If the idea was to introduce a different assault in Chapter 2 than in Chapter 1, the same basic observation would hold as well. Instead, what this concluding verse shows is that the locusts have been depicted in 2.1-11 as like an army (the foe from the north). The reason for this in the context of verse 25 is revealed in 2.28-3.21: the locust plague DOL is intended to be a figure of the end-time DOL, which is comprehensively one to do with national and military judgement. But the Book of Joel seeks to keep together the God of Creation and the God of History, much as we see the same instinct in the doxologies of Amos sitting alongside the scenes of a more obviously temporal/historical character (4.13; 5.8; 9.5-6). At the head of the army in Joel's present comprehension of the locust assault is the LORD himself. In a locust plague of unprecedented scale, the Day of the LORD is unfolding.

Extremely rare are allusions within the OT itself to Genesis 2–3[20] and rarer still direct references to the Garden of Eden (2.3). We have discussed the unusual use of fire/flame above (in the context of 1.19) as occasioned by a combination of factors: the locusts' devouring likened to fire devastation, so 2.5; the language of theophany; the judgement/DOL legacy of the prophets (Amos). In this context all

---

[20] Isaiah 65.20-5. See Seitz, Isaiah, NIB.

three are relevant. The realistic portrayal of locusts swiftly moving and consuming remains in the forefront. The creation/theophany motif is evidenced by the reference to Eden. God is un-creating. Eden is replaced by wilderness/chaos. The text never departs from the basic referential connection to natural disaster, but the prophet sees in this the theophany of the creator God in an unfolding Day of his making.

Verses 4-5 move to the images of warfare. The locusts are *like* horses/as swift *as* cavalry; noisy *as* chariots; *like* fire crackling; *like* a mighty army.[21] Indeed, verse 6 explicitly states that the warlike assaults of locusts are such that even nations fear before them. Their faces have gone ashen (suffix form) in consequence. Now, the frenetic depiction (using prefixed forms) ensues (vv. 7-9). Note the introduction with a double *kĕ* for clarity in which follows: *like* warriors running/*like* men of war. They move with military precision. They eat with resolve and do not worry about anything but what is in front of them; there is plenty for all. Their ranks are consequently orderly and no enemy or resistance rises to meet them (v. 8). The infestation described in verse 9 is not unlike what the plague of frogs

---

[21] Theodoret, who prefers the realistic interpretation, fairly introduces the commentary with an explanation of how 'like' might accommodate a military (Assyrian and Babylonian) interpretation – he calls it an intensive sense as against a comparative sense (he probably gets the idea from Theodore, where it is in evidence). But then he speaks of his own actual experience of locusts: 'any one carefully studying the head of the locust would find a close resemblance to the horse. And when it flies, you can see it is not inferior to horses in speed, easily flying over mountains and plains, and of course attacking crops like a flame devouring straw. It is like a vast number drawn up for battle, flying and crawling, doing what they do in packed masses, even presenting a military formation like shield-bearers massed together' (91). Cyril shifts ground a bit from his initial remarks in Chapter 1 (280-2), perhaps guided by the literal sense, and now leads with locusts and a realistic interpretation. The locusts 'are not less fearsome than a warlike horse'; 'stamping on the ground in such a way as to resemble the sound of chariots'; 'it is said, you see, that the consumption of the contents of a field is not done by them without noise'; 'like a wind fanning flames'. His reference to Assyrians and Romans (should you wish) is now therefore an extensional sense ('the Roman army, which like locusts devastated Israel for its ungodly crimes against our Lord Jesus Christ' (282). On our view, this is precisely the achievement of Joel: a realistic ground referent with extensional potential. Theodore moves quickly over these verses having already committed himself to the metaphorical sense. As I have argued elsewhere, Theodore is not allergic to allegorical or Christological-prophetic senses (rare though it may be). What he does not like is extended sense-making.

accomplished.[22] Truly this is an outstripping of even that first locust plague in intensity and result. The suffixed forms of verse 10 tell us what this has occasioned. Creation itself is being undone (*'ereṣ; šāmayim; šemeš; yārēaḥ; kôkābîm*). With a crescendo, we arrive at the final climatic verse. The voice that brought creation into being now arises in un-creation judgement, spoken in the form of his host. 'Mighty is He who gives forth his word'. The word spoken here is like the word spoken on the Days of Creation. On this un-creation Eighth Day the word that is breaking forth in 'let there be' is a word that brings one face to face with the LORD God, on His Day. The cry that arises from the heart of this portrayal is but two words (*umi yĕkilenu*):

וּמִי יְכִילֶנּוּ

And with that we are poised over the brink of Genesis 1's *tōhû wābōhû*.

Who can endure it? From within that same temporal space comes in response the divine Word of creation, made known at Sinai.

Direct Call to Return and Elaboration (2.12-14)

> [12] Yet even now, says the LORD,
>   return to me with all your heart,
> with fasting, with weeping, and with mourning;
> [13] rend your hearts and not your clothing.
> Return to the LORD, your God,
>   for he is gracious and merciful,
> slow to anger, and abounding in steadfast love,
>   and relents from punishing.[23]
> [14] Who knows whether he will not turn and relent,
>   and leave a blessing behind him,

---

[22] 'They shall come up into your palace, into your bedchamber and your bed, and into the houses of your officials and of your people, and into your ovens and kneading bowls.'

[23] Because this is a quotation from a formula we see in Exod. 34 and elsewhere, it would be possible to place the phrase in quotes, *viz.*, for 'he is gracious and merciful, slow to anger, and abounding in steadfast love, and relents from punishing'.

> a grain offering and a drink offering
> for the LORD, your God?

In the fifth chapter of Hosea the indictment of Israel begins with an address to the priesthood and alongside them to Israel as a whole and then the royal house (5.1). The wrath of God is to be unleashed upon a sinful people (5.10). God is likened to a lion who devours his prey (5.14) and here both Judah and Israel are victims. In the midst of the chapter the trumpet is sounded (5.8). The following chapter opens with a first-person plea, 'come, let us return to the LORD'. The book ends on the same note, with God himself ready to forgive, his wrath now set aside.[24] We know that in his roaring from Zion in the Book of Amos, though he looks for repentance and a turning to him, it is in vain. The relevant refrain is repeated over again in Chapter 4 (4.6, 8, 9, 10, 11). Israel should therefore 'prepare to meet your God' (4.12). He who turns dawn to darkness: the LORD God Almighty is his name. The Day of the LORD in Amos is therefore no day to be desired (5.18).

> Is not the day of the LORD darkness (*ḥōšek*), not light,
> and gloom (*'āpēl*) with no brightness in it? (5.20)

Joel opens with the assertion that something has happened that has no precedent (1.2). It is greater in intensity and scale than the unprecedented locust plague of old (Exod. 10.6) that Israel was never to forget and was to report to all future generations for time immemorial. The Day of the LORD is described again in just this way in 2.2, 'their like has never been from of old, nor will be again after them in ages to come'. The unit 2.3-11 places us firmly before this Day, when YHWH withdraws his creational 'it is good' and instead covers over earth, heavens, sun, moon and stars with a fourfold

---

[24] See the discussion of Jeremias, 'Function'.

blackness, such as the prophet Amos proclaimed in warning to his generation (5.20).

But what we hear in the horn blast of Joel and the clock tick of this unprecedented Day is an unprecedented – or so it might seem – *and yet* (*wĕgam-attâ*). This Day is also a Day when a return to YHWH – as Hosea besought and as Amos saw in forfeit – is still on divine offer. As has been noted, Joel's return 'with all your heart' evokes the repentance *to God* set out at the end of Deuteronomy.[25] There too Israel had been placed before blessing and curse, obedience and disobedience, but the final verdict is also in clear view: the curses had come upon God's exiled and cast off people. Though the motivation and logic of Deuteronomy has its own integrity and purpose, one cannot help but see the curses as bespeaking in their own deuteronomic idiom the darkness of the Day as we see it in Joel's own portrayal.

The LORD will send upon you disaster, panic and frustration ... The LORD will afflict you with consumption, fever, inflammation, with fiery heat and drought, and with blight and mildew, and they shall pursue you until you perish ... The sky over your head shall be bronze and the earth under you iron. The LORD will change the rain of your land into powder and only dust shall come down upon you from the sky until you are destroyed ... The LORD will afflict you with the boils of Egypt, with ulcers ... you shall grope about at noon as blind people grope in darkness (Deut. 28.20-29).

And yet. And yet, 'if you ... return to the LORD your God, and you and your children obey him *with all your heart and with all your soul*, just as I am commanding you today, then the LORD your God will restore your fortunes and have compassion on you' (Deut. 30.1-3). Bounty will be restored (30.9). The nations which destroyed will themselves come under the curse they inflicted, that is, 'the

---

[25] Jeremias, 'Gelehrte', 100; Müller.

adversaries who took advantage of you' (30.7). The 'turn to the LORD your God *with all your heart and with all your soul*' is repeated for emphasis in 30.10 as well. The *with all you heart* is in Joel followed by 'with fasting and weeping and mourning' – as befits the liturgical context so clearly in evidence in 1.15-20, 2.1 and 2.15-17. Rending the heart in Joel takes the form of turning, that is, the internal change God alone can bring about. Here it is, then, that the Sinai encounter of Moses is the Sinai encounter of the one made able to turn to God and in that turning to encounter him in his Day and ways.

One important feature we have yet to mention, is that the foundational Sinai event *precedes* the divine revelation vouchsafed to Moses, that is, his manifestation in the context of Moses' intercession and God's relenting from his decision not to accompany his people (Exodus 33–34), such as we see it repeated here in Joel and at various critical points in the Book of the Twelve. At the conclusion of Exodus 32 and the affair of the golden calf reference, is made to a time 'when the day comes for punishment, I will punish them for their sin' (32.34). The context is one in which the ultimate fate of the sinful people is far from clear. In the immediate aftermath of the calf debacle, the Levites have executed the righteous judgement over 'about 3000' (32.28). But what of the others? Here YHWH reserves for himself his own sovereign design. For them there remains a *yôm poqdî* (32.34). No relenting from or removal of this verdict is undertaken in the ensuing chapters. And of course we know of the visitation of judgement executed numerous times following, that will culminate in the verdict over the wilderness generation in Numbers 14.21-23.[26] The appeal to the character of God, by Moses, in Numbers 14.18 is a clear evocation of the foundational revelation as set forth

---

[26] See Dennis T. Olson, *The Death of the Old and the Birth of the New: The Framework of the Book of Numbers and the Pentateuch* (Brown Judaic Studies; Atlanta: Scholars Press, 1985).

in Exodus 34.6-7 and by means of it, Moses is able to preserve a new generation. That revelation runs:

> ⁶ 'The LORD, the LORD,
> a God merciful and gracious,
> slow to anger,
> and abounding in steadfast love and faithfulness,
> ⁷ keeping steadfast love for the thousandth generation,
> forgiving iniquity and transgression and sin,
> yet by no means clearing the guilty,
> but visiting the iniquity of the parents
> upon the children
> and the children's children,
> to the third and the fourth generation.'

Here it is on display in Joel's version, following the direct word of YHWH himself:

> Return to the LORD, your God,
>   for he is gracious and merciful,
> slow to anger, and abounding in steadfast love,
>   and relents from punishing.

As has been noted, the final phrase in Joel (wĕniḥām ʿal hārāʿâ; וְנִחָם עַל־הָרָעָה) is a plus over against the Exodus 34. Certainly it is an adaption perfectly suited to the context, where the rāʿâ in question is the un-creation itself of YHWH's Day. There is nothing that requires Joel, as it were, to reproduce the Exodus text as if it were strictly formulaic, brooking no adaptation; Numbers 14 already points to the flexibility that appears reflexive in that very first case of 'reuse' (14.17-19). It may be worth noting however, that the four generation motif has already been taken up in its own form in Joel 1.2-3. Four generations are to be told of the thing that has never happened before or will happen again. The point could well be that the report of YHWH's Day of mercy in the midst of a Day of nearing un-creation intends to release that same Day for future generations in mercy and new life

– just as the disobedience that made potent days of visitation extended in each instance over four generations (Exod. 32.34 and 34.7).

Jeremias has done the careful work around the theme of YHWH's wrath/repentance, here and in other OT texts and has attended to the different nuances attached to the theme.[27] He works with the assumption that Joel is composed in relationship to Hosea and Amos both, a conviction we share and that the wrath of God in Hosea has been set aside when we come to the end of the book, though with the cost borne by God himself (see the discussion in the Introduction above). So 'wrath' is not a prominent theme in Joel (where the word does not appear). When it comes to the verse in question (v. 14: 'Who knows? He may turn and relent …') he notes that the characteristic phrase in relation to possible divine relenting, such as we see it in Amos 5.15 and Zephaniah 2.3, does not appear here. In both of those texts the Hebrew word for 'perhaps' is *ûlay* and the context in both cases makes clear that the verdict is genuinely in doubt.[28]

> Hate evil and love good,
>   and establish justice in the gate;
> it may be (*ûlay*) that the LORD, the God of hosts,
>   will be gracious to the remnant of Joseph. (Amos 5.15)

The DOL context is crystal clear in the case of Zephaniah, as is the existence of divine wrath.

> Gather together, gather,
>   O shameless nation,
> ² before you are driven away

---

[27] *Der Zorn Gottes im Alten Testament: Das biblische Israel zwischen Verwerfung und Erwählung* (2nd ed.; Neukirchen-Vluyn: Neukirchener, 2011). On Joel more specifically, see most recently, 'Function', 82. See now as well, 'The Wrath of God at Mount Sinai (Exod. 32; Deut. 9-10)', *The Bible as Christian Scripture: The Work of Brevard S. Childs* (eds C. Seitz, K. Richards; Atlanta, GA: SBL, 2013), 21–34, where Jeremias provides a summary of his main thesis.

[28] See also Exodus 32.30, where Moses indicates his intention to confer with God after the sin in the golden calf, 'perhaps (*ûlay*) I can make atonement'.

> like the drifting chaff,
> before there comes upon you
>   the fierce anger of the LORD,
> before there comes upon you
>   the day of the LORD's wrath.
> ³ Seek the LORD, all you humble of the land,
>   who do his commands;
> seek righteousness, seek humility;
>   perhaps (*'ûlay*) you may be hidden
>   on the day of the LORD's wrath. (2.1-3)

In both cases we have a prophetic plea, as it were, representing the hope that against all odds God might provide some form of mitigation for a remnant. In the wake of God's wrath, that is all one might hope for.

But the situation presupposed in Joel is different. As such, the optative *'ûlay* is not found here but instead 'who knows?' (*mî yôdēa'*; מִי יוֹדֵעַ). The wrath of God is not in evidence in Joel. Amos and Zephaniah had reason to assume that there was no possibility of escape and in Joel the situation might appear to be worse. But in Joel, this language ('who knows?') is preceded by the divine voice announcing the character of God as wholly merciful – an emphasis that weights the original formula from Exodus in a distinctly favourable direction, including the feature unique to Joel in the final line ('who relents from punishing').[29] In the light of this divine word – which neither Amos nor Zephaniah have received – the response of Joel in 2.14 is different. So it is that Jeremias states it this way:

> This prophetic 'perhaps' has often been misunderstood, as if its meaning was: nobody knows for sure. His 'perhaps', is a sign of firm personal conviction intentionally leaving room for God's freedom in view of the knowledge of the terrible character of the Day of the Lord.[30]

---

[29] Compare the different weighting in Nahum 1.2-3.
[30] 'Function', 80. Theodoret, for his part, also sees this is a hopeful turning point. 'It is likely, he is saying, that he will leave the threats unfulfilled and give us the customary

We would add here, that the following unit also underscores this interpretation. Unlike Amos or Zephaniah, immediately following this verse is a summoning of people, elders, children, bride and bridegroom, with the priests in position to weep and intercede. The clear implication is that God's personal plea in 2.12 and the declaration of his favourable character are signs that the DOL holds within it the possibility of divine relenting and a dramatic change of fortune.[31] The blessing that may be left behind, consists of those offerings that the priests had been unable to bring in Chapter 1, as the locust plague and drought had cut them off.[32] God is not merely referred to as restoring the natural gifts that make life possible, given the devastations of the Day of the LORD. Rather, he is prepared to make the conditions for fellowship with him through liturgical offering again possible.[33]

Third Call to Assemble (2.15-17)

> [15] Blow the trumpet in Zion;
> sanctify a fast;
> call a solemn assembly;
> [16] gather the people.

abundance of good things so that we may offer the customary worship at the altar (by *a blessing* referring to the supply of good things). With this hope, then, he is saying, Sound the trumpet in Sion (v. 15) …' (93).

[31] In a recent work on Jonah, Moberly states his interpretation of 'who knows?' in this way: 'Most importantly, I suggest, the sense of contingency expressed by Joel's "Who knows?" is theologically sure-footed and is best read as classic prophetical theological insight. It represents what Jewish and Christian traditions have learned from this (and comparable passages) to be a right reading of the strong affirmation of divine mercy and responsiveness. God is indeed merciful and responsive, but although this can be relied upon, it should not be presumed upon. God's mercy remains His to give, and He interacts sovereignly and relationally but not mechanically' ('Educating Jonah', in *Old Testament Theology* [Grand Rapids, MI: Baker Academic, 2013], 195).

[32] 'Grain offerings and drink offerings are cut off from the house of the LORD" (1.10).

[33] So also Theodoret (in note 30 above). Theodore also sees the strong possibility of divine favour arising in v. 14 and he too notes that blessing takes the form of restoration of proper worship. 'The first token of this will be participating in the ritual of the customary offering of sacrifices and libations' (113).

Sanctify the congregation;
   assemble the aged;
gather the children,
   even infants at the breast.
Let the bridegroom leave his room,
   and the bride her canopy.

¹⁷ Between the vestibule and the altar
   let the priests, the ministers of the Lord, weep.
Let them say, 'Spare your people, O Lord,
   and do not make your heritage a mockery,
   a byword among the nations.
Why should it be said among the peoples,
   "Where is their God?"'

Strictly speaking this is now the third occasion for the prophet to call for a sacred assembly (1.13-14; 2.1-2). But this appeal is more auspicious, given the preceding text and so it is also longer and more comprehensive.³⁴ All are summoned and all will therefore be present, for the verdict when it arises. The horn sounded at the opening of the chapter, summoned those to tremble before a Day whose ensuing description would bring Israel before the very undoing of creation itself. Now the horn summons Israel for a sacred assembly, the clear prosecution of what had been declared in Chapter 1 (1.13-14) and which there led to the initial round of crying out in supplication, by people and prophet together (1.15-20). Here the prophet has already spoken his word and it is a word of hopefulness and encouragement (2.12-13). Now he addresses the people and calls for a sacred assembly.

The elders, who were the very first objects of Joel's address in 1.2 and who were to report an unprecedented occurrence to future generations, are the first group out of the generic people/assembly

---

³⁴ Seven imperatives and four jussives in the space of three verses generates a sense of urgency.

(2.15) to be named here. It cannot be coincidental that the very next group to follow is not a social group similar to them (farmers, et al., as in 1.5-12) but rather 'children' and 'infants at the breast'. The report to generations to come, is therefore about to be here set before them, elder and children together. Those whose vocation it will very shortly be to bring new life to birth are enjoined to cease ('let the bridegroom leave his room and the bride her canopy') in light of the new creation that is about to happen by divine fiat. The priests and ministers addressed in 1.9 and 1.13 are here given words to speak in a rite of lamentation (1.17). The language of 2.17 is very close in content and concern to Moses' plea in Numbers 14.13-16, when the question of Israel's existence after the disobedience in the affair of the Promised Land reconnaissance stretched God's patience to breaking point. Moses insisted that the destruction of the people would make Israel and God both a byword. Israel would be no more and God would be shown to have been impotent to achieve his purpose with them. We have an almost perfect digest of that same dual concern, here placed before God not by Moses but by the priestly intercessors summoned and scripted by the prophet.

Divine Response with Promises (2.18-20)

> [18] Then the LORD became jealous for his land,
>   and had pity on his people.
> [19] In response to his people the LORD said:
> I am sending you
>   grain, wine, and oil,
>   and you will be satisfied;
> and I will no more make you
>   a mockery among the nations.
>
> [20] I will remove the northern army far from you,
>   and drive it into a parched and desolate land,
> its front into the eastern sea,

and its rear into the western sea;
its stench and foul smell will rise up.

Surely he has done great things!³⁵

Standing at almost the precise middle of the Book of Joel, is the single verse response of YHWH. It consists of the verdict of mercy and forbearance and further promises in the light of that (2.19-20).

Temporal Issues in 2.18

The verb forms in this verse are clearly *wayyiqtol*, that is, indicating a completed action (the LORD *was jealous/took* pity). Nevertheless for a wide set of reasons the history of interpretation – ancient and modern – has been unconvinced the matter is so straightforward. We start with the modern period and allow the pre-modern to emerge in course.

1 For those who believe that the verse in question reports a completed verdict, it remained problematical why the important assembly called for by the prophet in verses 15-17 never actually assembled in the narrative depiction. To resolve this, the imperatives in 15-16 were repointed, so as to make them actions actually undertaken. The perfective sense of 2.18 is then properly anticipated.³⁶

2 Others sought to make a tidier movement (so they believed) from verses 15-17 to verse 18 (and following) by construing the

---

³⁵ The sense here, difficult to pick up in NRSV and other English translation, is 'surely he [the northern army] has acted haughtily'. This is in ironic contrast to the mighty act of YHWH in the following unit (2.21). This is also obvious in the translation of the Greek and Targum. Crenshaw in AB translates 'for he has acted reprehensibly' and notes, 'A more suitable contrast could hardly be contemplated than the one presented here: the rotting stench of one who has previously behaved in a grandiose manner. The verb and accompanying infinitive (*higdil la'asot*) ordinarily indicate impressive achievements, a meaning they have in the next verse with YHWH as stated subject. However, the context of 2.20 favours a pejorative nuance with the northerner as the implied subject ... just as both Assyria and Babylon are said to have gone beyond their assignment (Isa. 10.5-19 and Hab. 2.6-19)' (152).

³⁶ See the ICC commentary of Bewer, 107.

verbs in verse 18 as jussive (with conjunctive *waw*), *viz.*, 'that the LORD might be jealous/have pity'.[37]

3 A very popular interpretation – one finds it in the pre-modern period as well – is the idea that the perfective sense declared in 2.18 is so from the divine perspective only. So the future action of God pitying and being jealous is described for the prophet as a reality in God's time. This is the so-called 'prophetic perfect'.

4 A subset of this interpretation can be seen in Calvin. Given his well-known attention to the literal sense and his basic grasp of Hebrew, he read Chapter 1 as a realistic portrayal of a locust plague. So what to make of the drift of the latter chapters (3–4) and also of 2.19-27 which speak of future events? In the light of this, Calvin's instinct is to distinguish Chapter 1 and Chapter 2 and to let the latter move into a more general future perspective. That this is not without friction, is clear from the way he handles the problem of the obvious perfective sense of 2.19 ('he replied'). Having sought to read 2.18 as future declaration, 2.19 presents him with a problem.[38] Here it is that he has recourses to the 'prophetic perfect' conception described above (3). My point in distinguishing him is only to say that he gives indication of an obvious problem in sustaining a 'future' interpretation at 2.18.

5 The Antiochenes and Cyril commentaries require a particular sensitivity, because the former have a Greek text that arguably seeks to conform itself to the (present) MT tradition.

- The clue to Theodore's interpretation of 2.18 lies in the Preface to the commentary. There he makes Joel the contemporary

---

[37] E. O. Adalbert Merx, *Die Prophetie des Joel und ihre Ausleger von den ältesten Zeiten bis zu den Reformatoren. Eine exegetisch-kristiche und hermeneutisch-dogmengeschichtliche Studie* (Halle, 1879), 38.

[38] His translator wants to chide him to maintain consistently a future perspective without any recourse to prophetic perfect logic, though Calvin is better at accepting the challenge of the Hebrew text he is seeking to read and interpret, also via various translation media.

of Hosea and Amos, but more like the David of his Psalms commentary, he finds Joel inclined toward longer-term predictions (still within the history of Israel, however). So the general drift of Joel is historicized prophecy focused on the later developments in Israel's history, like the Babylonian exile. When it comes to the actual Hebrew of 2.18 his text renders a past tense, but he regards this as a peculiarity of the Hebrew upon which the Greek is based and thinks in terms of prophetic perfect. This allows the overall direction of Joel to remain focused on the future. He does not believe there was an actual historical (past time) verdict of divine favour, but one in the future, which was itself overshadowed by judgement. 'You see, the fact that he is not mentioning what happened [as an event in past time] is clear from the troubles that came upon them after this reference' (114). Here he does not mean 'after them' in the Book of Joel (since what follows is a very positive portrayal) but 'after them' in Theodore's historical timeline.[39]

- Theodoret picks up a tradition of relating the text to Hezekiah's deliverance (from Jerome or Julian of Aeclanum one might presume) under Sennacherib. This makes the actual text in question describe an accomplished fact ('the Lord accepts their repentance and promises to forgive them') somewhat consistent with his remarks on the positive character of 'who knows?' referred to above. Yet, while the tense being reflected is taken as perfect, the event to which it appears to refer is a future one. Reading Theodoret, it is not clear at this point whether he knows exactly what he is

---

[39] Unfortunately, the footnotes from the translator are not always reliable, though having the volumes accessible in English is an enormous help for general consumption. The Hebrew text is not 'prophetic perfect' but has been so taken by the interpreter (*Twelve Prophets*, n. 21, p. 114).

- describing. He prefers the natural over against the allegorical reading as we have seen, yet he is also compassed about by a history of interpretation that is more interested in future historical referents.[40]
- Cyril is more amplified than Theodoret, but basically adopts a similar view: a completed repentance and divine favour, with future historical colouration. 'Consider the speedy course of mercy: serenity outstrips grief, in my view; and the grace of the compassionate one, the tears of repentance. In other words, he not only has mercy on those faring miserably, but is also jealous and vents his wrath on the offenders who were responsible for the misery being inflicted upon them' – here quoting alongside Joel, Isaiah 47.6 and Zechariah 1.14-15.[41]

6 We find in Nogalski, a hybrid evaluation and also an interpretation nowhere present in the earlier history of interpretation. Because he views the opening *introitus* as declaring that the present generation of Joel has not and will not undertake the repentance called for by the preceding Hosea book, he will need to deal with 2.18 accordingly. It will need to speak of a future act of repentance.[42]

The challenge represented in the above inheres with the ambitious Joel portrayal, spanning as it does several temporal points of reference. There is a past locust plague (Chapter 1) and an opening up of its present logic and import, culminating in a concrete divine relenting (Chapter 2), which itself opens onto the future DOL (Chapters 3 and 4). Getting the proper balance and integration right,

---

[40] *Twelve Prophets*, 94–5.
[41] *Twelve Prophets*, 288.
[42] 'Joel 1–2 imitates the open-ended call to repentance that concluded the book of Hosea, the text where the people's response was also not narrated … This, Joel 2.18 portrays a future reality contingent on Israel's repentance' (*Hosea-Jonah*, 235). The difference between Hosea and Joel is precisely that Joel does enact what Hosea called for. On the rhetorical purpose of Joel, see Chapter 7 of the Introduction.

is not easily accomplished in Joel interpretation, with the tendency toward moving the direction of the entire book toward the future fulfilment – either as inspired predictive prophecy (so earlier history of interpretation) or as historically supplemented material from a later prophetic point of standing. The challenge of 2.18 is that its tenses so obviously point to an accomplished fact.

> Then the LORD became jealous for his land,
>   and had pity on his people.

Jealousy may well be that attribute of YHWH most associated with the Decalogue's commandment against image making (Exod. 20.5-6).

> … for I the LORD your God am a jealous God (*kî 'ānōkî YHWH 'ĕlōhêkā 'ēl qannā'*), punishing children for the iniquity of the parents, to the third and the fourth generation of those who reject me, but showing steadfast love the thousandth generation of those who love me and keep my commandments.

Striking is the reference again to the generational motif, such as we see it both in the compassionate formula and in Joel 1.2. In the former, the motif concludes the formula.

> Yet by no means clearing the guilty, but visiting the iniquity of the parents upon the children and the children's children, to the third and fourth generation (34.7).

It is of course this concluding phrase that is not included in Joel's rendition of the compassionate formula in 2.13, where instead we find the positive extension of Exodus 33.6 in 'who relents from punishing'. In Joel 2.18, the 'jealous' YHWH enacts that attribute now on behalf of his land. Rather than finding its association with the sin of parents distributed to the fourth generation in Israel, it speaks of the favour God reserves for his land and his people, upon whom he takes pity. It is this accomplished fact, that will constitute the basis of the report to be given by the elders to the generations yet to come, up to the fourth (1.2). Joel again creatively adapts the foundational Sinai revelation, in order to depict the unprecedented: within the midst of the cataclysmic DOL, God turns to his people in favour and in mercy.

Several important things require to be noted about the second half of the verse, 'and had pity on his people' (*wayyaḥmōl 'al-'ammô*). As with the phrase that concludes Jonah (*ḥûs*)[43] the verb here (*ḥml*), is not one directly referencing the compassionate formula of Exodus 34.6-7. As in Jonah, it may indicate a fresh action of divine mercy, that is, the character of God in a singular favourable intervention. So Jonah hears the divine verdict with which the book closes, 'should I not have pity on Nineveh' (*waănî lō' 'āḥûs 'al ninĕvēh*), just as he himself had pity on a plant sent to him singularly to comfort him (4.10). Moreover, *ḥûs* is in fact the verb used by Joel in his address to the priests.

> [17] Between the vestibule and the altar
>   let the priests, the ministers of the LORD, weep.
> Let them say, 'Spare your people, O LORD'.
> (*ḥûsâ YHWH 'al 'ammekā*)

In the divine verdict here, 'his people' (*'al 'ammō*) properly stands where 'your people' (*'al 'ammekā*) did in 2.17, now with the verb *ḥml* (*wayyaḥmōl*). This makes the compact divine response conform closely to the scripted priestly plea of 2.17.

Jonah and Joel

As stated above, in trying to understand what appear to be intentional cross-references in the XII, we take the view that there is limited value in an approach which relies on an absolute sequence of dependence (Jonah 'corrects' Joel or Joel 'constrains' Jonah). For one thing, such reconstructions are always speculative and there is

---

[43] 'Should I not be concerned about' (*waănî lō' 'āḥus*) is the NRSV rendering at 4.11.

no really good way to reach a solid conclusion given the nature of the evidence. But more to the point, we should not rule out the possibility that late witnesses mean to inform one another in a complementary way. To sharpen the point, what does it mean, for whatever witness is held to be subsequent, that they now exist alongside each other, with no editorial clue as to their relationship? One strong possibility, is that the intention is to fill out the picture the one provides by setting alongside it a second, related witness.

In the case of Jonah, it is striking that, for the lesson Jonah is made to learn from, the author has chosen an example from nature (the plant). Like the great fish, it is a singular exemplar (the *qîqāyôn*). God's sparing of Nineveh is analogous to his bringing up a plant to provide graceful shade over Jonah, as the lesson concludes. God has pity: on Nineveh and on his faithful servant. The King of Nineveh somehow intuitively grasps the possibility of divine mercy, as the author portrays it. 'Who knows if the God (*hāĕlōhîm*) will turn and repent?' Joel 2.17 exists within a welter of associations it shares with Jonah. Perhaps yet another one is the divine pity: a pity that brings up a surprising natural gift of grace for Jonah and which also spares a repentant nation.

It has already been noted that some feel the repentance enactment has been short-changed in Joel and in comparison to the lavish rite of the Ninevites, that is indeed so. But what is for the Ninevites certainly required by the narrative, is not true as well for the Book of Joel. By indicating what is to be done and by then showing the display of divine favour enacted, all future generations will hear this report and stand before the same possibility of divine grace in the DOL that is to come. The 'plant' that God brings up over his own people as he has become jealous for his land is the grain, wine and oil of Hosea. It was forfeited there in judgement, but it was always assured if Israel would but 'take words with you and return to the LORD' (14.2). Then the verdict of divine favour would ensue:

> They shall again live beneath my shadow
> > they will flourish like the grain,[44]
> they shall blossom like the vine (14.7[8])

The fate of Joel and Jonah in God's singular pity will be theirs. And so it is, in Joel's depiction.

Verse 19 moves from the verdict of divine mercy to an elaboration of the promises of God. Hosea's 'grain, wine and oil' will be restored in lavish form. The nations will take note, as they took note over the DOL above in 2.6.

But now we begin to experience a more pronounced shift in the Joel discourse, as we prepare for the next and final main Section (2.28–3.21). In 2.6 the nations were to be in anguish in the face of the dramatic assault unfolding. Yet, they were clearly incidental to the main action. We noted in the preceding unit, that the priestly intercession material stands very close to the original Sinai intercession of Moses (Exod. 32.11-13) and its extension in the reconnaissance of the land (Num. 14.13-19). Moses was concerned for the integrity of YHWH's public pledges to his people if they were destroyed by God.

> But Moses said to the LORD, 'Then the Egyptians will hear of it, for in your might you brought up this people from among them, and they will tell the inhabitants of this land. They have heard that you, O LORD, are in the midst of this people; for you, O LORD, are seen face to face, and your cloud stands over them and you go in front of them, in a pillar of cloud by day and in a pillar of fire by night. Now if you kill this people all at one time, then the nations who have heard about you will say, "It is because the LORD was not able to bring this people into the land he swore to give them that he has slaughtered them in the wilderness."' (Num. 14.13-16)

---

[44] Reading MT *dagan*.

Joel's version of this is compactly stated at 2.17

> and do not make your heritage a mockery,
>   a byword among the nations.
> Why should it be said among the peoples,
>   'Where is their God?'

Up to this point, the natural assault unfolding into the DOL has not developed with attention to the nations in any sustained, non-metaphorical sense. But tapping into the primary context of intercession and revelation at Sinai, for the purpose of the Book of Joel and the divine relenting integral to its central panel, occasions as well a transition to this larger theme. And so we see it gaining traction here as well. The bringing of grain, wine and oil in surfeit is accompanied by a promise – not developed except as part of the use of exodus material by Joel for his Day – that Israel will never again be made an object of scorn among the nations (2.19).

This transitioning is more fully extended in 2.20. The verse sits perfectly poised over the natural/literal and national/extensional senses, the first fully developed and the second up to this point still under-determined. The 'northern army' is the natural assault under the image of the foe from the north – the national threat seen elsewhere in the prophetic material (Assyria and Babylon). Yet, residually the plague *topos* remains. Driving into the sea is reminiscent of the defeat of Pharaoh and the stench imagery is closely associated with the plague tradition. The frogs that found their way into the houses of the Egyptians – like the locusts of 2.9 – die and are heaped up, and their stench rules the land (Exod. 8.10). Realistically, the locust hoard is removed by driving it into 'parched and desolate land' – that is, into a place where it has nothing to eat, which resembles the kind of land it has created through its own gorging invasion (1.7, 11-12, 16-17). To eliminate the hoard altogether, it is driven further east and west into the Mediterranean and into the Dead Sea, where its stench is mitigated, but still arises. We have here a marriage between a reminiscence of the destruction of the 'Egyptian hoard' and the extinguishing of the locust assault of the present, thereby foreshadowing the defeat of the nations which is to follow.[45] With that intimation in place, the prophet returns to conclude the main central section of the book, where the locust removal and the joy that ensues from YHWH's deliverance in the DOL are celebrated. The joy that withered away along with the produce of the land (1.16) returns in surfeit.

Response to God's Verdict (2.21-4)

[21] Do not fear, O soil;
   be glad and rejoice,
      for the LORD has done great things!
[22] Do not fear, you animals of the field,
      for the pastures of the wilderness are green;
   the tree bears its fruit,
      the fig tree and vine give their full yield.[46]

[23] O children of Zion, be glad
      and rejoice in the LORD your God;
   for he has given the early rain[47] for your vindication,
      he has poured down for you abundant rain,
      the early and the later rain, as before.
[24] The threshing floors shall be full of grain,
      the vats shall overflow with wine and oil.

The MT and Versions properly see the final line of verse 20 as referring to the northerner ('he has acted reprehensibly') in ironic

---

[45] Both the Egyptian host and the locusts met their fate in the Sea. 'And the LORD changed the wind to a very strong west wind, which caught up the locusts and carried them into the Red Sea. Not a locust was left anywhere in Egypt' (10.19).
[46] MT has *hayil* '(strength)' which in parallel with fruit (*peri*') means 'yield' or 'produce'.
[47] NRSV translation of *hammoreh* following Ps. 84.7. G and OL appear to read another word related to Hebrew food (*ma'acol; ta bromota; escas*) while Vulgate heads in the direction of 'teacher of righteousness' (*doctorem iustitiae*) based presumably on the root *yrh*.

anticipation/contrast with the final unit of verse 21. The 'northern hoard' presumed to do 'great things'. The locust assault was sent by the Lord himself and indeed represented his own DOL intervention. The theme of seeking to act independently and presumptuously is hinted at here, such as we find it in relation to the national agents of judgement sent by YHWH (e.g. Assyria and Babylon in Isa. 5–14). This sets up the 'great doing' of YHWH in delivering his people from the midst of the DOL (2.21) and also the wondrous doing of the final unit (2.26), where the language of the wonder-working of Exodus is evoked. 'Fear not, be glad, rejoice' is the language of divine encouragement, such as we find it in Deutero-Isaiah, in relation to the reversal of the exile. There too we have all the images of a creation restored and made fruitful again (Isa. 40.4; 41.18-20; 42.15-16; 43.15-21; 44.1-5; 45.8, 18).

Verse 22 carefully returns to Chapter 1's depiction of animals in mourning and crying out in anguish (1.18, 20). The wilderness is blossoming – Hosea's natural crisis and Deutero-Isaiah's rejuvenated wilderness brought together in the conclusion of Chapter 2. Not only are things restored to their pre-assault state, we are meant to see ongoing fruitfulness and bounty as well. Grain, new wine and oil will return and indeed overflow the vats. Taking words and returning to YHWH (as called for in Hos. 14.2) reverses the painfully registered judgement the prophet there described.

Who is speaking here? We must assume that the prophet is the one announcing this new reality and encouraging the people of Zion. The latter are not ranged according to vocation or status, but are the whole people of God in longed-for rejoicing over the LORD's great pity and great provision. This sets up the final climax of Section Two, the direct divine speech that wraps up this central and dramatic portion of the Book of Joel.

Divine Reply for the Present (2.25-7)

²⁵ I will repay you for the years
    that the swarming locust[48] has eaten,
the hopper, the destroyer, and the cutter,
    my great army, which I sent against you.

²⁶ You shall eat in plenty and be satisfied,
    and praise the name of the LORD your God,
who has dealt wondrously with you.
And my people shall never again be put to shame.
²⁷ You shall know that I am in the midst of Israel,
    and that I, the LORD, am your God and there is no other.
And my people shall never again be put to shame.

We come full circle in this final climatic text. The locust tetrad of 1.4 is distinctly brought back into focus and set before our eyes. But there is, in addition, a fresh durative feature that operates presumptively and also moves us forward at the same time. Mention is made here not of the fundamental temporal integer of the opening chapters – *yôm*, in its temporal richness in what has preceded – but instead 'years'. Have the locusts been at work for years? Here the realistic portrayal spills out into its extensional sense-making: the text urges us to see the dramatic assault and its release in terms of a wider future implication. The promise of bounty and indeed surfeit, continues the language of the preceding units. But now we see an anticipated future consequence. Here the perspective of 1.2-3 is joined. The wonder working of the past – as in the recital psalms or as in Exodus 10 – is to be the occasion for future praise in remembrance.

But the final repetition seems to want to say more than this as well ('my people will never again be put to shame'). For the recognition formula that concludes this main section is but the first such text of

---

[48] See the discussion of 1.4 above. Here is an obvious *inclusio* anticipating the denoument of 2.27.

its kind and it will be repeated in the same form at the conclusion of the next and Final Section (3.17). Our eyes are being directed to the future even as the denouement of Chapters 1 and 2 is jubilantly described. This act of forgiveness and new life is meant to occasion a knowledge of God that is yet on the horizon. In the context of the promise of a shame-free existence ('never again') Israel will know the LORD. Here, for the first time, we have reference to 'other gods' (in the form of their inconsequentiality), though we may say that the general logic was intimated at 2.17. This again serves the purpose of moving us forward into the Final Section, where the nations (and one assumes, their gods) are in central focus.

Undeniably, we find in 2.27 the stunning and clear conclusion of the well-crafted first two Main Sections of Joel: 'The Day Upon' and the 'Day Unfolding'. The recognition formula serves to accomplish a conclusion (much as it functions in Exodus and in Ezekiel), but at the same time it suggests that more is to come.

Part Three

Finale (2.28–3.21)

Introduction: Literary Coherence and the Book of Joel

For those disinclined to believe the proper approach to interpreting the Book of Joel – much less one that can actually succeed, given the nature of the material before us – requires us to reconstruct the social and religious forces that allegedly produced the work, there remains nevertheless an objection to the book in its entirety as coming from a single hand/author.[1] Ironically, the evidence for this consists in the extremely well designed character of the first two chapters as a literary product. One is tempted to speak of the symmetry and coherence of these chapters as unrivalled.[2] This conclusion also sits congenially alongside the reality that in Joel 1–2 we are dealing with literary prophecy in the first instance and indeed a written work, carefully drawing upon other works and assuming their intertextual perception by readers. The final unit of Chapter 2 shows us a fitting conclusion that draws together themes introduced earlier. It is hard to miss this crowning denouement and indeed we should not. So what then of the following chapters?

One feature of Chapters 1–2 we have identified is the interweaving of national/military imagery alongside the natural/realistic. For the

---

[1] Jeremias holds this view in the ATD commentary over against his teacher Wolff (Hermeneia; BK).
[2] The paucity of text-critical issues in Joel – especially given some of the eccentric language – bears testimony to this in the earliest reception history of Joel in the form of translation. A quick glance at the bottom annotation of BHS confirms this.

bulk of these chapters, this aspect belongs to the literary level as ingredient allegorical extension (locusts like an army). But as we approach the conclusion of Part Two, we see this aspect as more realistic and primary in character. We have argued this is due to the use of the Exodus motifs to portray the intercession of the priests on analogy with that of Moses. We have in view here the references at 2.17 and 19.

> 'Why should it be said among the peoples,
> "Where is their God?"'
>
> and I will no more make you
> a mockery among the nations.

We have argued above that these serve the intentional purpose of anticipating the theme of the nations as the primary level of discourse in the Final Section of the Book. We have also argued that the dramatic intervention in the DOL of Part Two, leads to forgiveness and new bounty in unprecedented terms. As such, it is intended to serve as exemplary for future generations and not in general terms only, but on the terms of the future DOL, as this is elaborated in the final Joel section (Part Three). This Final Section also anticipates the DOL as we find it in the ensuing books of the XII and has been crafted to do just that.

One could of course argue that an imbedded theme of the nations – as against a redactionally supplemented one *à la Duhm* – can work sufficiently well on its own and that the final chapters simply develop that by means of a secondary elaboration. On our view, this kind of finding is not wrong in itself; it is consistent with a literary approach that attends carefully to distinctive style, themes and overall intention. One can hold this view and not regard as critical a laying bare of the social and religious forces that produced it, if indeed this is possible or desirable.[3] It would simply be the case that deeply ingredient in

---

[3] So the literary and theological argument of Jeremias, ATD, 4, 7, 41.

the 'original discourse' was a potential for immediate extension and elaboration. We regard the line between this conception and the one we adopt here as very thin indeed. On our view, a later work like Joel, with so clear a density of intertextual association with earlier works, is difficult to separate further into discrete 'layers' (original and supplemental). Perhaps, this is the force of a canonical approach and where it begins to part company with an otherwise compelling and careful evaluation of what are held to be primary and secondary layers of text.

So we take it as unresolved and unresolvable, whether in the Final Section of Joel we are dealing with a secondary elaboration that must be understood on those terms only. To conclude this, is to ask and answer a question we do not believe is primary for interpretation as the text itself portrays this. On those specific grounds, we will take the Final Section as an intentional extension of the first two main parts. We see no compelling reason to invoke secondary editors and prefer to think of a single organic conception.[4]

Species of Historical Reading and Allegory

James Barr once referred to allegory as an instinct in interpretation guided by what he called a 'resultant system'.[5] What he meant, was a heavy *a priori* whose tendency was to reduce the literal sense to a set of clues for a larger conception already in place in the interpreter's mind (Christological, tropological, ecclesiological, eschatological). Obviously, all interpretation involves a degree of circularity in that the reader brings some kind of hunch to the task of line-by-line reading based upon a larger grid into which that will finally (it is hoped) fit. Good readers may in fact be those who operate in this way and then subsequently adjust their working conception in the

---

[4] The case of 3.4-8 will be addressed in course.
[5] J. Barr, *Old and New in Interpretation: A Study of the Two Testaments* (London: SCM, 1966), 108–10.

light of the *circumstantia* of the words as they make their force felt serially.

Allegory may be more immune to this kind of sequential adjustment.[6] It allows the working system to be resultant in as far a range as is possible. In this sense, the literal sense is a cipher for the resultant system, which is in reality what the interpretation is finally about *tout court*. In the present period, for example, the individual witnesses of the XII may only be relevant insofar as they can be used to outfit a scaffolding, which purports to describe the Book of the Twelve as its own work, greater than the sum of its (otherwise clearly demarcated) book-parts.

Another kind of historical reading believes that the final literary work, in its given order and presentation, is rather like crude oil or uncooked ingredients. The text's given form has rich potential (perhaps) but it is raw and unable to be put to any kind of use. It needs mixing and cooking or a refinement process of some kind. *And that is its baseline reality as text*. On this view, the text *is* its sociological or religious-development re-description.[7] This is not a mere aspect of its reality, bound up with a text's lived life within Israel and within a world of genuine historical referentiality. It is its *only true reality*. On this account, the re-description of the text's origins and coming-to-be is incumbent and in truth has no other larger alternative. The literal sense is a starting point only and, beyond that, means very little as a hermeneutical fact.

It would be our view that the actual distance between more radical forms of allegory and this species of historical reading is in fact very close in hermeneutical approach, if not result. The text is something

---

[6] See the interesting essay by Morwena Ludlow, 'Theology and Allegory: Origen and Gregory of Nyssa on the Unity and Diversity of Scripture', *International Journal of Systematic Theology* 4:1 (March 2002): 45–66. See also the discussion in Seitz, 'Mistake-Making' (2014): 286–7.

[7] See my review of Blenkinsopp, Isaiah 56–66, in *Scottish Journal of Theology* 60 (2007): 476–8.

other than itself. The other thing *(allegoria)* is the real thing and once one has hold of this, then and only then can the text be 'put to use' in interpretation. It is an extreme irony that a historical-critical approach that sought to improve on the limited history of interpretation that preceded it, in fact produced something of the same external apparatus as the allegory being condemned, but now in the form of historicism.

The Day of the LORD in Part Three

For various reasons, Joel has emerged in recent research on the Twelve as the most prominent work in the collection. This is because of the density of the theme of the DOL, which is a critical thread running through the Twelve and because the work is regarded as sufficiently late in composition to know the other works and to serve as a commentary on them. Why Joel was not then placed first is then explained as due to its critical location between Hosea and Amos, with which it is most directly related and for which it seeks to provide a transition.

Though this view is shared by a good number of recent commentators, they are not in agreement as to what this means. Nogalski, who is rightly credited for developing the idea (it is more latent in Wolff), tends to read Joel in such a way that it gathers to itself the individual witnesses to follow. It eschatologizes the oracles of Amos, for example, because of the character of the DOL with which it concludes.[8] Others speak of it as softening the blow of Amos, by providing a more optimistic portrayal of Israel's ultimate fate.[9] In our view, both accounts fail to allow the historical referentiality of

---

[8] *Redactional Processes*, 45–8. He writes, '… Joel introduces a new frame of interpretation, which intends to reinterpret judgment against the nations from this eschatological perspective. Essentially, Joel creates his own oracles against the nations which play off the oracles of Amos' (45). 'Joel 4.1ff. actualizes and eschatologizes Amos' oracles against the nations' (48).

[9] T. Collins, *Mantle of Elijah* (see note 40 below).

the individual works to continue to sound their notes in their own day and for their own day, such that the reader continues to see them primarily in this light (and not drawn up into the gravity pull of subsequent levels of intentionality).

One reading of Joel that has been put forward in a similar light is that of Rendtorff.[10] He takes the basic insight of Plöger and others, that Joel contains three DOL scenarios. He cuts loose the socio-religious dimension, however, and puts the literary-critical suggestion to work hermeneutically. On his view, Joel is a container of three different DOLs and this is its literary and hermeneutical intention as a complete work (in canonical form, as he means that term). Now the reader, aware of this, is to make his way through the Book of the Twelve and observe when this day, and then that one, is being set forth. Joel has drawn up his work on the basis of noting the existence of different accounts of the Day in the witnesses of the Twelve. He therefore anticipates them and presents us ahead of time, with a kind of overview of coming attractions. The hermeneutical significance of this is not entirely clear, however, when all is said and done. It would appear that the DOL tableau in Joel, serves to constrain the reader against making any unbalanced assessment of any individual depiction to come.[11]

We refer to this account and others, because it is obvious that one task of interpretation is determining the DOL functions in Joel and certainly one challenge is to see if there is an integrative purpose at work, or one that has simply left three different DOL ranged alongside one another for no real purpose in Joel as such, but rather to guide the reader in some way *vis-à-vis* books yet to be encountered. At

---

[10] R. Rendtorff, 'Theological Unity'.
[11] See now the more recent offering of Rendtorff on Joel in *The Canonical Hebrew Bible: A Theology of the Old Testament*. (David E. Orton, trans.; Tools for Biblical Study, 7; Leiden: Deo Publishing, 2005), 275–9.

issue, is Joel as one witness among Twelve and not as one witness with a strong asterisk next to it.[12]

The issue is further a critical one, because of the way the DOL unfolds within the narrower compass of the first two chapters themselves. Already there we see not two different Days (one having to do with a past locust plague and a second one somehow bringing alongside it a new and distinctive presentation), but one Day being further explored hermeneutically. (One might equally have spoken of four distinctive DOL scenarios in Joel if the theory of Plöger and others were to be consistently applied.) So the real question is how the first two main sections are related to the Third and whether we have found sufficient cause in them for an integrative reading – a view widely held by recent interpreters (H. W. Wolff, Beck, Schwesig) with some exceptions – that might track with what is happening in the Final Section.

Most critical in this regard, is the transition represented by 3.1. We see no evidence to suggest that the Day being described is intended to be viewed as different from the Day in 2.28-32. On our view, the rubric intends to describe the same Day but from a different angle of vision. The effect of 3.1 is to ask us to double back and see a further aspect of the same Day not yet explored in 2.28-32, but fully integrated with it. There would be a range of ways to communicate that Joel means to describe yet another Day out beyond the temporal indicator of 2.28. This is more so the case,

---

[12] The same concern is operative in Watson's (otherwise insightful) treatment of Habakkuk in the Twelve. History is 'stalled' and lies flat and one-dimensional, locked in its pastness. Habakkuk kick-starts it back into action by releasing a fresh breathe of historical air, that makes active the past through a single subsequent prophetic work. See *Paul and the Hermeneutics of Faith*, 129–38. The obverse of this reading can be found in representative historical-critical sequential approaches. Jonah is the final work. It brings a note of critique of what precedes and offers a whimsical and almost cynical appraisal of God's work in time, or our ability to comprehend it (Blenkinsopp, *History of Prophecy*, 240–5; Seitz, *Prophecy*, 140–6).

given the way in which Chapter 1 and Chapter 2 now accomplish something of the same thing and as such prepare us for the final main section.

Stylistics

A cursory survey of the DOL *topos* in these final chapters, shows it to be more uneven, looser in terminology and more complicated in depiction. Gone is the uniform 'Day of the LORD' language, such as we find it in the first two main sections. Here, also is likely the reason for the development of two different versification systems in the Hebrew and Greek traditions. In the one associated with the Greek tradition and typically represented in English printed Bibles, it appears as though the verses that follow 2.27 are intended to be taken as an enlargement or continuation of what proceeds. To know the LORD in days ahead and never to be shamed (2.27), is explored through the lens of the distribution of the prophetic spirit in this future time. Israel will praise the name of the LORD (2.26) and the terms under which this is so are then dramatically explored (vv. 28-32). The reference we find in this unit is to *days* (v. 29, *yāmîm*) suggesting a protraction of the concept as we last saw it earlier in Chapter 2. The reference to the DOL ('great and terrible') speaks of it in terms of actions prior to it (*lipnê bô*').

In the final chapter, we do find more straightforward use of the DOL language such as we have seen it thus far (3.14, 18 [Eng.]). The notice at 3.1 appears to want to file this Day under the same rubric as we had in 2.29 (*bayyāmîm hāhēmmâ*; בַּיָּמִים הָהֵמָּה) adding 'and at that time', as though to make this clearer.

One way of accounting for this uneven portrayal, is to break it into reasonable parts and seek to describe a redactional or tradition-historical development. This is the strategy of Plöger, who wants to bolster the literary-critical conclusions by recourse to a socio-religious reconstruction of various apocalyptic groups.[13] In his view, the latest piece of the literary puzzle that is now Joel is the middle section (3.1-5 [Heb.]). Jeremias holds to this view as well, while sitting easy to the history-of-religions argument of Plöger.[14] Our view is that when working with later texts, it is best to avoid overly complicated theories of development as far as that is possible, since the usual form-critical depth is now differently to be conceived.[15] One way to account for the different stylistics of these final chapters, is to lay the complexity at the feet of the ambition of the author, who is trying to describe the final DOL in the same way he described the DOL previously: by opening it up and exploring its inner dimensions. This is even clearer in these last chapters, where the terms appear to emphasize protraction. Twice we hear 'in those days' and not, as in Chapters 1 and 2, a single descriptor 'Day of YHWH'.

The Spirit Poured Out (2.28-32 = 3.1-5 MT)

[28] Then afterward
I will pour out my spirit on all flesh;
your sons and your daughters shall prophesy,
your old men shall dream dreams,
and your young men shall see visions.
[29] Even on the male and female slaves,
in those days, I will pour out my spirit.

[30] I will show portents in the heavens and on the earth,[16]
blood and fire and columns of smoke.
[31] The sun shall be turned to darkness, and the moon to blood,
before the great and terrible day of the LORD comes.
[32] Then everyone who calls on the name of the LORD shall be saved;

---

[13] *Theocracy and Eschatology*, 96–105.
[14] ATD, 41.
[15] Note by contrast the simple chart provided by Schwesig, for example, describing Joel in two main parts (*Rolle*, 117).
[16] NRSV type-sets this (3.1-3) and what follows (3.4-8) as continuous text, which leans toward a critical judgement that here we have a secondary addition.

> for in Mount Zion and in Jerusalem there shall be those who escape, as the LORD has said,
> and among the survivors[17] shall be those whom the LORD calls.

One reason Jeremias holds to a different hand/s at work in these final chapters, is that he believes we are witnessing a significant departure from the portrayal thus far.[18] The prophet Joel is a singular recipient of God's revelation, but here the prophetic office is distributed to all. The DOL here requires an individual decision, but this aspect is missing in previous chapters. At issue, then, is the character of development in the overall portrayal and how the depiction here is to be understood as a creative continuation of the preceding material.

There can be little doubt that this section of Joel is related to DOL texts elsewhere in the Twelve. The challenge for present interpretation is understanding how best to characterize this relationship. Two texts in particular show remarkable similarity to the depiction here, even as we can use them to show Joel's own creativity in adapting them for his own presentation. That this is the proper way to understand the direction of influence finds confirmation in the notice at Joel 2.32 ('as the LORD has said'). On our view, this indicates an intention to refer to a text already in circulation, here Obadiah 17. The fact that Joel is likely presenting the DOL in this Final Section by means of a reading of other prophetic texts, also explains the different stylistics in the Final Section, as compared with what precedes. Here the prophet is not relating a dramatic locust plague in the present to the end-time DOL, as otherwise known to him. Rather, he is letting the end-time DOL stand, but is at the same time exploring its contours by comparing prophetic texts available to him.

---

[17] Greek has *kai euanggelizomenoi*, apparently reading *ubebaserim* for MT *ubasseridim*.

[18] ATD, 41. 'Erstmals deutet sich im AT das Ende der Prophetie an. Wenn künftig all Glieder des Gottesvolkes mit Gotts Geist begabt sind und dieser Geist ab ein spezifisch prophetischer Geist darstellt is, der befähigt, die Zukunft Gottes zu erkennen, dann bedarf es der gesonderten Institution der Prophetie nicht mehr. Jeder Einzelne ist sein eigener Prophet.'

In Zephaniah we find the collocation of three themes that appear in Joel: purified lips, calling on the name of the LORD and the promise not to be put to shame. There as well is the idea of a remnant left that is humble and lowly.[19]

Zephaniah 3.9-13a

> [9] At that time I will *change the speech* of the peoples
>   to a pure speech,
> that all of them may *call on the name of the* LORD
>   and serve him with one accord.
> [10] From beyond the rivers of Ethiopia
>   my suppliants, my scattered ones,
>   shall bring my offering.
>
> [11] On that day *you shall not be put to shame*
>   because of all the deeds by which you have rebelled against me;
> for then I will remove from your midst
>   your proudly exultant ones,
> and you shall no longer be haughty
>   in my holy mountain.
> [12] *For I will leave in the midst of you*
>   a people humble and lowly.
> They shall seek refuge in the name of the LORD—
> [13] the remnant of Israel;

Twice in the brief space of 2.26-27 we found the prophet referring to shame (*bôš*) being vanquished. In Zephaniah, the shame is linked to past wrong-doing on Israel's part, while in Joel it arises in the context of the nations and their (possible) rebuke of Israel (2.17). That said, the ideas may not be finally distinct: the national assault in Zephaniah was the consequence of Israel's sins. In Joel, the concern is more extra-mural: if Israel is extinguished by plague or consumed in the

---

[19] Schart mentions the use of Zephaniah by Joel more broadly (*Entstehung*, 269–70), citing with approval E. Bosshard, 'Beobachtungen zum Zwölfprophetenbuch', *BN* 40 (1987): 37.

DOL, it would bring shame upon them (Joel using the exodus *topos* in his own creative way). The lack of shame in Joel also appears in the context of proper praise and knowledge of God, as this has been gifted by him. It belongs to proper religious deportment (2.26-7).

The Zephaniah text opens with reference to purified lips, made so in the future by God, with the effect that Israel might then 'call on the name of the LORD' (3.9). In consequence, 'on that day', Israel will bring proper offerings, will worship and will be free of shame (3.11). So the same theme of proper religious deportment is at work in Zephaniah's DOL tableau.

It would appear, that Joel has taken the recognition formula crucial to his own depiction (2.28 and 3.17) and on the basis of other DOL texts, has explored what it means to say that 'you will know that I am in the midst of Israel and that I am the LORD your God'. Zephaniah's 'shoulder to shoulder' service of God, implies a comprehensive solidarity whose counterpart in Joel 2.28 is 'all people'.

But here we touch upon a critical issue at the heart of proper interpretation of this passage. Does Joel speak here – and does Zephaniah before him – of 'all people' and by that mean also those outside of Israel? In Zephaniah, the reference to 'peoples' would seem to move in this direction. Yet, as we read on the text would appear to focus on Israel ('my worshippers/my scattered people') and the remnant left on God's holy hill could only with difficulty refer to the 'nations' – not least because their fate is being held up in contrast (3.6-8). In the context of Joel (2.32), we find a quote directly from Obadiah where the distinction between the nations and a deliverance on Zion is front and centre.

Obadiah 15–17

> [15] For the day of the LORD is near against all the nations.
> As you have done, it shall be done to you;

> your deeds shall return on your own head.
> [16] For as you have drunk on my holy mountain,
> all the nations around you shall drink;
> they shall drink and gulp down,
> and shall be as though they had never been.
> [17] *But on Mount Zion there shall be those that escape,*
> *and it shall be holy;*
> and the house of Jacob shall take possession of those who
> dispossessed them.

It is crucial to get the Joel version right – for its own sake and in relation to the texts with which it is in association – because if its depiction is indeed 'universalist' – the term is not without considerable problems[20] – this has also served to distinguish the present passage (2.28-32) from what follows, enabling three DOL scenarios to emerge in consequence, which are in sharp contrast with each other. This is the view of Rendtorff, for example, seen above. It would then set the text in sharpest opposition to 2.26-7 which precedes it.[21] It is for this reason that many hold the view that if 2.28-32 is supplemental, it must represent the last stage of Joel's development, later than 3.1ff. and its portrayal. As such, it softens or mitigates the force of what follows by showing the final Day to be one that has accommodated the nations and their possible 'conversion'.[22]

---

[20] Bewer seems to want to have it both ways. He writes 'All flesh may mean all mankind, and we should interpret it thus, if the following context did not restrict it to the Jews, cf. also Isa. 66:22' (123). Yet, he continues by quoting with approval G. A. Smith, 'But within Joel's Israel the operation of the Spirit was to be at once thorough and universal'. Barton takes a full page to swing to and fro and leaves the matter fairly unresolved at the end. He acknowledges that part of the reason for this, is that he believes the oracle is an anonymous creation from another context (*Joel and Obadiah*, 96). The stipulation in 2.28 that follows ('your sons and your daughters') tips the verdict in favour of Israel only for Wolff (Hermeneia, 67), Crenshaw ('all Judahites' *Joel*, 165, 171) and Weiser (kleinen Propheten, 103).

[21] Robinson is typical in declaring that with 3.1 [Heb.] 'beginnt der eigentliche apokalyptische Teil des Buches'. Sweeney is rare in taking 3.1ff. as a continuation of the preceding unit (*Twelve Prophets*, Vol. 1, 173).

[22] Jeremias takes a slightly different position (ATD 24/3, 40-4). The effect of the interposition of this material is to clarify that salvation is not automatic for Israel. He does not take 3.1-5 as referring to those outside of Israel, but he will allow that the text has

Because we believe Joel is drawing on both Obadiah and Zephaniah here and because the possibility of a more 'universalist' reading is on offer with the latter (and not the former), we should also inquire about its own take. Adele-Berlin holds that a universal reading is to be preferred in 3.9 ('peoples'), based upon what she takes is a comparable text in 2.11. Sweeney follows suit, but not without underscoring that what Zephaniah depicts is such a purified speech made possible only through the fire of judgement.[23] Vlaardingbroek, noting that the 'peoples' play no genuine role in what follows, assumes the text must originally have read 'my people' (*'ammî*) instead of 'peoples' (*'ammîm*). He therefore reckons with a later adjustment.[24] One is tempted to wonder if the same confusion, or lack of clarity, confronted Joel himself, if we are correct that he has this text in view. If so, he has resolved the matter via the medium of 2.28-32, where there is no staging envisioned as Adela-Berlin and Sweeney must assume. Instead, the prophet introduced the idea of 'purified lips' on his own terms and directs his remarks to the same Israelite audience assumed in the preceding chapters.

On our view, the problem introduced in the secondary literature (going back to Duhm and bent to purpose by Plöger), is the failure to keep the same intertextual field of association at work in these five verses as previously. We have seen the prophet carefully negotiate two frames of reference: the DOL legacy from the prophetic literature (and kindred texts in Jeremiah) and critical tradition from the original Sinai and wilderness literary deposit. We have every reason

---

set out the conditions whereby even the nations might be saved. It is not clear how this balance is struck. For the explanation, we must wait for his treatment of 3.5, which he distinguishes from the unit as a later gloss. It speaks of a universal calling of God – the elect – without reference to Israel/Gentile distinctions.

[23] His lengthy discussion aims as well, at setting aside the view that the oracle is a later supplement. It belongs rather to the purification theme the prophet unfolds – for Israel as well as for the nations (*Zephaniah*, 182-4).

[24] *Zephaniah*, 192.

to believe that dual context of influence is operative here. We have mentioned Zephaniah and the directly 'quoted' Obadiah. But what of the exodus material?

We believe the most obvious intertextual association in 2.28-32 is the account of Numbers 11.[25] Moses opines, on hearing that the spirit has fallen, not only on the assembled elders around the tent, but also in the camp on Eldad and Medad, 'would that all the LORD's people were prophets, and that the LORD would put his spirit on them!' (11.29). 'Elder' is a key word in Joel as we have seen, appearing three times at critical junctures in the dramatic flow (1.2, 14; 2.16). It appears again here ('your elders will dream dreams'). Darkness and blood (28.30-1) are reminiscent of the plagues of Egypt (10.21-3; 12.21-7) and fire and columns and smoke, belong as well to the events unfolding in the same plague context and its aftermath. Much of this colouration, has already been on display and for similar reasons, in the preceding two chapters.

One possibility is that Joel is drawing on Numbers 11 because it describes a spirit endowment of special character – it comes from Moses and rests on them – that precedes the fateful reconnaissance disobedience (Numbers 13–14). The verdict of judgement divided the generations – one would die, one would take their place (14.31-5) – and this in spite of Moses' intercession. Yet, there had been a moment when the spirit lavishly rested on the elders and on those in the camp, even as it was a one-off (11.47). Now the spirit does not momentarily – if wondrously – rest (11.25, 26), but is rather poured out (2.28) 'on all flesh'. As many note, the 'all flesh' used here aims to describe an encompassing by the spirit that is not restricted to a single 'prophet' – as Moses had wished. The generations are not divided, but brought under one spiritual dispensation (the elder and younger). Surely this was the main point of 1.2-3, which began the

---

[25] See also the compact treatment of Deissler.

Joel presentation: the generations are not to be divided but united by virtue of God's unprecedented action, which forms the content of the elders' report to the younger. The portents of Egypt (2.30) are again on display, as the DOL unfolds in this 'afterwards' of Joel's main portrayal preceding.

In the light of this, one may ask what the import of the final verse (v. 32) actually is. Does it describe a general capacitating by the spirit that as such allows the calling on the name? That does not seem likely. Instead, we hear of a deliverance and an escape. As the DOL breaks upon Israel in the 'afterwards' of Joel's now future vision, already prepared for them is the record of Joel preceding. In that DOL, Israel is bidden to call on the LORD (2.12-14, 17) and the light of that Israel is delivered. 2.28-32 forms the logical continuation of the dramatic portrayal of Chapters 1–2 by describing a DOL, inside of which the generations are held together by the spirit and the wish of Moses is fulfilled in time and space. The intercession of priests and prophet are effective, as was that of Moses in his day. Now we have a prophetic intercession that unites all the people and brings the generations under the steadfast love of YHWH. [26]

Far from representing a curtailment of the prophetic office, by means of exodus/wilderness texts, Joel sees into its eschatological/protological reality. Moses wishes that all God's people would be prophets. Joel understands that under the conditions of divine favour within the DOL, an eschatological reality is breaking in and he speaks of this as a coming reality. Joel, for now, is the prophet in the role familiar from earlier prophets. But even his vocation operates now under their shadow and within their authoritative legacy. Little

---

[26] Does the reference to 'daughters' and 'women servants' mean to provide a positive gloss on the transgression of Miriam in presumptively encroaching on the prophetic spirit of Moses (Num. 12.2). Now women and women servants receive the same spirit that was Moses' alone. Elizabeth becomes the positive counterpart to Miriam.

wonder he can see a day when the spirit given to Moses will be shed upon all God's people, given the generationally received word to which he bears witness in his day.

Acts and Joel

The early witness of the Church fathers moves this text fairly briskly into conjunction with the Gentile reception of the Holy Spirit in the Church. Joel's 'all flesh' means a breaking down of the boundaries between Israel and the wider world. It is worth noting, that in this they move more quickly than does Acts. The Joel text under discussion is cited in its entirety as testimony that the Spirit's descent on 'all who with one accord in one place' (Acts 2.1) is not the babel of drunkenness, but conforms to the promise of Joel 2.28-32. But, of course, all those gathered in Jerusalem at the feast of Pentecost are Jews, 'devout men, from every nation under heaven'. To be sure the march of the Spirit will move to the Gentiles in time, but not until eight full chapters within the household of Israel and only then to an Ethiopian proselyte, who 'had come to Jerusalem to worship' (8.27) and who confesses Christ as Lord by the preaching of Philip. The first explicit reference to the Holy Spirit's descent upon Gentiles comes only with the tenth chapter of Acts (10.44). Perhaps this is what G. A. Smith meant when he commented, 'But within Joel's Israel the operation of the Spirit was to be at once thorough and universal'. That is, 'was to be' in time and by means of 'Joel's Israel'.

At the beginning of the Luke/Acts narrative and inside of 'Joel's Israel', we do see the Holy Spirit speaking through old men (Zechariah and Simeon) and women (Elizabeth) and, of course, the descent of the Spirit on the young maiden Mary in fullest measure. Here the faithful Israel manifests the life of the Spirit as it has become, to break down older frames of reference, as Joel foresaw.

The Great Day Elaborated (3.1-3 = 4.1-3 MT)

> ¹ For then, in those days and at that time,
>   when I restore the fortunes of Judah and Jerusalem,
> ² I will gather all the nations and bring them down to the valley of Jehoshaphat,
>   and I will enter into judgment with them there, on account of my people and my heritage Israel,
>   because they have scattered them among the nations. They have divided my land,
> ³ and cast lots for my people, and traded boys for prostitutes,
>   and sold girls for wine, and drunk it down.

Introduction

We are convinced that Joel is working on the basis of a textual witness available to him in the Sinai/wilderness narratives but also in the DOL material in the prophetic legacy and here, chiefly Zephaniah 3. This explains the character of the transition to the final chapter, such as we see it in the opening unit above and also in the overall content of this final chapter. The gathering of the nations, the 'restoring of fortune', the centrality of Zion, the motif of retributive justice and especially the concern with 'the LORD in the midst' of Zion/his people – these are features shared in the last chapter of Joel and the conclusion of Zephaniah.[27] Obadiah and Joel may both have this key text in mind in their respective presentations.[28]

In Zephaniah, the priests and prophets are portrayed in a negative light, consistent with the frame of reference in the pre-exilic prophets – the priests have profaned what is holy and have done violence to the

---

[27] Restoring fortune (Zeph. 3.20); gathering the nations for judgement (Zeph. 3.8); retribution (Zeph. 3.19); 'in the midst' (Zeph. 3.5, 15, 17 [3, 11, 12]).

[28] It is beyond the scope of the present work to offer a reconstruction of the direction of influence, but our general sense is that Joel and Obadiah are being composed at roughly the same time and perhaps with the knowledge of one another. Both texts play a critical role in the shape of the first half of the Twelve. Schart has spoken of 'bookends' around Amos. We prefer to think more broadly of the shape of Hosea to Micah. See also van Leeuwen.

law (3.3). They are joined by lupine judges and princes like roaring lions (*ărāyôt šōăgîm*; שְׁאָגִים אֲרָיוֹת). In consequence, Zion's fate is before her, such as Jeremiah, Lamentations, Ezekiel, Isaiah will tragically chronicle it. In our view, Zephaniah does not seek to contest this portrayal but rather to pick up where it leaves off. So he takes the final phrase of Zephaniah – which speaks of a future reversing of captivity – and explores it from the standpoint of prophecy after the Fall. What Zephaniah described as a future purification, judgement of the nations and the LORD in the midst of a restored Zion, Joel assumes and extends for the purpose of his own portrayal.

This consists of seeing in the dramatic locust plague of his day a proleptic rendition of the final DOL. More dramatically still, he depicts the favour of YHWH for his people, in such a way that a generation is forgiven and given new life and the future generations are to be healed in the wake of that action. Now he is turning his attention to the DOL, as the prophetic legacy described this from an earlier, pre-exilic standpoint and seeking to explore it on the basis of his own back-dated one. The restoring of fortunes has begun already for him, practically speaking. The exile plays no role in his depiction, because it is now in the past. What is incomplete are the 'Last Things', as these have been set forth in judgement and in hope, in the prophetic legacy (called by Zechariah 'the former prophets'). So the main lineaments of DOL language and proclamation exist now to help him elaborate his own inspired rehearsal. The themes he inherits are alive and are calling forth a new extension and elaboration.

Structure

I agree with the basic conclusion that in 4.4-8, we have a portion of text that 'interrupts' an otherwise smooth transition from 4.3 to 4.9ff. It appears to be a contemporizing footnote of some kind, offering a learned historical notice on the theme of booty and retribution as this arises in 4.3 (and in different form at the conclusion in vv. 19-21). Less clear is where the unit ends. This does not amount to a major issue, as it is more to do with proper units for discussion than a form-critical determination as such. The recognition formula in 4.17, is a good candidate for the unit's conclusion. The DOL scenario that here unfolds, leads up to the conviction that in these events the critical matter is recognizing the LORD's sovereignty and presence in Zion. Moreover, it finds a clear counterpart in the denouement of the second main section of Joel (2.27) and is a significant textual marker for this reason. The final 'in that day' unit, serves to contrast the fate of Judah with Egypt/Edom and serves as a fitting transition to Amos. Amos returns the favour by recycling the refrain of 4.16, but its context has a more ominous tone than in Joel, where it linked explicitly to divine favour for a protected people.

It has become something of a commonplace to categorize phrases such as we find in 3.1 (and 2.28), when they appear in pre-exilic prophecy, as signs of secondary elaboration.[29] 'In those days', need not refer to exilic supplementation wherever it appears, insofar as the prophets cannot be denied the capacity to have any future vision at all; that would be too restrictive. But often such language does mark an enlargement, even if built upon the more general drift of the prophets' message to contemporaries. But, in the case of Joel, the basic presuppositions are entirely different. His entire book is an exploration of the DOL *topos*, from beginning to end. His book is a 'post-exilic supplement' *tout court*, *vis-à-vis* the prophetic legacy with which he is in dialogue. For this reason, we judge the usual criteria and wider logic to be far less relevant in the case of Joel.

On our view, the basic starting point for the prophet is the final scenario of Zephaniah. He picks up the language – familiar more widely, especially in the Psalter – of 'reverse the exile', 'return the

---

[29] Jeremiah 50.4, 20.

turn away of', or as we have it commonly in translation, 'restore the fortunes'. 'In those days and at that time' suggests already a protracted series of happenings, which is what we have both in Zephaniah and in Joel's depiction to follow. However, Joel sees the latter days not from the perspective of purifying judgement over Israel, as befits the perspective of Zephaniah and kindred early witnesses. For that purification is a fact, on the ground in his own portrayal of the DOL in the two-stage presentation of Chapters 1 and 2. There it is that, from within the all-encompassing DOL unfolding in day, that already the conditions are present for the verdict of divine favour and new life. So that particular aspect of Zephaniah's vision will fall from view, as Joel elaborates on the final day/s from within the perspective peculiar to his own temporal location.

The aspect of Zephaniah fully alive and carefully anticipated, in what precedes in Joel through the metaphorical extensions of locusts as militia, is the destiny of the nations. The nations are indeed a tetrad of assault, as Israel has experienced them in Assyria, Babylon, Persia, Greece and the list continues (the tetrad of locusts implied thoroughness of assault, not one-to-one correspondence, however much that may indeed fit). Assyria overreached (Isa. 10.5-10) as did Babylon after her and Isaiah's DOL promised her defeat (Isa. 13; 46-7). The same notes sound widely in Habakkuk, Nahum, Zephaniah, Ezekiel and all the way down to the Book of Daniel. So Joel here stands on firm ground. The urgent gathering/assembling of Joel 2.15-17, here gives way to the gathering of nations, such as we see it in Zephaniah 2–3.

The prophet's vision of the nations assembled for judgement is generalized so as to be comprehensive in character. Here the specific enumerations of Isaiah, Jeremiah, Ezekiel, Zephaniah and Zechariah stand in contrast. This is consistent with the tetrad conception, which aims at comprehension and with the general imagery of locusts, as a mighty nation amassing for battle in the

DOL in Chapter 2 (2.1, 11). Now, the nations are huddled in what the prophet calls *'ēmeq yĕhôšāpāt* – as the verse explains, the valley where 'I will put them on trial' (*wĕnišpaṭtî 'immām šām*).[30] The charges are likewise comprehensive: mistreatment of YHWH's heritage in the form of scattering the people and dividing the land. It is the more specific charge of (sexual) slavery in verse 3, that occasions the lengthy footnote of 4.4-8. Tyre and Sidon are singled out in this connection. They are well known in the 'Oracles Against Nations' for ruling the seas, for commerce, for great wealth and for godlike self-regard. If the oracle comes from the hand of Joel, it would be notable for interrupting what is usually a smooth flowing style. The next strophe following the notice of 4.4-8 will continue the imagery of nations gathering, clarified then as mustering for battle (4.9). The trial, we will learn, takes the form of allowing the nations full scope for self-destruction and in that, rendering a full judgement in the Valley of Jehoshaphat.

But before we move to that next episode we find a specifying notice regarding Tyre, Sidon and the regions of Philistia.

Internal Footnote (3.4-8 = 4.4-8 MT)
> [4] What are you to me, O Tyre and Sidon, and all the regions of Philistia? Are you paying me back for something? If you are paying me back, I will turn your deeds back upon your own heads swiftly and speedily. [5] For you have taken my silver and my gold, and have carried my rich treasures into your temples.[6] You have sold the people of Judah and Jerusalem to the Greeks, removing them far from their own border. [7] But now I will rouse them to leave the places to which you have sold them, and I will turn your deeds back upon your own

---

[30] I hold the general view that Zechariah 14 is later than Joel. He also has the Valley imagery in his DOL, but in a more detailed and personal way; YHWH himself makes the valley.

heads. ⁸ I will sell your sons and your daughters into the hand of the people of Judah, and they will sell them to the Sabeans, to a nation far away; for the LORD has spoken.

The note opens onto the theme of tit-for-tat, or retributive logic. This seems a bit abrupt and not a clear transition from what it purports to explain. But it does anticipate in a way the final verses of Joel, which speak of vengeance and pay-back, using a different vocabulary. Our assumption is that the language of trade and exchange is here used, because of the fame of these regions in wealth and commerce. The note explains that a crime has been committed – selling of Israelites and looting of gold and silver and treasures, so as to adorn their own temples – and offers the excuse given, that this was somehow deserved: that the God of Israel is being paid back for some crime he has committed. But, of course, this is to the obvious rhetorical effect of denouncing the notion altogether and promising divine retribution. God's own people will be mustered (and brought home?) while the actual criminals will be fairly sold as they sold and exchanged illicitly. They will find themselves scattered to the distant land of Saba, a locust hoard sent packing and rendered null.

In Zephaniah, the scattered Israel are also brought back from afar, the land of Cush (3.10), with which Saba is frequently associated (Isa. 45.16). The nearest textual referent for Joel may well be Amos. 'For three sins of Tyre, even for four, I will not relent/Because she sold whole communities of captives to Edom'. This would also help explain the special attention to Edom found at the end of Joel and also in the Book of Obadiah.

The Coming Day Dramatically Depicted (3.9-17 = MT 4.9-17)

⁹ Proclaim this among the nations:
Prepare war,

>   stir up the warriors.
> Let all the soldiers draw near,
>   let them come up.
> ¹⁰ Beat your plowshares into swords,
>   and your pruning hooks into spears;
>   let the weakling say, 'I am a warrior'.
>
> ¹¹ Come quickly,
>   all you nations all around,
>   gather yourselves there.
> Bring down your warriors, O Lord.
> ¹² Let the nations rouse themselves,
>   and come up to the valley of Jehoshaphat;
> for there I will sit to judge
>   all the neighbouring nations.
>
> ¹³ Put in the sickle,
>   for the harvest is ripe.
> Go in, tread,
>   for the wine press is full.
> The vats overflow,
>   for their wickedness is great.
>
> ¹⁴ Multitudes, multitudes,
>   in the valley of decision!
> For the day of the Lord is near
>   in the valley of decision.
> ¹⁵ The sun and the moon are darkened,
>   and the stars withdraw their shining.
>
> ¹⁶ The Lord roars from Zion,
>   and utters his voice from Jerusalem,
>   and the heavens and the earth shake.
> But the Lord is a refuge for his people,
>   a stronghold for the people of Israel.
>
> ¹⁷ So you shall know that I, the Lord your God,
>   dwell in Zion, my holy mountain.

> And Jerusalem shall be holy,
> and strangers shall never again pass through it.

One of the most brilliant artistic features of this dramatic finale is the reintroduction of agricultural and natural imagery, such as we had in Chapters 1 and 2. At the end, all comes full circle. There, it constituted the realistic base upon which the metaphorical extensions were developed. Now in a scene which reverses the realistic base to warfare and national aggression, the language of nature is the metaphorical extension. Here is but one of the biblical loci the American 'Battle Hymn of the Republic' draws on for its famous line 'he is trampling out the vintage where the grapes of wrath are stored'.[31] Verse 13 speaks of a bounteous harvest such as we expect from the conclusion of the main central DOL section. But now it joins up with imagery of overflowing vats of wine – either to be drunk down to the dregs of God's judgement (so in Jeremiah's rendition), or representing the wine press of divine judgement, where the grapes are symbols of violent excess and also of deserved judgement/blood (see Isa. 63).[32] The locust plague that devastated – only to be stopped and reversed – gave rise to a bounty (2.19, 21-4) that for its final Day correlates with a bounty of violence in judgement on the 'plague' of the nations. As then, so now, the final purpose of both events is Israel's full knowledge of the LORD (2.27; 4.17). In this, it tracks seamlessly with the divine purpose in the plague and exodus narratives of Exodus 6-15. The sustained point of this foundational plague encounter, ending in defeat at the Sea, was always: 'then you will know that I am the LORD'.[33] The character of the LORD, as faithful through time to

---

[31] More directly, of course, Revelation 14 and Isaiah 63 are in view. But they share much of the same conceptual ground as here.

[32] Vast storehouses of divine blessing (2.19) find their counterpart here: the full winepress of accumulated wickedness (2.13).

[33] C. Seitz, 'The Call of Moses and the "Revelation" of the Divine Name: Source-Critical Logic and Its Legacy', in *Theological Exegesis: Essays in Honor of Brevard S. Childs* (eds C. Seitz, K. Greene-McCreight; Grand Rapids, MI: Eerdmans, 1998), 145–61.

an obedient people, would be displayed. And as foundationally then, so now as well in this Day (4.17). This finale matches the one found at 2.27. Here the emphasis is on the abiding presence of the LORD, 'dwelling in Zion, on my holy hill'.

Two other clear links back to the earlier DOL scenario require to be mentioned here, for they illustrate the way Joel's finale makes its sense in association with the Day as already unfolding.[34] The description of the Day in 3.15 is a precise – and we believe for that reason intentional – recycling of 2.10. The mighty army of locusts now finds its national counterpart in the final DOL. The description at 2.10 intentionally anticipates 3.15 and the latter recalls the former.

The second major link can be observed in the way Joel takes the Zion tradition of national assault, familiar in Isaiah and the Psalms, combines it with reflections on Zephaniah's Day, to produce his own version appropriate as the conclusion to his well-crafted work. The main novelty is the specific way the nations are in fact judged. We are already on alert to this, in the brilliant way Joel utilizes the *sprichwort* of Micah and Isaiah and bends it to his purpose. There swords and spears are beaten into agricultural implements suitable for a time of bounty and peace.

Micah's version[35] reads

> ³ He shall judge between many peoples,
>   and shall arbitrate between strong nations far away;
> they shall beat their swords into plowshares,
>   and their spears into pruning hooks;
> nation shall not lift up sword against nation,
>   neither shall they learn war any more;

---

[34] The same trend can be identified in the final verses as well (3.18-21).
[35] Isaiah's lacks the vine and fig tree line, an image of equitable shalom; otherwise it is identical at the relevant point.

⁴ but they shall all sit under their own vines and under their own fig trees,
and no one shall make them afraid;
for the mouth of the LORD of hosts has spoken.

It is not hard to see the relevance of this text for Joel's utilization: judgement, nations, sword against nation, vine and fig tree are the working ingredients he now takes up for a dramatic reversal. Nations are gathered for war, as they undo the hoped-for disarmament and bring on themselves the judgement that was to have led to just settlement.

But Joel has not finished. The introduction of the agricultural imagery into the tradition of nations coming against Zion – undeveloped in Micah and Isaiah, except for the purpose of disarmament – is in fact a crucial, sustained motif in Joel. Pruning hooks and ploughshares are the implements of cultivation necessary for sustaining the picture of bounty with which the Day of Chapter 2 closes (2.19, 21-4). This clue allows us access to what is otherwise the strange image we find at verse 13. Because this verse sits at what should arguably be the denouement associated with the national assault as such – what follows in verses 14-17 belongs to the effect achieved by this climax – it is important that we understand what the prophet is endeavouring to communicate. If we bring Zephaniah into play, the matter is even more focused. The actual final fate of the nations in his depiction is never clarified, in specific terms (3.19). We have instead a general promise that those who afflict God's people will be dealt with.

Clearly, the agricultural dimension is front and centre in 3.13. We are poised and ready to see what form the judgement of God (3.12) in the Valley of Jehoshaphat will take. The text has been moving us in this direction steadily and dramatically from 3.2 onwards. The climatic verse reads:

¹³ Put in the sickle,
   for the harvest is ripe.
Go in, tread,
   for the wine press is full.
The vats overflow,
   for their wickedness is great.

Again we have a reference back to the earlier Day, though it is more subtle than what we find at 3.16 (cf. 2.10). The two portions of texts we are comparing for enlightenment as to Joel's purpose are:

²⁴ The threshing floors shall be full of grain,
   the vats shall overflow with wine and oil. (2.24)

¹³ Put in the sickle,
   for the harvest is ripe.
Go in, tread,
   for the wine press is full.
The vats overflow,
   for their wickedness is great. (3.13)

The first speaks of the reversal of judgement in Hosea's portrayal, in the light of YHWH's verdict and promises in Joel's day. The second plays on this text by referring to a full winepress ('full of grain'), overflowed vats ('vats will overflow') and the main image of wine/vineyard. Up to this point the addressees have been clear: the ten imperatives/jussives of 3.9-12 have the nations as their object.[36] That they are not addressed here, is apparent from the final third-person plural ('so great is their wickedness'). We should think of an

---

[36] Verse 9 does not alter this (address to unknown, likely heavenly, heralds), though Barton seizes on it as suggesting a problem in a sustained address to the nations (*Joel and Obadiah*, 103–5). Compare Deissler and Jeremias (who see the imperative to a heavenly cohort in 9a, but without disturbing the main addressees: the nations being assembled, as in the Zion theologumenon; ATD 24/3, 50). Also Rudolph, Wolff. Crenshaw likewise suggests an addressee 'heavenly heralds' in 9a (187), but then immediately states: 'The summons goes out to the nations' (*Joel*, 187).

intentionally unknown agent: this allows the sovereignty of God in executing the judgement to remain unconstrained.[37]

What is being depicted is a harvesting and treading (of vines and wine). These exist in abundance (full/overflow) – the motif we see in a positive connection in Chapter 2. God has driven away the locust plague and brought instead a marvellous bounty intended to sustain the generations and bring joy (2.23-6). Here the superabundance motif is linked to the amassed and well-equipped nations and the weakness turned to military strength (3.10). Israel was to 'know that I am the LORD' (2.27) and never be shamed again. The recognition motif is firmly rooted in the defeat of Pharaoh at the Sea and the run-up to that in Exodus 6-15. That is the ultimate purpose here as well, as the concluding verse of this unit, following this charge in verse 13. In sum, we do not see a concrete unfolding in realistic terms that reveals the precise end of the nations; what we have instead is a recycling from 2.17 intended to make clear that God will deliver as he has previously done. So the text does not end here, but proceeds further with the concluding verses of 3.14-17. The conditions that obtained previously in the Day of Chapter 2 (2.10) are here on view again, as the nations are amassed as were once the locusts. We know the verdict and fate of the former. The prophet reassures us by reference backwards, to a future victory as well in the final Day.

So we hear the final refrain of reassurance.

> [16] The LORD roars from Zion,
>   and utters his voice from Jerusalem,
>   and the heavens and the earth shake.
> But the LORD is a refuge for his people,
>   a stronghold for the people of Israel.

---

[37] So also Wolff, in his manner. 'Hier werden wie in 9a Ungenannte aufgefordert' (BK XIV/2, 97).

Unsurprisingly, given the interest in interrelationships amongst the Books of the XII, verse 16 has come in for entrenched scrutiny. The same opening phrase appears in Amos 1.2 – the proximity is striking as is the linguistic match. Does Joel use Amos, Amos use Joel, both use a common source and so forth? Which is better situated (form-critically) and suited (content-wise) in its respective context? Is there a possibility of mutual reinforcing and how does one characterize that? Additionally, mention should be made of the final verses of Joel, with the theme of wine dripping from mountains also finds a place in Amos, at the book's conclusion (9.14). On our view, this makes it unlikely that the framing of Amos with these texts is to be explained on the basis of common tradition lying below Joel and Amos both, even as it is likely that both books have gone their own way in a manner suitable to their respective contexts. On this account, we have a mutual influencing of Amos and Joel, with an expectation that this is intended to have us attend to both contexts and their present association as well.[38]

In Joel, the LORD roaring from Zion is filled out with the image of heaven and earth shaking. This establishes a link backward to the redolent DOL imagery of 2.10, similar to the effect of 3.15 immediately preceding. God roars in his sovereign might and shows himself able to save his people, as he has done in Joel 2. So we do not miss this sovereign intention of blessing, the verse concludes, 'he will be a refuge for his people' inside the DOL. As he was, so he will be. This is yet again the ground logic of the revelation of the Name in Exodus 3. God will act faithfully through time, through trial, through the Day of his encounter with Pharaoh, on behalf of those people to whom he has chosen to display his mercy. He will be as he will be and in that manner, 'You will know that I am the LORD": you will know who the LORD is as revealed in his faithfulness and mercy through time with you. These revelatory manifestations, are sufficient to portray in all

---

[38] Crenshaw mentions Jer. 25.30. See the discussion to follow.

necessary fullness who God is, while at the same time always insisting there is more to be said in the realms of sovereignty and mercy through time. That is why the phrase can be repeated in Joel and not be redundant. The emphasis here is on the LORD being known in Zion, his hill, in his final rebuff of the nations and in his providing refuge for his people.

The use of the phrase in Amos cannot be taken in isolation from this depiction in Joel, in the manner of earlier treatments of the prophetic books; this seems to me the minimal consequence of seeing the Minor Prophets as in intentional association, however that is now to be defined. The fact of their proximity, is built into decisions that now result in the Book of the Twelve as a collection. I would agree with the basic premise that one reads Amos 1.2 now in the light of Joel and of the extremely positive portrayal of YHWH's thundering sovereignty, for his people, as the last verses of Joel describe that. But what is at issue is how we understand that 'in the light of'.[39]

In my view, it is totally incorrect to hold that Joel somehow softens the blow of Amos' opening 'for three yea four' denunciations of the nations and of Judah/Israel.[40] The theory holds that because we know

---

[39] 'Das Joelbuch steht im Zwölfprophetenbuch unmittlebar vor dem Amosbuch und soll dem verständigen Leser als hermeneutischer Schüssel zu dessen Verständnis dienen. Gleichzeitig gilt allerdings, dass das jüngere Joelbuch viel zom älteren Amosbuch gelernt hat' (Jeremias, 'Gelehrte', 105). He offers a sensitive reading of this Joel–Amos relationship in summary (107). Without a proper appreciation of the reciprocal character of relationships in the Twelve, one can produce a monochromic result. This is why a combination of diachronic and synchronic sensibility is required, as well as an understanding of editorial work as mutually reinforcing the sum of two distinctive perspectives. One can also see this sensibility at work in Jeremias' recent essay on Exod. 32 and Deut. 9–10 ('Wrath', 32–4).

[40] Collins carefully notes the parallel between Joel 3.18 and Amos 9.13 ('the mountains shall drip sweet wine') and also concludes that 'the ending of Joel seems to be a deliberate anticipation of the beginning of Amos, so that the positioning of Joel in between Hosea and Amos once again appears purposeful' (*Mantle*, 68). And so he draws this conclusion: 'The effect of all this, in the context of The Twelve, is that the dire threats against Israel which dominate Amos are softened when read in the light of the more optimistic ending of Joel' (68). On our view, this is a species of reading the Twelve which has eliminated the historical dimension, as purposefully maintained. The individuality of the witnesses and their marked historicality, is absorbed into a post-exilic reader response in which 'happy endings' are the final word. See my discussion of 'Temporality and Canonical Hermeneutics' in *Prophecy and Hermeneutics*, 118–22.

the ultimate fate of the nations in Joel, the stinging rhetorical effect achieved in Amos, whereby Israel is lumped with the nations in crime (Amos 1.3–2.8) is blunted. We know that their fate and that of Israel, will in point of fact go decidedly separate ways. That may, of course, be said in an eschatological sense, *but not one that evacuates the historical time that Amos and his Israel occupy.* When we hear the LORD roaring from Zion as Amos opens, we are put in mind of his sovereignty over the nations. For Israel and Judah to be included in the roll call of crimes is then to sharpen the message of Joel for readers of Amos, not to loosen it. We will watch a patient YHWH seek to spare his people, but in vain.[41] The effect of Joel on our reading of Amos is to show the 'perhaps' dimension of Joel 2.14 go forfeit, in spite of Amos' historical intercession (Amos 7.1–8.3) in the days of 'Uzziah king of Judah and in the days of Jeroboam the son of Joash, King of Israel, two years before the earthquake' (1.1). The roaring voice of the LORD (1.2) will not exempt a disobedient generation, as we grimly observe in the Book of the Prophet Amos to follow.

Finale and Transition to the Twelve (3.18-21 = MT 4.18-21)

> [18] In that day
> the mountains shall drip sweet wine,
>   the hills shall flow with milk,
> and all the stream beds of Judah
>   shall flow with water;
> a fountain shall come forth from the house of the LORD
>   and water the Wadi Shittim.
>
> [19] Egypt shall become a desolation
>   and Edom a desolate wilderness,
> because of the violence done to the people of Judah,
>   in whose land they have shed innocent blood.

---

[41] See the careful evaluation of Jeremias on the relationship between Joel and Amos ('Gelehrte', 105–7).

²⁰ But Judah shall be inhabited forever,
   and Jerusalem to all generations.
²¹ I will avenge their blood, and I will not clear the guilty,
   for the LORD dwells in Zion.

For the approach adopted in this commentary, *totality* becomes a significant index for consideration in interpretation. This corresponds to the concerns of earlier interpreters with overall coherence (*hypothesis*), order and arrangement (*taxis* and *hermon*) and larger thrust (*scopus*). In the light of this set of priorities, the Final Section of Joel – rather than representing a departure from a pristine original or an obscuring gloss – requires careful attention. This remains true however one judges the presence of redactional or secondary hands at work, as has been argued for by historical-critical labour from the last century. A good example of this can be seen in Wolff, who judges the final verse both secondary and also a serious departure from the thrust of 'authentic' Joel. Working with his own effort to retain the MT at 3.21 ('and I will declare exempt from punishment their blood which I had not wanted to declare exempt'), he writes:

> The divine speech does not fit the context. It is the aim of this gloss to adduce a final theological clarification. If the Day of Yahweh was announced to Jerusalem earlier (1.4–2.11) as a day of judgement, then that meant precisely that the people of God was 'not exempt from punishment'. But the reversal that has now occurred – whereby Egypt and Edom are punished for their violence against Judah – shows that the sons of Judah are now 'declared exempt from punishment' by their God. In the rest of the book of Joel no similar theological trends of thought can be found. They scarcely derive from Joel (34).

Of course, at the heart of this judgement lies a very serious problem concerning how one properly renders the last verse of Joel.

I introduce the discussion of the Final Section (3.18-21), consisting of four verses, with attention to the final verse of Joel, because proper interpretation of it turns on grasping the intertextual character of the unit as a whole, within which the final verse makes its point as the conclusion to the entire Joel presentation. So I propose to begin at the end and then approach the interpretation of the unit as a whole.

By way of anticipation, we are not operating with a view of the final unit (3.18-21) as specifically to be set apart from what precedes.[42] The voice roaring in 3.16 roars from Zion. God dwells in Zion, both 3.17 and the final verse (3.21) declare. In Jeremiah 25 – where judgement over the nations is the main theme, beginning with Egypt (25.19; compare Joel 3.19) and including Edom (25.21; compare Joel 3.19) – we see the extended depiction of the LORD's voice roaring from his holy habitation, with language already noted in Joel 3.16 (and Amos 1.2). But we also see there clear reference to the language of (not) declaring innocent, such as we find it in Joel's final verse (3.21). Addressing the nations who are to be dispatched for judgement against God's people, including the city 'called by my name', and just prior to the anticipated prophesying concerning the LORD's roaring voice, in judgement against the nations (Jer. 25.31; compare Joel 3.1), we read:

> And you, shall you go unpunished (*wĕʾattem hinnāqēh tinnāqû*)? You shall not go unpunished (*lōʾ tinnāqû*). ... You therefore shall prophesy against them all these words and say to them, 'The LORD will roar (*yišʾag*) from on high and from his holy habitation utter his voice' (Jer. 25.29-30).

Joel (4.16) and Amos (1.2) declare that prophetic word, anticipated in Jeremiah's framework, to be presently and actively in force at Zion/Jerusalem. The LORD roars from Zion.

When we turn to the textual challenge of Joel's final verse, then, we confront not simply a problem of proper interpretation of the MT

---

[42] Compare the remarks of Scolarick, 'The literary context indicates a connection of Joel 4.19 with Joel 4.1-17. There the judgement of the nations has already been described as well as its outcome (Joel 4.17). Joel 4.18-21 adds a look at the results. Why then does Judah's paradisiacal future have to be contrasted with the bad fate of Edom and Egypt? Joel 4.19b, 21a implies that the cause is past misdeeds against Judah that will be dealt with by God' ('The Case of Edom in the Book of the Twelve', *Perspectives*, 49).

and Versions, but a wider nexus of intertextuality and the theological pressure of numerous key texts. As has been widely noted, chief among these is the compassionate formula of Exodus 34.6-7. As such, we must enter, along with this key text, the landscape of its usage within the Book of the Twelve where it plays such a critical role. We noted above, the crucial character of the fundamental revelation of God's Self and Name in Exodus for the interpretation of Joel 2.12-14 and Joel as a dramatic whole. The completion of that revelation was missing in Joel's central declaration, because not germane to the message in that context. God forgives iniquity, transgression and sin, he solemnly declares in Exodus 34.6, but as the revelation continues (Exod. 34.7):

> He will by no means clear the guilty (*wenaqqēh lō' yĕnaqqeh*) visiting the iniquity of the fathers upon the children and the children's children, to the third and the fourth generation.

The opening refrain of Joel comes to mind, where a report is to go forth across three generations and beyond (Joel 1.3), constituting in our view the dramatic word of Joel as existing now in the present work before us. It is a word of repentance and forgiveness from inside the DOL. But the LORD's character is also intrinsically concerned with guilt, especially blood guilt. The exit of Joel serves as a contrast to the entrance due to the concern here with the nations and blood 'shed in their land' (3.19; 3.21).[43]

The portrayal of active deployment of God's character in vengeance is to be seen as well at the opening verses of Nahum.

The LORD is a jealous God and avenging (*wĕnōqēm*), the LORD is avenging (*nōqēm YHWH*) ... the LORD takes vengeance on his

---

[43] Crenshaw proposes moving the final verse after 3.19 to make the link clear. This is not necessary, as the reference to blood in both verses makes that clear enough as it stands.

enemies (*nōqēm YHWH lĕṣārāyw*)⁴⁴ ... the LORD will by no means clear the guilty (*wĕnaqqēh lō' yĕnaqqeh YHWH*).⁴⁵

The strong vengeance introduction of Nahum (where the unceasing violence of Nineveh is the theme) stands in contrast to the final verses at the conclusion of Micah (7.18-20), where the compassionate character in relation to Israel is on display.⁴⁶ That same contrast is on clear display at Joel's conclusion (vengeance in relation to the violence and shedding of innocent blood by enemies; YHWH as compassionate refuge for his own people). However, we account for it diachronically, a clear theme of the Twelve is being reinforced at the conclusion of Joel, fully in line with the message of Joel *vis-à-vis* a repentant Israel. Micah speaks of the pardoning, forgiving, steadfast love of YHWH for the remnant of his inheritance (7.18-19) and in the canonical shape of Joel this is enacted. The final verses of the presentation only underscore the wider implications within the context of the XII's unfolding account of God's history with Israel and the nations. That Amos and Obadiah follow Joel and attend to the fate of Edom (in anticipation in Amos 1.11-12 and 9.12, and in detail in Obadiah) is hardly accidental, given Joel's final verses (3.19).

We are now in a position to address the translational problem at Joel's final verse, mindful of the density of appearance of the compassionate/vengeance motif elsewhere (Exodus, Jeremiah, Hosea, Jonah, Micah, Nahum) and the theological significance it bespeaks as rooted in the very character of YHWH foundationally manifested at Sinai. The problem is compounded somewhat by the verb at issue. To fail to declare innocent, or not to clear of guilt (as in Exod. 34.7

---

⁴⁴ The verse continues by stressing the greatness of, not *ḥesed* (Exod. 34.6), but power (*koakōaḥ*).
⁴⁵ A direct citation of Exodus 34.7, with infinitive absolute, negative and piel of *nqh*.
⁴⁶ Casting Israel's sins into the sea depths (*wĕtašlîk bimĕṣulôt yām*) is reminiscent of Jonah's watery grave (*wattašlîkēnî mĕṣûla bilbab yammîm*); see Micah 7.19 and Jonah 2.4 (Seitz, *Prophecy*, 238).

and Jer. 25.29), is the English rendering of the verb *nqh* in a three-part formula: infinitive absolute, negative *lō'* and finite verb (*piel* in Exod. 34.7; cf. Exod. 20.7; *niphal* in Jer. 25, due to the passive-voice context). To 'exact vengeance' (in the active sense) translates Hebrew *nqm* (so repeated three times in Nahum, before the final solemn *nqh* formula from Exod. 34.7).

Verse 21 would appear to read: 'and I will hold innocent their blood' (so note in RSV) followed by 'I will not hold innocent', that is, a repetition of the exact same verb but in the second case, with the negative particle. Wolff tries to retain this reading ('and I will declare exempt from punishment their blood which I had not wanted to declare exempt') with the result that the 'blood' or 'bloodguilt' then needs to be Israel's – a position Wolff adopts and also declares at odds with the message of Joel as such.

A further difficulty is the accentual implication of the MT which joins 'their blood' with the second verb. 'I will not declare innocent their bloodguilt' makes sense in relation to other texts where the Exodus formula appears (see references above) and keeps the blood-guilt that of the nations (3.19); the first verb is however stranded.[47] Perhaps, as in Jeremiah 25.29, we were supposed to take this as an implied question: 'Shall I declare innocent? Their blood guilt I shall not so declare innocent.'[48] When one notes the solemn formula in Exodus, moreover, one might have expected the first verb to appear in infinitive absolute, followed by negation and then the finite verb it serves to intensify. The position of Jeremias is close to this, one might conclude, for he notes the clear association with Exodus 34.6-7 and translates in consequence '*aber ganz und gar ungestraft kann Ich ihr*

---

[47] Crenshaw offers as one solution elimination of the first verb, as causing the confusion in the verse. He opts for influence from Exodus 34.7 (where we would expect infinitive absolute and negative, followed by finite verb).

[48] See the excellent discussion of Scolarick, 'The Case of Edom', 49. Joel 4.21 is notoriously difficult, but probably speaks of not leaving bloodshed in Judah unpunished ('And I should leave their blood unpunished? I will not leave [it] unpunished') (49; compare *Gottes Güte*, 174–5).

Blut nicht lassen.'[49] Consistent with our view above, he offers this view in a footnote: '*Vielleicht ist mit dieser Aussage auch schon im Horizont des Zwölfprophetenbuches eine vorwegnehmende Anspielung an Nah.1,3 intendiert*'.[50]

Our view is that some combination of influence from Exodus 34.7, or a possible question implied at the beginning of the verse best explains what is intended as the final word of Joel. This would be consistent with the rendering in Greek and Syriac as well, which make clear the bloodguilt of the nations is being referred to and also remains under God's final judgement.[51] If so, the final verse serves to remind the reader of the character of God manifested at Sinai and his sovereignty over the nations. This theme is a major one now to unfold in the drama of the Book of the Twelve. Verse 20 has stated positively that Judah and Jerusalem would dwell secure for all generations (*lĕdôr wādôr*). But what of the bloodguilt referred to in verse 19, spilled in their land? Exodus 34.7 declares that the LORD's sovereignty over generations to come and the Book of the Twelve, shows that to be so for the nations as well. Jeremiah 25 repeats the identical theme and does so with reference to the LORD's voice roaring from his holy habitation. Joel ends and Amos begins on that same note of sovereignty, grounded in YHWH's presence in Zion.

In the final verse transitioning from the preceding unit, the familiar formula of Exodus 3–15 appear (3.17). 'Then you will know that I am the LORD your God' referred in Exodus to the dramatic manifestation of the LORD's Name and Character in the unfolding drama, from burning bush to victory at the sea.[52] In the context of

---

[49] ATD 24/3, 47.
[50] ATD 24/3, 55, n. 121. See also R. Skolarick, *Gottes Güte*, 175.
[51] LXX: καὶ ἐκδικήσω τὸ αἷμα αὐτῶν καὶ οὐ μὴ ἀθῳώσω, 'I will avenge their blood and will not put it away' (*wĕniqqamtî* for the first verb; *lōʾ ănaqqeh* for the second).
[52] C. Seitz, 'The Call of Moses and the "Revelation" of the Divine Name: Source-Critical Logic and Its Legacy', in *Theological Exegesis: Essays in Honor of Brevard S. Childs* (eds C. Seitz, K. Greene-McCreight; Grand Rapids, MI: Eerdmans, 1998), 145–61. 'God has not been truly known as YHWH because this involves the mighty deliverance yet to

Joel, the emphasis is on knowledge of God's Character and Name in forgiveness and new life (2.18-27), which takes form in God's own eternal life with his people. The promise of 2.27 is repeated here. The locusts of creational undoing and martial assault, both will be halted for good.

In verse 18 we enter a developed contrast between the pronounced fertility of Judah and the desolation of Egypt and Edom (v. 19). For the latter's fate, a locust devastation would not be a sufficiently strong image, even as it is clear that Judah's paradisiacal life marks a strong reversal of the opening chapters' threat. Commentators have noted the various possibilities for the images of wine, milk and water in verse 18. Abundant fountains issuing from Zion/Jerusalem point us to kindred texts from the same period (Zech. 14; Ezek. 47) which are themselves derived from Psalm language (e.g. Ps. 46.6) and the garden of Eden (Gen. 2.10-14). The reference to violence (*ḥamas*) and innocent blood (*dām-nāqî*), as marking the crimes of Egypt and Edom, is likewise reminiscent of the life East of Eden in Genesis 4–11 (innocent blood at 4.10 and violence at 6.11). Hills flowing with milk may evoke the bounty of the Promised Land which Israel entered in spite of Edom's refusal to give passage (Num. 20.14-21). *Shittim* likewise plays a role in this period, as a place of plague and judgement (Num. 25.9). Now it is irrigated by the abundance of water coming from the house of the LORD (Joel 3.18).

We have probably begun to answer the question as to why Egypt and Edom are paired in 3.19, which is a singular occurrence. Egypt

---

be accomplished. Such a reading is consistent with the presentation in Chapters 7–14, which centre on YHWH making himself known before the Egyptians (7.5), before Pharaoh (7.17), above or beside other gods (8.10), in the midst of the earth (9.29), throughout all the earth (9.16), in all creation (9.29), as distinguisher of Israel (11.7) and before Pharaoh's host (14.4). The recognition formula which appears in 6.7 runs like a red thread through all the subsequent scenes, until the denouement at the sea … the author of the unit at 6.2-9 knows that YHWH appeared to the ancestors and sometimes referred to them as God Almighty. But God reveals to Moses that he was not known to them as he is about to make himself known' (158).

and Edom play a role in the Exodus and the latter, though Israel's brother, is famously responsible for bloodshed 'in their land' at the time of Zion's destruction (Obad. 11; Ps. 137.7; Isa. 34.5-7; 63.1-6; Lam. 4.21). The great fountain imagery in Zechariah's final Day of the LORD passage, speaks of a massive plague against those who fight against Jerusalem (14.12-15) and the only nation mentioned by name is Egypt. Malachi follows and makes singular reference to Edom (1.1-5).[53] A final vindication at the close of Joel targets an ancient foe (Egypt) and one with more recent currency (Edom), as both live on as historical and more figural extension. The plagues on Egypt, as we have noted, play a major role in the formulation of the day of the LORD theme in Chapters 1–2 of Joel.

We have already noted the repetition of the imagery of Joel 3.18 ('the mountains shall drip sweet wine') at the close of the Book of Amos (9.13), book-ending the roaring voice of the LORD at Amos 1.2 (Joel 3.16). There too reference is made to Edom (9.12) in the context of the fallen booth of David. The crimes of Edom in Amos 1.11 make reference to his being a 'brother'. The restoration of an Israel doomed for judgement in Amos complements the picture of Judah and Jerusalem in Joel 3.1-17 and the shared image of bounty and mountains dripping with sweet wine reinforces this. What is said of the everlasting habitation of Judah and Jerusalem, is said again *vis-à-vis* Israel in the final verse of Amos (9.15).

The Ending that Begins

As presently constituted and so as we believe composed for this purpose, the Book of Joel represents the response to the final plea of Hosea to 'take with you words and return to the LORD'. The Book of Joel is a solemn, dramatic presentation of the DOL in which

---

[53] See R. Scolarick, who writes: 'It may be noted that the devastation of Egypt and Edom is mentioned once more in the Twelve – at the end of Zechariah and the beginning of Malachi, of the two texts are read in sequence' ('The Case of Edom', 50).

the generation depicted and all generations to come, are to find a template of repentance, a turning to the LORD and in consequence the promise of forgiveness and deliverance. This durable enactment is played out in the context of a locust plague unlike any other, which at the same time serves both to imitate and anticipate every dramatic military assault sent by God, for the purpose of maintaining his sovereignty over history and creation, as two sides of his self-same providential character with Israel, the nations and the world he has made. Every generation to come is to hear this story of judgement and mercy and see within it the ways of the LORD.

So the movement from Hosea to Joel. But equally Joel has been designed to open onto the remaining chapters of the Book of the Twelve. There the dramatic, locust-like march of the nations will unfold, as sent by God for his purposes of judgement and also for their own recognition of his ways. Amos opens with its own national roll-call and this anticipates in broad strokes the encounters of Israel, with the nations brought to judge and to learn: to acknowledge the One God's ways with all people. Joel solemnly warns at its close, that those who refuse to acknowledge will find the ways of judgement only to be their fate.

In many ways, a prayerful place where these notes coalesce can now be seen in Psalm 25. The 'ways' the penitent desires to walk in are the markers of God's own character as revealed to Moses' generation, for all ensuing generations. The sins that have brought about God's righteous judgement are acknowledged by the humbled one and this reveals the pathway opening onto his mercy and steadfast love, whose range is longer than any single individual or generation.

> [1] To you, O LORD, I lift up my soul.
> [2] O my God, in you I trust;
>   do not let me be put to shame;
>   do not let my enemies exult over me.

³ Do not let those who wait for you be put to shame;
  let them be ashamed who are wantonly treacherous.

⁴ Make me to know your ways, O Lord;
  teach me your paths.
⁵ Lead me in your truth, and teach me,
  for you are the God of my salvation;
  for you I wait all day long.

⁶ Be mindful of your mercy, O Lord, and of your steadfast love,
  for they have been from of old.
⁷ Do not remember the sins of my youth or my transgressions;
  according to your steadfast love remember me,
  for your goodness' sake, O Lord!

⁸ Good and upright is the Lord;
  therefore he instructs sinners in the way.
⁹ He leads the humble in what is right,
  and teaches the humble his way.
¹⁰ All the paths of the Lord are steadfast love and faithfulness,
  for those who keep his covenant and his decrees.

¹¹ For your name's sake, O Lord,
  pardon my guilt, for it is great.
¹² Who are they that fear the Lord?
  He will teach them the way that they should choose.

¹³ They will abide in prosperity,
  and their children shall possess the land.
¹⁴ The friendship of the Lord is for those who fear him,
  and he makes his covenant known to them.
¹⁵ My eyes are ever toward the Lord,
  for he will pluck my feet out of the net.

¹⁶ Turn to me and be gracious to me,
  for I am lonely and afflicted.
¹⁷ Relieve the troubles of my heart,
  and bring me out of my distress.
¹⁸ Consider my affliction and my trouble,
  and forgive all my sins.

[19] Consider how many are my foes,
    and with what violent hatred they hate me.
[20] O guard my life, and deliver me;
    do not let me be put to shame, for I take refuge in you.
[21] May integrity and uprightness preserve me,
    for I wait for you.

[22] Redeem Israel, O God,
    out of all its troubles.

To say this prayer is to walk into the heart of Joel and the access he provides to God's grace. It is the unspoken prayer that all the same belongs to the nerve-centre of Joel's 'turning to' YHWH, occasioning his jealousy and his mercy for the people whom he loves (2.18-27). The unspecified form of this prayer in Joel does not mean it did not happen, but that it cannot be scripted in any way except as those in every generation might come to speak it, in whatever specific circumstance of distress they might find themselves. And that includes us today who still recite Psalm 25 and who continue to meditate on the Book of Joel.

What will be left to view as we move forward through the Book of the Twelve is the range of that divine character extending not just in judgement but also in mercy toward the nations. The unnamed foes and enemies of Psalm 25 are not described specifically as outside the household of Israel. That is also true of what is to follow, as the encounter of Amos with Amaziah will demonstrate, or indeed in Israel's confrontation with brother Edom. But as those foes and enemies do take on national dress, such as we find them fully anticipated in Joel, it will be the message of the fifth Book of Jonah, that reminds us of God's compassion and ultimate concern for them as well 'who do not know their right hand from their left, and also much cattle'. The Gentiles, who are today's Christian readers of Joel, are of course the enemies brought near by the One Cross. Whatever will remain to be accomplished of God's sovereign purposes, with Israel and the nations beyond the horizon of the Book of the Twelve itself, God's final messenger hands over to the messenger who is to come in God's good time, for which he is but the obscure harbinger with a pregnant name (Malachi).

The Book of Joel, then, situates the reader of every generation within the DOL, which is the final Day now brought into temporal, figural reality. In something of the same manner, the synoptic Gospels all describe the final day of the LORD, not as the last word of their respective literary witnesses, but prior to the passion narratives which take up where they leave off (Matt. 24; Mk. 13; Lk. 21). Abandonment, betrayal, tribulation, the wracking of creation, national enmity – all these mark the end times. But, equally, they constitute the conditions that One Cross and One Lord embody at the middle of time. Inside an act in the middle of time, the end times are played out in judgement by the Lord of time and life upon the Lord of life and time. We enter the redoubled heart of 'the LORD, the LORD, compassionate and merciful, slow to anger, abounding in steadfast love, but who will by no means clear the guilty'. The sting of those end times is not thereby withdrawn but embodied, in full judgement and mercy, granting those who take refuge in that Lord new life on the other side of betrayal and abandonment. The new life that Joel grants in the middle of the Day of the LORD is likewise a durable and lasting earnest, intended to withstand all that will finally be accomplished when the final Day of the Lord draws down the curtain of time.

In Joel we are witnesses to a type of that Day which is Good Friday, Easter and the final Day,

וְהָיָה יוֹם־אֶחָד הוּא יִוָּדַע לַיהוָה
(Zech. 14.7)

Appendix I: *NY Times*, 6 March 2013

A Locust Plague, Shy of Biblical Proportions, in Israel

JERUSALEM – For many Israelis, the biblical comparisons were irresistible: locusts were swarming across the border from Egypt three weeks before Passover, like a vivid enactment of the eighth plague visited upon the obdurate Pharaoh. Others with a more modern sensibility, said it felt more like Hitchcock.

Israel first announced that it was on 'locust alert' on Monday, after large swarms were spotted in the Cairo area. The Food and Agriculture Organization of the United Nations warned that wind and climate conditions increased the chances of an entomological cross-border invasion.

The Ministry of Agriculture set up a hot line for swarm sightings. By Tuesday, grasshoppers the size of small birds were reported on balconies and in gardens in central and northern Israel. But the largest concentration, an ominous black cloud of millions, settled for the night near the tiny rural village of Kmehin in Israel's southern Negev desert, not far from the border with Egypt.

Potato farmers in the area complained that their fields were being ruined. Drivers said they could not see through their windshields for all the bugs flying in their direction.

Uriel Sinai/Getty Images
According to one researcher, the locusts had originated from the deserts of Sudan and had moved north in search of food.

On the up side, some considered the curse almost a blessing. The popular Channel 2 television news showed delighted Thai agricultural workers frying up locusts for a crunchy snack. The Israeli television crew munched on a few too, noting that locusts are considered kosher.

The Agriculture Ministry said it was the first time that Israel had seen locusts since 2005 and recalled an even worse invasion in the 1950s.

Stav Talal, a researcher from Tel Aviv University who went south to gather samples of the invaders, told the Hebrew news Web site 'Ynet', that the locusts had originated from the deserts of Sudan and had moved north in search of food. But, he added, that the conditions in Israel were not ideal for the locusts, the relative cold making it hard for them to multiply.

'As I understand it,' Mr. Talal said, 'they did not come here in droves.'

However, as in the time of Moses, Egypt was deeply afflicted. While the country's political chaos has been grabbing international attention, the Egyptian Ministry of Agriculture has been combating locust swarms countrywide: in Cairo, Upper Egypt, the Canal area, the Red Sea governorate, El Arish and other border areas in the Sinai Peninsula.

Monitoring stations have been established in areas suspected as possible destinations for the locusts, the state newspaper 'Al-Ahram' reported. While the ministry maintained that there were no material losses, the Bedouin of Upper Egypt said the locusts had destroyed their cumin crop and asked the government for compensation.

The Jewish holiday of Passover commemorates the biblical story of the Israelites' liberation from slavery in Egypt. Divine punishment in the form of ten plagues afflicted the Egyptians, as the Pharaoh refused the entreaties of Moses and Aaron to let their people go. An east wind brought the locusts that devoured what was left of Egypt's crops. Locusts also appear in the Koranic version of the tale.

Modern Israel, however, has a greater range of tools to fight off this plague. On Wednesday, the Ministry of Agriculture said in a statement that spraying pesticide from the ground and air had reduced the size of the swarm considerably.

Mayy El Sheikh contributed reporting from Cairo.

From *The New York Times*, © The New York Times. All rights reserved. Used by permission and protected by the Copyright Laws of the United States. The printing, copying, redistribution, or retransmission of this Content without express written permission is prohibited.

Appendix II: Temporality in Joel 2.3-11: The interchange of prefixed and suffixed forms

לְפָנָיו אָכְלָה אֵשׁ וְאַחֲרָיו תְּלַהֵט לֶהָבָה כְּגַן־עֵדֶן הָאָרֶץ לְפָנָיו וְאַחֲרָיו מִדְבַּר שְׁמָמָה וְגַם־פְּלֵיטָה לֹא־הָיְתָה לּוֹ	ג	3	A fire has devoured before them, and behind them a flame blazes; the land is as the garden of Eden before them and behind them a desolate wilderness; indeed rescue has become impossible. [S,P,S]
כְּמַרְאֵה סוּסִים מַרְאֵהוּ וּכְפָרָשִׁים כֵּן יְרוּצוּן	ד	4	The appearance of them is as the appearance of horses; and as horsemen, so they run. [P]
כְּקוֹל מַרְכָּבוֹת עַל־רָאשֵׁי הֶהָרִים יְרַקֵּדוּן כְּקוֹל לַהַב אֵשׁ אֹכְלָה קָשׁ כְּעַם עָצוּם עֱרוּךְ מִלְחָמָה	ה	5	Like the noise of chariots, on the tops of the mountains they leap; like the noise of a flame of fire that has devoured stubble; like a mighty people set in battle array. [P,S]
מִפָּנָיו יָחִילוּ עַמִּים כָּל־פָּנִים קִבְּצוּ פָארוּר	ו	6	Before them peoples are in anguish; all faces have gathered blackness. [P,S]

ז	כְּגִבּוֹרִים יְרֻצוּן כְּאַנְשֵׁי מִלְחָמָה יַעֲלוּ חוֹמָה וְאִישׁ בִּדְרָכָיו יֵלֵכוּן וְלֹא יְעַבְּטוּן אֹרְחוֹתָם	7	Like mighty men they run, like men of war they mount the wall; and they move on, every one in his ways; and they do not entangle their paths. [P,P,P,P]
ח	וְאִישׁ אָחִיו לֹא יִדְחָקוּן גֶּבֶר בִּמְסִלָּתוֹ יֵלֵכוּן וּבְעַד הַשֶּׁלַח יִפֹּלוּ לֹא יִבְצָעוּ	8	Neither does a man jostle his neighbour, each warrior marches on his (own) highway; and they break through the weapons, and they suffer no harm. [P,P,P,P]
ט	בָּעִיר יָשֹׁקּוּ בַּחוֹמָה יְרֻצוּן בַּבָּתִּים יַעֲלוּ בְּעַד הַחַלּוֹנִים יָבֹאוּ כַּגַּנָּב	9	They leap on the city, they run on the wall, they climb up into the houses; they enter in at the windows like a thief. [P,P,P,P]
י	לְפָנָיו רָגְזָה אֶרֶץ רָעֲשׁוּ שָׁמָיִם שֶׁמֶשׁ וְיָרֵחַ קָדָרוּ וְכוֹכָבִים אָסְפוּ נָגְהָם	10	Before them the earth quaked, the heavens trembled; the sun and the moon became black, and the stars withdrew their shining. [S,S,S,S]

Appendix II

11 יא וַיהוָה נָתַן קוֹלוֹ לִפְנֵי חֵילוֹ כִּי רַב
מְאֹד מַחֲנֵהוּ כִּי עָצוּם עֹשֵׂה דְבָרוֹ
כִּי־גָדוֹל יוֹם־יְהוָה וְנוֹרָא מְאֹד וּמִי
יְכִילֶנּוּ

And the LORD gave voice before His army; for His camp is very great, for he is mighty who declares His word; for great is the day of the LORD and very terrible; and who can abide it? [S,Prtc,S]

Summary: 9 S forms; 16 P forms
Verses 7, 8, 9 – *all prefixed form*
Verses 10, 11 – *all suffixed forms*
Verses 3, 5, 6 – mixed forms

Index

a priori 185
Acts 199
Africa, Saharan 125
Ahaz 69
allegory 184, 185–7
Amaziah 25, 64, 113, 134, 225
Amos 5, 7, 8, 9, 13, 14, 15, 16, 18, 20,
    21, 23, 25, 26, 27, 39, 42, 43,
    44, 51, 56, 63, 64, 67, 72, 79,
    112, 113, 116, 123, 124, 125,
    128, 134, 135, 143, 146, 151,
    158, 161, 162, 165, 166, 167,
    172, 187, 205, 212, 213, 214,
    216, 218, 222, 223, 225
  doxologies of 158
  visions 28
analogy 152
Antiochenes 3, 15, 23, 171
apostasy, cultic 134
Ash Wednesday 52, 86
  Collect for 89
Ashkenazim tradition 92
assembly 139, 168
Assyria 56, 68, 69, 178, 180, 203
Assyrians 127
audience 3, 52
authorship 3

Babylon 69, 172, 178, 180, 203
Babylonians 127
Baruch 45
Bethel 134
blight 143
blood 218, 219
blood guilt 217, 219, 220
Book of Common Prayer 86, 89
Book of the Twelve 1, 6, 9, 13, 18, 28,
    34, 33, 38, 41, 49, 52, 54, 62,
    63, 73, 163, 186, 188, 213, 217,
    220, 223, 225, 226

analysis 34
booty 201
bounty 46, 54, 67, 130, 162, 180, 181,
    184, 207, 208, 209, 211, 221,
    222

Cairo 126
Caleb 45
call narrative 40, 49, 112
Calvin, John 3, 19, 25, 51, 114, 171
Chaldeans 127
chaos 159
Chronicles 40, 127
Church fathers 199
commentaries 15
commerce 205
Common Prayer, Book of 86, 89
confession 45, 55, 60, 92
Cranmer, Thomas 86, 89, 90, 91, 93
creation 82, 159
crop devastation 124, 126
Cross 85, 225, 226
cross-reference 40
cult 14
cultic apostasy 134
Cush 205
Cyril 22, 23, 24, 114, 127, 171, 173

Damascus 16
Daniel 17, 203
dating 3, 38
David 40, 172, 222
Day of darkness 151, 162
Day of judgement 83
Day of mercy 164
Day of the LORD (DOL) 7, 8, 21–2,
    26, 27, 28, 33, 35, 36, 39, 41,
    42, 43, 44, 46, 56, 57, 58, 60,
    61, 62, 63, 64, 67–83, 90, 93,
    128, 129–46, 147–82, 184,

187–90, 191, 192, 194, 195, 198, 201, 202, 203, 204, 208, 212, 217, 222, 226
Decalogue 174
deliverance 73, 223
destroyed fruit 124, 136
Deuteronomy 56, 80, 87, 112, 162, 180
diachronics 5
DOL, *see* Day of the LORD
doxologies
    Amos 158
drought 7, 35, 72, 124, 135, 143, 144
drunkenness 137

Easter 85
Ebed-Melech 45
Eden, Garden of 158, 159, 221
Edom 16, 27, 202, 216, 218, 221, 222, 225
Egypt 56, 124, 125, 198, 202, 216, 221
    plagues 152, 197
Eldad 197
elders 168, 175
Elijah 85
Elizabeth 199
Elohim 64, 65
Empty Tomb 85
Ephraim 15
eschatology 61, 141, 154, 187, 198
exchange 205
exegesis 22, 23
exile 201
    Babylonian 172
Exodus 47–8, 54, 63, 66, 73, 75, 76, 77, 78, 79, 80, 81, 83, 93, 117, 128, 140, 143, 161, 163, 164, 166, 174, 175, 181, 182, 184, 207, 211, 212, 217, 218, 219, 220, 222
    plague traditions 151
exodus texts 198
Ezekiel 17, 40, 123, 138, 182, 201, 203

false worship 14
fasting 86
fig destruction 136
fire 143, 144, 158, 159
forgiveness 45, 59, 60, 83, 91, 135, 184, 217, 223
frog plague 159–60, 178

Garden of Eden 158, 159, 221
Gaza 16
Genesis 158, 160, 221
golden calf 163
Gomer 53
Good Friday 85
Greece 203
Gregory the Great 86, 90
guilt 218

Habakkuk 17, 21, 37, 62, 203
Haftarot 91, 93
Haggai 17, 64
Hananiah 61
Hermeneia 32
hermeneutics 52, 53, 60, 61, 62, 63, 114, 119, 186, 188, 189
Hezekiah 69, 172
historical reading 185–7
historicism 187
Holy Spirit 16, 199
Holy War traditions 67
Holy Week 85
horn 168
Hosea 9, 10, 13, 14, 15, 18, 20, 23, 26, 35, 37, 39, 46, 47, 51, 53, 54, 55, 56, 57, 58, 60, 64, 78, 81, 92, 111, 112, 113, 115, 116, 125, 128, 133, 134, 135, 136, 146, 161, 162, 165, 172, 173, 176, 177, 187, 210, 218, 223

Idumæa 16
image making 174
imagery 159, 183, 203, 207, 209, 212, 221, 222

Index

stench imagery 178-9
incomparability 73, 74, 76
India 125
iniquity 217
intercession 80, 178
interpretation 170-1, 186, 187, 188
intertextuality 217
Isaiah 5, 18, 26, 29, 39, 41, 45, 52,
    62, 63, 68, 72, 79, 132, 142,
    151, 173, 180, 201, 203, 208,
    209, 222
Israel 16, 43, 48, 53, 54, 55, 56, 61,
    62, 65, 77, 81, 90, 93, 122, 123,
    124, 126, 137, 143, 147, 161,
    169, 172, 174, 176, 182, 186,
    190, 198, 205, 207, 213, 214,
    218, 221, 222, 223, 225
  indictment of 161
  sin 193

jealousy 174, 176
Jehoshaphat, Valley of 204
Jeremiah 17, 18, 19, 39, 42, 43, 44,
    45, 48, 52, 55, 63, 72, 136,
    146, 196, 201, 203, 216, 218,
    219
Jerome 15, 18, 19, 20, 23, 114, 123,
    127, 172
Jerusalem 216, 221, 222
Jezreel 15
Jonah 8, 16, 23, 24, 26, 37, 38, 40,
    64-5, 66, 81, 123, 137, 139,
    175-9, 218, 225
Joseph 15
Joshua 45
Judah 16, 42, 43, 113, 161, 202, 213,
    214, 221, 222
Judaism 90, 91
judgement 117, 124, 125, 137, 143,
    145, 147, 152, 158, 197, 203,
    204, 207, 216, 222, 223, 226
Julian of Aeclanum 127, 172
justice 63
  retributive 200

Kings 127

lamentation 145-6, 147
Lamentations 201
lectionary texts
  Jewish 91
Leo the Great 85
Levites 163
Litany 86, 90
literary structure 115
liturgy 33, 163
locust plague 7, 31, 35, 46, 47, 51,
    60, 61, 71, 72, 73, 74, 76, 80,
    116-17, 118, 120-2, 123, 124,
    125-6, 127, 130, 132, 136, 137,
    142, 143, 144, 147, 149, 150,
    152, 153, 155, 156, 157, 158,
    159, 160, 167, 171, 173, 178-9,
    180, 181, 192, 203, 208, 211,
    221, 223
Luke 199
Luther, Martin 62, 78

Macedonians 127
Malachi 17, 62, 222, 226
manuscript tradition 19-20, 25
Mark 226
Mary 199
Masoretic Text 99
Matthew 226
Medad 197
Medes 127
mercy 177, 223, 226
messenger formula 49
metaphor 50, 120-1, 123, 132, 144,
    152, 155, 158, 203, 207
Micah 15, 16, 20, 23, 26, 37, 41, 56,
    81, 92, 111, 112, 113, 114,
    208-14, 218
military assault 152
militia 203
ministers 169
Moab 16
mortification 139

Moses 28, 38, 44, 45, 54, 57, 58–9, 74, 75, 77, 78, 79, 80, 83, 85, 93, 138, 139, 140, 146, 163, 164, 169, 177, 184, 197, 198, 199

Nahum 16, 26, 37, 38, 49, 81, 203, 217–18
nature 207
Nebukadnezzar 127
New Revised Standard Version (NRSV) 99, 156–7
New York Times 125, 227–9
Nicaea, Council of (325) 86
Nineveh 37, 38, 65, 176, 218
  King of 8, 64, 139, 176
Northern Kingdom 19, 113
NRSV, *see* New Revised Standard Version
Numbers 78, 83, 163, 164, 169, 197

Obadiah 15, 16, 20, 21, 23, 24, 26, 27, 29, 37, 38, 40, 50, 56, 81, 192, 194, 196, 197, 200, 205, 218, 222
original sin 137

parents
  sin 174
Passion 85
Passover 76, 85
Paul 62
Pentateuch 11
Pentecost 199
Persia 203
Persians 127
pestilence 124
Pharaoh 74, 75, 77, 82, 178, 211, 212
Philip 199
Philistia 204
plague traditions 56, 151, 178
  Egypt 152
priesthood 135, 161
priests 145, 169
Promised Land 44, 169, 221

prophecy 4, 14, 41
Prophetic Speech 33
Psalms 40, 63, 68, 89, 117, 128, 144, 172, 202, 208, 221, 223, 225

Quadragesima 86

reception history 23, 51, 52, 93
recital psalms 181
recognition formula 73, 74, 77, 121, 181, 194, 202
reconstruction 13
redaction 34, 155
remembrance 82
repentance 38, 46, 55, 65, 165, 217
Resurrection 85
retribution 201
retributive justice 200
revelation 77, 178, 192, 212, 217
righteousness 14, 93
Romans 127

Saba 205
Salmanassar 127
salvation 62, 69
Samaria 15, 16
Samuel 146
Sennacherib 127
Sephardim pairing 92
Shabbat Shuvah 91
Sidon 204
Simeon 199
sin 78, 81, 91, 92, 93, 122, 137, 174, 217, 223
  Israel 193
  original sin 137
Sinai 38, 66, 73, 77, 80, 81, 82, 92, 125, 138, 160, 163, 175, 177, 178, 200
social justice 14
Somaliland 125
Song of the Vineyard 132
Spirit 16
stench imagery 178–9

stylistics 190–1
Suffrages 89
syntax 150, 156–7, 170–1

temporality 231–3
Theodore of Mopsuestia 15, 18, 23, 114, 127, 171, 172
Theodoret of Cyrus 15, 18, 23, 114, 127, 172, 173
theophany 144, 158 159
Tiglathpilesar 127
trade 205
tradition 4, 34
transgression 217
trumpet blast 149
Tyre 16, 204

Unleavened Bread, feast of 76

Valley of Jehoshaphat 204
vine destruction 136
Vineyard, Song of the 132
vision 62–3
vocation 14, 139
voice of God 9

warfare images 159

wilderness 85, 159, 180, 198, 200
wisdom 55, 57
witness 27, 48, 176
Word of creation 160
word of the LORD 126

YHWH 28, 58, 60, 64, 65, 67, 69, 71, 75, 77, 78, 79, 80, 81, 82, 83, 91, 111, 119, 135, 136, 138, 139, 142, 161, 162, 163, 164, 170, 174, 177, 180, 191, 201, 204, 210, 213, 214, 218, 220, 225
wrath 165–6
yôm 82–3
Yom Kippur 91

Zechariah 17, 41, 42, 123, 173, 199, 201, 203, 222
Zephaniah 8, 17, 21, 26, 39, 40, 43, 44, 45, 56, 63, 64, 72, 79, 111, 112, 113, 137, 151, 165, 166, 167, 193, 194, 196, 197, 200, 201, 202, 203, 205, 208, 209
Zion 16, 68, 148, 149, 180, 194, 200, 201, 202, 208, 209, 213, 212, 214, 216, 220, 221

www.ingramcontent.com/pod-product-compliance
Lightning Source LLC
Chambersburg PA
CBHW062138300426
44115CB00012BA/1966